Mission in the Gospels

Mission in the Gospels

R. Geoffrey Harris

EPWORTH PRESS

0 7162 0577 7

British Library Cataloguing in Publication data

A catalogue record for this book is available
from the British Library

Typeset by Regent Typesetting, London
Printed by Biddles Ltd, *www.biddles.co.uk*

Contents

Acknowledgements

This work has been a glint in my eye for some years now, but turned into a labour of love, blood, sweat and tears in the last two years. It began to take shape in the form of words and sentences when I was fortunate enough to take three months' sabbatical leave in 2001 from my work as minister of two Methodist churches in Lincoln, and from the East Midlands Ministry Training Course – both of which at the time were supposed to be half-time jobs. I am grateful to St John's College, Nottingham, where I spent a good deal of that time, both in residence and on day trips. The librarians of St John's, Evelyn Pawley and Christine Ainsley both offered their expertise and assistance, along with patience, friendship and a cheerful demeanour.

I am also much indebted to Gerald Burt and to Natalie Watson at Epworth Press, whose encouragement and careful examination of the script, with detailed suggestions for improvement, have proved to be an invaluable form of motivation, and have preserved me from some foolish misjudgements.

My colleagues at the East Midlands Course, based at Nottingham University, in particular the Principal, Canon Michael Taylor, and the Vice-Principal, Revd Jenny Morton, have been most understanding when I have disappeared for days – and occasionally weeks – on end to work on my pet project. They have shown interest even in the most arcane ideas relating to this work, and have discussed various aspects of it without even realizing that I was picking their brains.

My wife Jane has also been a great support, and my children,

Joe, Ruth and Katie, have shown an understanding of computers that is well in excess of my own. To all members of my family I dedicate this book.

I hope that this work will not only be a small contribution to the field of New Testament scholarship, but will also inspire and stimulate those who are seeking to renew and revitalize the mission of God's Church in the twenty-first century.

September 2003 Feast of the Blessed Virgin Mary

A brief introduction

There is now a growing number of books on mission, and there is certainly a vast library of books on the Gospels. Yet, strangely enough, there is comparatively little writing to date which brings these two important subjects together. Many of the writings on mission are either about the theology of mission in general, or about the practicalities (or otherwise) of mission in a postmodern world. There are some writings on the biblical bases of mission, but they tend to focus very much upon the Acts of the Apostles or on the writings of the Apostle Paul. Anything to be found specifically on the Gospels usually runs to a chapter, an article or perhaps a few pages – rarely amounting to a full-length work.

And yet the Gospels are very much preoccupied with mission. The coming of Jesus, his ministry and work on earth and then all that followed on – his death, resurrection and ascension – are all interpreted as the climax of God's mission to the world. In addition, the Church at the time the Gospels were finally edited and produced was wrestling with the problems of mission to the Gentile world starting from a largely Jewish base and background. The Gospels' own questions and concerns over mission are therefore bound to be reflected in the way their authors understand Jesus' own mission and his relations with different groups of people. Did Jesus really only interest himself in the lost sheep of the house of Israel, or did he come with a wider purpose in mind? Did Jesus' ministry in an Israel influenced and affected by Hellenistic culture yield lessons for a Church operating in a multicultural and pluralistic society? Was Jesus' faithfulness to the practices of Judaism and to the teachings of the Jewish

Scriptures an obstacle to the Gentiles in their reception of the
message of salvation and understanding of the living of the
Christian life? These and many other questions must surely have
been at the forefront of the minds of the Gospel writers as they
undertook to write up the story of the coming of the Messiah
from their own very different but equally real and challenging
contexts.

In addition, the Gospels reflect the fact that mission is the
essence of the Church's life and not just an aspect of it. The life
of Jesus is invariably represented as being enacted in the world at
large (and not in religious settings), among ordinary people of all
sorts (and not just among believers) and, in particular, as reaching out to those beyond the normal scope and influence of the
religious establishment. Jesus' early nickname, 'friend of sinners',
is transformed in the Gospels from a term of abuse into a badge
of honour and respect.

The Gospels also have an underlying theology of mission. In
the Synoptic Gospels, the writers draw on the prophecies of
Isaiah in particular as a key to the understanding of mission as
God's plan of salvation for the messianic age. In other words,
they regard mission as a phased series of eschatological events
culminating in mission to the Gentile nations. This plan, conceived in the mind of God, would begin with the reformation and
renewal of greater Israel, but, going through several subsequent
stages, would culminate in the recognition by the Gentiles of the
God of Israel as the one, true God, and the pilgrimage to
Jerusalem as to their spiritual home.

In John's Gospel, the perspective is somewhat different. There,
mission is seen primarily as God's mission (*missio dei*) – a plan
conceived from all eternity and stemming from God's personal
interest in and love for the world he created. The words of John
3.16 are crucial to the concept of God's reaction to the needs of
a world gripped by the power of evil: 'For God so loved the
world that he gave his only Son, so that everyone who believes in
him may not perish but may have eternal life.' In John there is no
dualistic notion of a God saving his chosen few from the world
by taking them out of the world physically or by lifting them out

of it spiritually. Instead, there is an insistence on God's desire to redeem the world: 'Indeed, God did not send the Son into the world to condemn the world, but in order that the world might be saved through him' (3.17).

It might be feasible to call this *missio dei* – the mission of God which begins with God's own initiative and comes from the nature of God as a fountain of self-giving love; but it is probably more accurate to say that John's theology is that of *missio trinitatis* – the mission of the Trinity. Admittedly, this is a bold stroke, for the doctrine of the Trinity is not explicitly formed or articulated in John's Gospel. However, the process of mission is seen in John as a series of 'sendings': the Father sends the Son (1.11); the Son sends the Holy Spirit (14.15); and finally the Holy Spirit sends and empowers the disciples and, through them, all believers (20.21–3). Thus, the ultimate aim of the Father is to establish a community willing to serve his purposes.

Having said this, it is important to add the rider that although mission is seen in all of the Gospels (in their different ways) as a commissioning of the disciples – and, by extension, of the Church community – nevertheless, mission is not regarded as the exclusive activity or right of the Church: there are others who are touched by God or who unconsciously co-operate in his designs for the world. The Gospels furnish clear examples of this, in the story of the 'strange exorcist' (Mark 9.38–41) and the story of the Roman centurion's slave in Luke 7.1–10. In this latter case, the crowd tell Jesus that the Gentile centurion 'is worthy of having you do this for him, for he loves our people, and it is he who built our synagogue for us' (7.4–5).

In what we have said so far, then, it is clear from the Gospels that Jesus' own mission forms the starting point for the mission of the Church later on. The Gospel writers are certainly interested in the real historical life and work of Jesus. In many instances they attempt to fix it in the Jewish context of the time. But the Gospels also contain theological insights into the significance of that life and work for the mission and life of the Early Church. This is a perspective which has been neglected, or even often lost to sight. Critical approaches to the Gospel over the past fifty years have laid emphases on other things, things such as the pre-history of the text, the historicity of the Gospel accounts, the self-understanding of Jesus, the representation of Jesus by the Early Church as Messiah, the theological aims of the Gospel writers, the literary construction of the Gospels, along with the Gospels' use of rhetoric and techniques of persuasion. Critics have analysed the Gospels in the light of the social and political conditions of Jesus' day: at the other end of the spectrum, they have thought about the present-day reader's own interests and point of view, in examining the reader's response to the Gospels. But the time has perhaps come for another focus, and one which was of particular importance to the Gospel writers themselves – the focus on mission.

So it is my aim in all that follows to show that when the Gospels are examined from the perspective of the Early Church's mission – that is to say, the context out of which they were written – then the reader will be able to see stories and discourses from a new angle: new meaning will be cast on obscure sayings and new light shed on shadowy places.

I might go so far as to say that certain misconceptions might be cleared up and find a more accurate interpretation. However, I should refrain from sounding ambitious to the point of pretension. The aim is really more modest; namely, to take a fresh look at the Gospels as whole books, conceived as literary units with a single overall plan – and not as a collection of *pericopes* – units of tradition – completed by a passion narrative.

The idea of trying to perceive, or even to glimpse, aspects of the Church's mission in the later part of the first century by reading between the lines of the Gospel accounts may seem speculative at best, dangerous at worst. It will certainly be viewed with some suspicion in certain quarters. My defence is simply that the setting of the Early Church's mission among Jews and Gentiles is a real, historical and well-documented context. Even in the pages of the New Testament we have the testimonies of Paul and Luke (in Acts) to the Early Church's mission activity. Conclusions in my account hardly ever depend on detailed guesswork about the veracity or historical accuracy of individual sayings or narratives. It also seems self-evident on reflection that the communities from which the Gospels emerged were fully engaged with their mission to the world and with all the concomitant problems, decisions and changes connected with that engagement. The overriding importance of that work for the Early Church has led me to have confidence that it is a profitable exercise to examine and analyse the Gospels from such a perspective.

The various Churches of the first century – and there were certainly quite a variety – all had common roots and origins in the life and faith of the Jewish people. This was not a monolithic faith in the early first century, but rather was tolerant of a range of beliefs and practices. The Jewish religious life, and the life of the synagogues and the Temple in particular, is explored in the opening chapter. Thereafter, each Gospel is analysed in some detail, by looking at what is distinctive about each rather than at those things they share in common. In this way, I have attempted to avoid too much overlapping of topics and themes. In addition, I have attempted to highlight the fact that different social and cultural contexts give rise to different presentations of Jesus' mission. This is something which can be seen very clearly in the difference between John's Gospel and the Synoptic Gospels. It is also more subtly evident in the differences between Matthew and Mark, between Matthew and Luke, or between Mark and Luke.

Perhaps the most significant aspect of the Early Church's mission is its astonishing capacity to hold together in unity very disparate groups of people: Jews who came to believe in Jesus as Messiah; Samaritans who were the sworn enemies of such Jews; and Gentiles, who were feared and reviled in turn by both groups, and who had a very different philosophy of life and understanding of God and Jesus. The reconciliation that was forged in these early years of the Church's life almost defies belief: it was perhaps the most significant achievement of the Church in its entire history; and it leaves us with a great legacy – an example to follow and a pattern to imitate – as we in the present day struggle to bring together in harmony different groups and factions which have hitherto been at loggerheads with one another. This applies as much within the Church, with all its splintered fragments of different denominations, as in the world at large, with its ethnic divisions and its histories of oppression and mistreatment of one group or race by another.

Reconciliation in this sense is not just about people deciding to tolerate one another and to live together in peace: it is about different groups with different agendas forming part of the same community; learning to merge their identity and give up their individual ambitions for the sake of a common ideal and vision. The Church's way of mission is in this way the remedy or cure for all manner of conflicts – from the evils of racism and nationalism to all forms of exclusive behaviour, and the demonization or marginalization of particular people. If this kind of reconciliation can be combined with the Pauline ideal of diversity within an overarching unity, then many rich cultural and social expressions could flourish under the same umbrella.

In this way the mission of the Early Church has much to teach us today. In the final chapters, I have attempted, through a brief overview of the life and worship of the Early Church, and then through an examination of the principles of mission in the Gospels, to bridge the gulf between then and now, and to offer a few radical suggestions for mission today.

I

Jewish mission as the springboard for Christian mission

At the time of Jesus Christ, whatever one may think of the remote and inconspicuous position of Palestine, it is true to say that the Jewish people as a community or 'nation' (ethnos) were very well known and very visible. Pagans were well aware that the Jews had a long and illustrious history, possessed ancient Scriptures and had spread all over the Roman Empire, especially around the Mediterranean seaboard. The Jewish population was, in the words of William Horbury[1] 'unmistakably vast'. He goes on to say, 'To speak only of the Roman Empire, the Jews formed a very large minority, perhaps eight or nine per cent, a bigger proportion of the total population than was attained by the Jews in pre-1939 Europe.' Even post-Constantine, in the fourth century, Jews probably outnumbered Christians and exceeded them in strength and influence. The Jewish influence on Hellenistic society was also marked, judging by the fact that most of the Roman world adopted the Jewish week. Josephus' exaggerated comment on this was that 'There is not one city, Greek or barbarian . . . to which our customs have not spread.'[2] The unsympathetic Seneca also grudgingly conceded that 'the customs of this accursed race [the Jews] have gained such influence that they are now received throughout the world. The vanquished have given laws to their victors.'[3]

From the time of the Jewish exile in Babylon, Jewish communities began to settle all over the Mediterranean world. The communities in Babylon itself and in Alexandria were extremely sizeable by Jesus' lifetime. Many other Hellenistic cities also gave hospitality to large Jewish colonies; so much so that many Jews saw themselves in the same light as the Greeks, spreading their culture and religion all over the civilized world. These centres of the Diaspora or dispersion became bases for the Jewish way of life and, by extension, for the spread of Judaism among Gentiles. And there is considerable evidence to suggest that the Jews managed to arouse the curiosity of many Gentiles, some highborn or wealthy or influential in their society. The Samaritans – of mixed race and, in the eyes of Jews, a heretical group – were also adept at spreading their influence around the eastern Mediterranean, and had colonies in places such as Tripoli, parts of Egypt, Damascus and Rome.

Yet Jerusalem remained the spiritual capital where pilgrims gathered from all over the Diaspora. Jews considered themselves duty-bound to make the pilgrimage to Jerusalem from time to time, although not everyone felt so obliged. In Acts 2 we read of the Diaspora communities from all over the known world (arranged in an idealized pattern) visiting Jerusalem for the Festival of Pentecost:

> Now there were devout Jews from every nation under heaven living in Jerusalem . . . Parthians, Medes, Elamites, and residents of Mesopotamia, Judea and Cappadocia, Pontus and Asia, Phrygia and Pamphylia, Egypt and the parts of Libya belonging to Cyrene, and visitors from Rome, both Jews and proselytes, Cretans and Arabs – in our own language we hear them speaking about God's deeds of power. (Acts 2.5, 9–11)

It is sometimes imagined that a purer form of Judaism existed within Palestine itself, and that all manner of Hellenistic ideas infiltrating Diaspora Judaism were resisted by a rather monochrome Judaism within the Holy Land. This notion would better reflect the situation after the destruction of Jerusalem, as we shall see, but applying it to the early or mid-first century will not stand up to close scrutiny. Palestine itself was part of the Hellenistic world. It had Gentile cities within its borders, like Sepphoris – only six miles from Nazareth – and Tiberias, the new city built in honour of the Emperor Tiberius. In addition, many other towns and regions had a large population of Gentiles living alongside Jews. Galilee was one of these areas, and can with justice be named 'Galilee of the Gentiles' (Matthew 4.15 quoting Isaiah 9.1–2). It was the settlement of the tribes of Zebulun and Naphtali, on the north-west of the Sea of Galilee, and Jesus himself lived at Capernaum in this area. According to Matthew's quotation, it says in Isaiah that 'the people who walked in darkness have seen a great light'. Presumably, in the prophet's mind is the idea that Zebulun and Naphtali were the first tribes to go into exile (2 Kings 15.29); so they would be the first to be restored. But this quotation also indicates that the restoration will take place in the sight of the Gentiles as well, and will affect them too.

The use of the vernacular

The lingua franca most Jews could speak and understand was presumably *koine* (or common) Greek. In the Acts of the Apostles Luke has Peter address the crowd, not in Hebrew, but in Greek, even though Peter himself, in common with the Jews of Palestine generally, spoke a form of western Aramaic as his first language, just as Jesus did.

Much of the Hebrew Bible was loosely translated into Aramaic, in the form of *targums*. However, the translation of the Hebrew Scriptures into Greek became increasingly necessary among the communities of the Diaspora, for the common language of the Roman Empire was Greek, although Latin was also widely spoken in the west and Aramaic in the extreme east. The various Greek translations were standardized into the one Septuagint (LXX), purportedly the inspired work of 70 Jewish scholars – which meant that all Jews could read the Scriptures and hear and understand them in synagogue worship. This translation also became the Scriptures of the early Christian community – even when the churches had a majority of Gentiles. A little observed fact about the Septuagint is that it was understood not only by Jews and Jewish Christians, but also by Gentiles. The

Jewish Scriptures could clearly be read and accessed far beyond the Jewish community – and all over the Empire. What arose from necessity – a translation for a Diaspora community who had lost their facility for reading Hebrew – became something far more significant and far reaching than originally envisaged.

The Greek language gave the Scriptures a new and more wide-ranging readership, just as the subsequent writing of the New Testament documents in Greek made Christianity a religion accessible to the whole Empire. Thus, the production of the Scriptures in Greek gave a great impetus both to Jewish and Christian mission among the Gentiles. It is doubtful whether either mission could have enjoyed any degree of success without the translation of the Scriptures – and the worship of God – in the vernacular. And once the Scriptures had been translated into Greek, there was no reason for other Diaspora communities not to have material for worship and devotion translated into their own vernacular languages. *Targums* (paraphrases of Scripture with commentary notes), appeared in Aramaic, other renditions appeared in Coptic, Median, Iberian, Arabic, Persian and other more minor tongues.

Such translation work inevitably led to a greater accommodation of both Jewish and Christian life and thought to the Hellenistic cultural world. This is especially evident in the work of the first-century Jewish philosopher Philo and the Jewish historian Josephus, as well as in the writings of the Christian theologians such as Justin and Clement of Alexandria. But in some areas Jewish rabbis resisted accommodation to Hellenistic culture in all its forms. Elsewhere, accommodation brought about cultural differences between Hebraizing Jews and Hellenistic Jews, as we shall see. In the former case, the Hebrew language was taught and the Hebrew Scriptures inculcated and the Jewish way of life assiduously guarded and protected. Undue mingling with Gentiles was discouraged. But the spread of Hellenistic culture meant that the power of the Temple and Jerusalem establishment (the priesthood, Sanhedrin and party of the Sadducees) was widely viewed with suspicion and regarded as corrupt. All the same, certain aspects of Hellenistic culture – especially its philosophy and literature – were admired and adapted to Jewish thought, as the historian W. H. C. Frend makes clear:

> Hellenistic civilisation as it developed under the Ptolemies and Seleucids became increasingly attractive to the Jews. It was not merely that the great majority of those settled in Syria and Egypt became Greek-speaking (and to some extent Greek-thinking also), but in Palestine itself the prescriptions of the Law began to be watered down as Greek trade and Jewish interest in Hellenistic culture, at least in its cultural forms, increased.[4]

Herod the Great undertook the rebuilding of the Temple in Jerusalem, but elsewhere, in his new cities of Sebaste (near Samaria), Sepphoris (in Galilee) and Caesarea (on the coast) he was able to include the usual trappings of Graeco-Roman civilization: baths, colonnades, pagan temples, fountains and gymnasia. The evidence of Hellenistic culture was widespread – even in the apocryphal work of Ecclesiasticus by Jesus ben Sirach, written in Hebrew around 200 BC (but translated into Greek), there is a kind of synthesis of traditional Jewish and Hellenistic Greek morality.

The developments in the use of the vernacular and adaptation to the Hellenistic world gave the Christian mission a flying start, but it should be borne in mind that these were developments first and foremost within the Jewish world of the Diaspora. Yet the use of the vernacular was later readily accepted in the churches, and translations of New Testament books and letters took place from an early date.

The life of the Temple

The great difference between Christian mission at the time of the Apostle Paul – the AD 40s to 60s – and the time of the writing of the Gospels – AD 70–95 – was that, in the time of Paul, the holy city of Jerusalem and its Temple were central to the life of Judaism; and the Jerusalem Christian Church held the place of honour and respect among all Christian communities and was

consulted on all controversial issues. In the time of the Gospels,
Jerusalem and the Temple were in the process of being or had
already been completely destroyed and the Jerusalem Church
was forced into exile and lost its role of leadership among the
churches. The impact of these events on the Jewish psyche cannot easily be measured and can hardly be overestimated. It was a
catastrophe of the first order. But it also changed the balance of
power in the Christian world as well, and must have made a deep
impression upon the early Christians especially in the light of the
fact that Jesus had prophesied such an event in his lifetime, as the
evangelists remembered (Mark 13.1–2; Matthew 24.1–2 and
Luke 21.5–6).

Before its destruction, the Temple drew pilgrims to its major
festivals, especially to the Passover Festival and the Day of Atonement. These pilgrims came not only from Palestine itself but also
from throughout the Jewish Diaspora around the Mediterranean
and also in the ancient region of Mesopotamia. To those ap-
proaching Jerusalem from a distance the Temple rebuilt by Herod
would have appeared like a radiant mountain constructed from
white stone and embellished with large quantities of burnished
gold. The reconstruction of the second Temple of Jesus' times –
with its surrounding buildings and courtyards – began in 20 or
19 BC and was not completed until AD 62–4, after Herod's death
in 4 BC. Not long after its completion the Temple was utterly
demolished. This happened near the end of the Jewish Wars for
independence, which were crushed by Roman armies led by
Vespasian and then his son, Titus.

The Temple was roughly a thousand feet long on each side
and dominated the city as the Muslim Dome of the Rock (on the
same site) does today. Its magnificent porticoes with great
marble pillars entirely filled the Temple mount. The stoa called
Solomon's portico on the east side was the location of the early
Christian community in Jerusalem (Acts 3.11; 5.12). A low stone
wall divided the surface area of the mount into an inner and
outer courtyard. Inscriptions along the wall – in Latin and Greek
– prohibited foreigners from passing beyond the wall – on pain
of death. Samaritans as well as Gentiles were debarred from the

inner courtyard and the Temple proper. The first courtyard beyond the wall was the court of the women. They could enter this far but no further. Beyond lay the court of Israel, open only to Jewish men, and inside that was another court open only to the priests. Within that court was the altar of sacrifice and, beyond, the sanctuary itself, covered with gold plate. Above its golden doors were golden vines and a great Babylonian tapestry depicting the universe. The sanctuary contained two chambers. The first – decorated with a 'menorah' or seven-branched candle-stick – had a table for shewbread (constantly replenished) and an altar for incense. A thick 'veil' or curtain separated that from the Holy of Holies, empty of all decoration, where the lost Ark of the Covenant would have stood. The space was only occupied by the presence of God's glory – the *shekinah*. Only the High Priest could enter therein, and then only once a year, on the Day of Atonement, to offer sacrifices for the sins of all the people. One unblemished goat was burnt on the altar, another released and sent into the desert, as the 'scapegoat'. Thus, the sins of the people could be 'carried away' and destroyed. In this way the forgiveness of God was made a visible reality.

The priesthood – both permanent and levitical (from the tribe of Levi called up individually on a rota basis) – had their own private quarters, from which led a walkway over the rooftops directly into the Temple. They could not risk defilement by contact with any impurity. This priesthood, along with the ruling aristocracy of the Sadducees, disappeared after AD 70 and lost all influence over the national life at a single stroke. Israel – and the Diaspora Jews – must have felt bereft both of the focus of their worship and cultural life and of leadership and the voice of authority in Jerusalem. In due course, another influential sect from among the people, the Pharisees – the 'separated' – so-called because of their scruples about ritual purity – moved into the vacuum of power created by the destruction of the Temple, to provide new leadership and a new direction for the way of life called Judaism. The Pharisees were essentially a lay movement around 6,000 strong, but included an increasing number of rabbis in their number.

In the Temple, sacrificial offerings had been made twice daily: early in the morning, accompanied by the sound of trumpets; and in mid-afternoon. In Acts 3.1 Peter and John went to pray at the ninth hour. This meant that even as Christians they attended the service of sacrifice and priestly blessing, and did not meet just for prayer. In the Letter to the Hebrews, for example, it is clear that early Jewish Christians understand the high priest's role in offering the sacrifice of atonement, which suggests first-hand experience of the rite (Hebrews 5.1–4). The sacrificial cult had been focused exclusively on the Temple since the days of Josiah the King (in the seventh century BC) and his discovery of the Book of the Law, in all likelihood the book of Deuteronomy. All of this came to an abrupt and traumatic end. There were serious economic consequences. The Temple tax, levied on every male adult Jew, and money from the purchasing of unblemished animals and birds for sacrificial purposes had enabled the Temple and its officials to enjoy a prosperity and prestige which had impressed even the might of Rome and its emperor.

There were even more serious religious consequences. The sacrificial cult had, in the minds of all Jews wherever they lived, related the chosen people to God in a special way. What did it now mean, in the Temple's absence, to be a child of the Covenant? What could take the place of the daily Temple rites by which ordinary people could keep in a right relationship with God and know their sins forgiven and their gratitude recognized? What would happen if the great festivals of Judaism were left uncelebrated, and the Jewish people were no longer linked together as 'one nation' by common religious practices and a common way of life? What would become of the Jewish people if they no longer atoned for their sins and sought God's forgiveness? What would become of the Jewish sense of God's presence and blessing if the glory had departed from the Temple and from the Holy City?

The impact of the events of the Jewish Wars is described by the historian Josephus, but in a manner sympathetic to Rome and to Hellenistic culture. He regarded the siege and sack of Jerusalem as God's judgement upon the people's rebellion, and saw the Roman general (later emperor) Vespasian as an agent of God's will.[5] But for the ordinary Jew, to whom Rome was a pagan and brutal occupying power, the destruction of the Holy City and the desecration and demolition of the Holy Place must have been a very bitter pill to swallow. Better had an earthquake razed the buildings of Jerusalem to the ground and swallowed up the Temple in an abyss. But the invasion of the city by a marauding army and the molestation of holy objects by idolaters with unclean hands must have seemed like violations of everything devout that Jews had held sacred.

The Temple was thus a place where, through sacrificial offerings, individual sins were purged, the people's sin was atoned for and the Covenant between God and the people was maintained intact. In addition, it was also a place where religious teaching and learned discussion took place. The Torah, or guidance of God – the Law, was always a subject for debate and interpretation. It was at no time viewed as a fixed and rigid imposition upon the lives of ordinary people. Rather, it was more like a living, evolving organism. The opening tractate of the *Mishnah* (called *Avoth*) – committed to writing around the second or third century AD but containing earlier traditions – put it this way: 'Moses received the Torah at Sinai and transmitted it to Joshua, Joshua to the elders, and the elders to the prophets, and the prophets to the men of the great synagogue.' So the written Torah comprised the five books of Moses (the Pentateuch), but there was also the tradition of an oral law or, better, interpretation of God's will, which was commented upon, understood in new contexts and applied to different situations, so that the Law as a whole became an open-ended and flexible subject for discussion. Torah was viewed in Jesus' time not so much as a code of rules but as guidance for right behaviour, and that guidance needed new exposition and a return to first principles in every new generation.

Jesus' own teaching, and his gathering of people to himself in the Temple courts was the typical practice of a great rabbi who could impart his own understanding of the principles of Torah. We see this kind of approach reflected in Matthew's presentation of the Sermon on the Mount.

So the removal of the Temple and the city of the great king at one fell swoop took away the two great foundations of Judaism as they existed in Jesus' day. The Temple was the focus of God's very presence among human beings. It also provided from among the priests and ruling Council the leadership of Israel's religious life. It was viewed as the place where worship was properly conducted and the people could join themselves to their God. It was the very focus of God's presence among human beings, the sign of his interest in earthly life and love for his people. It represented a major strand of Israel's hope for the future; for a time was expected when a new king like David – a man after God's own heart – would return and rule in righteousness and establish God's kingdom. He would re-establish the holy city as the place where God could be found and where God's light would shine out to the nations and draw them to Jerusalem.

After the destruction of the Temple and the Holy City two things were lacking: a focus for Jewish religious life, a meeting place and place of pilgrimage for all seeking God; and godly leadership to provide guidance for the people and an example of how to live and worship in the absence of the centrepiece of the nation's faith.

The life of the synagogues

Just as there remained one focus for the religious and cultural life of Judaism – its Holy Scriptures, there also remained one institution where the people could still hear the word of God, where they could read and learn, where they could meet in fellowship and where they could worship. That institution was the synagogue, which existed not only in Palestine itself but also in every Jewish community all over the known world. Sometimes the synagogue was a purpose-built centre, but often was simply a meeting place in a building adapted for the purpose of prayer and instruction.

The origins of the synagogue as the centre of Jewish life and worship are lost in obscurity, although the common legend that they went back to the time of Moses is farfetched. It is possible that the synagogue served a useful role from the time of the Babylonian exile, holding the community together, preserving its faith and its distinctive way of life. After the return from Babylon, as places for meeting for prayer, instruction in Hebrew and the study of Scriptures, the synagogues might well have found their *raison d'être* and so continued in the towns and villages. They performed a function which complemented the role of the Temple, with its festivals and sacrificial rituals. The first certain testimonies to the existence of synagogues come from the third century BC among the dispersed Jewish communities of Egypt. Then in the second century BC a synagogue in Antioch is mentioned. It seems that the synagogues arose first in the Judaism of the Diaspora, and, once conceived, the idea caught on very fast and synagogues became numerous very quickly. Whatever the case, certainly, by the time of Jesus, synagogues were extremely common and their life well developed. There are no less than 56 references to synagogue (*sunagogos* – gathering together) in the New Testament and there were several hundred synagogues in Jerusalem alone at the time of Jesus.

In the Diaspora, every Jewish community had its own synagogue, and often there were more than one. They could be instituted simply along the lines of a neighbourhood, or alternatively serve a particular interest group. Although some of the historical evidence in Acts may be suspect, there is no reason to doubt that when Luke indicates different synagogues serving different groups this was the case. In Acts 6.9 he mentions Cyrenians, Alexandrians, Cilicians and people from Asia as having their own synagogue, known as the synagogue of the Freedmen, serving slaves freed by Rome (or their descendants). It is also quite possible that groups such as people in a particular trade or type of work had their own synagogue, along the lines of the guilds or associations which were very common and popular in the Roman Empire. Isaac Levy[6] mentions the synagogue of the Alexandrians in Jerusalem, the synagogue of the Babylonians in Tiberias, as well as the synagogue of the copper-workers in Jerusalem. This means that Gentiles who travelled a lot could well have been attracted to synagogues not only out of admiration for the Jewish religion but also in order to meet their compatriots, or members of the same guild or trade.

In addition, the synagogues of the Diaspora seem to have been very open to Gentile culture, for in Rome there were synagogues of Augustus, of Agrippa, of Volumnius, of Herod and so on. It became customary among Diaspora Jews to confer traditional Gentile honours, such as a crown or a special seat, and to record these on inscribed *stelae* in the synagogue – or even in the amphitheatre. Sometimes slaves, presumably of wealthy Jews, would be freed, with the proviso that they would be dedicated to the synagogue, would attend its worship and honour it. This paralleled the pagan practice of selling a slave to a temple.

Archaeologists have revealed differences in the structure of synagogues from one period to another. The purpose-built synagogue was a long rectangular building facing Jerusalem, at whose entrance were pitchers of water for the purpose of ritual washing and cleansing prior to entry. In the main room for worship, at first a portable wooden shrine carried the Scripture scrolls; at a later stage this became an alcove built into the wall. In the first century, the Scriptures were probably read from an elevated podium – the *bema* – where scholars and officials were seated facing the people (cf. Matthew 23.2), and the people would be seated on built-in masonry benches, set in two- or three-stepped rows along the walls. Others may have sat on mats or rugs on the floor. Those attending or, better, participating could easily follow the reading and exposition or discussion in the centre and could see the faces of almost all the other members of the congregation. In this way, interaction among worshippers was facilitated, and this can be confirmed in the story about people reacting to Jesus' words in the synagogue in Luke 4 for instance.

This said, in theory the women present were meant to listen and to keep quiet, although such an injunction might have been suggested by rabbis discontented with the noise levels in worship, and blaming the group most easy to criticize; for women were generally not well educated in the synagogue schools – if at all – and were not allowed to be witnesses in the law courts. In addition, for the setting up of a synagogue or for the enactment of a service of worship, the consent of ten male adult Jews was required.

Later basilical synagogues (from the second century AD) rarely had more than one bench along the walls – perhaps indicating more of a classroom arrangement. The head of the synagogue (the *rosh hakeneset* or Greek *archisynagogos*) determined who would read the Torah and the Prophets and spoke a word of interpretation or delivered a sermon. The leader was assisted by a 'servant of the synagogue' who actually ensured the smooth functioning of the services and also chose people to be responsible for the collection of alms and distribution of charity. He also carried out any punishment inflicted on wrongdoers or heretics, up to 39 lashes. In addition, the servant had a most important role, that of schoolmaster in chief, taking responsibility for the education of children. At a later stage, the synagogue school could be a separate building and be a 'house of instruction' not only for children and beginners but also for advanced students and scholars of the law – those training to be rabbis. The possibility of a good education made the synagogue schools attractive to Gentiles. Sometimes the synagogue, or its house of study (*beth ha-midrash*), deliberately sought to serve the educational requirements of all sections of the community at large, and saw their role as the establishing of the principles of Judaism among the Gentiles as well as among its own people.

Priests and rabbis did not hold any special office in the community or the synagogue government, although the lecture of a rabbi was always gratefully heard, and people would gladly invite a priest who lived locally or who was visiting to pronounce a blessing. The Scribes and Pharisees of Jesus' day had an authority of respect, not of office. They could not impose their views, but had to compete with others for the hearts and minds of the people. It was only much later, after the destruction of the Temple, that the pharisaic rabbis exerted greater influence at local level and were eventually able to rule the life and worship of the synagogues.[7]

The reading of Torah and instruction upon it would have been the most important activities of the synagogue, but a typical service would also include prayer, Psalm singing and discussion. The usual liturgy would begin with the Confession of the One God, using three passages of Scripture (Deuteronomy 6.4–9; 11.13–21; and Numbers 15.37–41). Prayer would follow, with the Eighteen Benedictions (much later the twelfth Benediction would exclude 'Nazarenes and heretics'). There were also prayers of praise and petitions. Then readings from Scripture would follow – from the Torah (the five books of Moses) and from the Prophets; then would follow the instruction (an exposition of the Scripture passage later called *midrash*). The service would end with a formal blessing.

There were various other activities undertaken in the synagogue day by day. First, there were regular community meals; and many synagogues had a separate eating area or dining room. There was the collection and keeping of communal funds, particularly used for almsgiving and for helping those in need. There was general education – and not only in the learning of Sacred Scripture, but also often in the reading and writing of Hebrew, basic mathematics, astronomy, literature and philosophy. Then the synagogue also served as a communal law court. It is not an exaggeration when Jesus refers to corporal punishment – 'beatings' – in the synagogues (Mark 13.9; Matthew 10.17); for punishments as well as sentencing could be carried out in the synagogues. There would be meetings of the General Assembly of the synagogue when policy decisions would be taken. And then the synagogue could also be used as a place of hospitality and as a lodging for travellers and visiting teachers. One of the most remarkable features of the synagogue system was the way in which the whole Jewish 'nation' was linked together and connected via a network of relationships, visits and other means of communication.

Clearly, the synagogue was used during the week as well as on the Sabbath, and could boast many functions other than worship. It was a community hall, a friendly society, a guest house, a council chamber and a school or even an academy. In short, it was a true community centre. In many cases this meant an open centre for the use of Gentiles as well as Jews. Almsgiving could include proselytes and even 'outsiders' like Gentile widows, or orphans in need. Works of charity gave the Jewish faith a human face and a practical outreach or mission.

This rather long explanation of synagogue life is actually relevant – even in its detail – to the life and customs of the early Christian Church. The practices of the synagogue were not lost on the earliest Christian Church. First of all, the worship had a similar format in many respects, including prayers (adoration, thanksgiving, confession, petition); Scripture readings from the Greek Septuagint (and in the course of time readings from Gospels and letters); the sermon or teaching; and the blessing. Jewish baptism and rites of cleansing also had their counterpart in Christian baptism (with important differences, of course – see Chapter 6), and the communal meal after the service could well have influenced the form of the 'agape' meal. The commemoration of the Lord's Supper, or the Eucharist, was something quite different and new, and we will return to the transformation from synagogue to church in Chapter 6. The collection for almsgiving also has its counterpart in the Early Church. The collection of funds crops up in Paul's exhortations to the congregation at Corinth to take up a relief collection for the victims of famine in Jerusalem (1 Corinthians 16.1–4).

The churches also developed as centres of education and learning – the Johannine community is often considered to be a kind of 'school', as described in Oscar Cullman's *The Johannine Circle* (1976); and the great churches of Antioch and Alexandria were soon rivalling one another with their schools of philosophical theology.

The churches, like the synagogues, had their communal leadership (although practices varied considerably at first), and were able to convene 'councils' in order to take decisions. Barnabas and Paul were sent to Antioch at the behest of a group decision in the Jerusalem church (Acts 11.22–6). The churches also took on a role in pastoral discipline of members and acted as law courts in given situations (see Matthew 5.25–6).

Finally, the churches were held together in a regional and a

universal network – through visits from apostles and teachers
(bringing letters of commendations with them); through letters
and sermons and other forms of communication, and through
acceptance of the Jerusalem leadership (and later the leadership
in Rome). Just as the Jewish Diaspora still saw itself as 'one
nation', despite considerable regional variations, so individual
churches or regional groupings regarded themselves as part of
the Church Universal. A good deal of Paul's letter writing has the
aim of holding together in unity fellowship not only in his own
churches but also in the Christian Church as a whole.

It is quite feasible that the Gospels – although written within a
particular Christian community or regional grouping – were
intended to be circulated, read and used among all the other
churches of the Christian 'Diaspora'. In other words, they were
written for all Christians.[8] Thus, the concept of a new 'People
of God' or of a new 'Israel' was directly borrowed from the
Jewish concept of a 'Holy Nation' spread all over the world, but
connected together with spiritual (and, to a lesser extent, racial)
bonds.

The Jewish nation in the Roman Empire

Not only were the Jews tolerated in commercial and political life
– even though viewed with suspicion in some quarters – but also
the Jewish religion enjoyed a privileged status throughout the
Empire. From the time of Julius Caesar, Jews were allowed to
worship freely and to practise their traditional customs, such as
keeping the Sabbath free from work, refraining from eating pork
and other unclean foods, and requiring those of Jewish race and
Gentile proselytes to submit to circumcision. Such matters of
religious observance gave the Jews a visible difference, separat-
ing them from other peoples; but in social life and in the world of
work, Jews were able to mix freely and they were indeed active
in most professions and trades.

The early Christian mission could take advantage of the
widespread infiltration of Judaism into all major cities, and could
easily be regarded as a Jewish splinter group or sect; but when in

the end Christians became 'persona non grata' in the eyes of the local synagogue authorities then the Christian position became exposed and precarious and Christians were sporadically subjected to persecution. In an atmosphere of competition it must have been tempting for certain Jewish leaders to 'betray' fellow Jews as Christians. Nevertheless, the Christian mission throughout the first century mainly concentrated not on outreach to Gentiles in Roman society at large but on 'inreach', that is, on winning the hearts and minds of Jewish compatriots and of Gentiles attached to the synagogue, most notably those married to Jews as well as proselytes and the more loosely affiliated 'God-fearers'. Not only did the earliest Christians see themselves as Jews for whom the Messiah had come, or as a Jewish reform movement, but also they cherished the hope that the whole 'nation' of the Jewish dispersion would come to accept Jesus as the Christ and that a renewed 'messianic Judaism' would then become a light to the Gentiles, drawing all peoples into the heart of the life of 'Israel'.

The traditional and older theory that Christian mission was first and foremost outreach to the Gentiles is expressed starkly by Richard De Ridder in the following terms: 'Centuries ago an unrecorded step was taken by some unknown "follower of the Way" across the national boundaries of Israel into the vast Gentile world.'[9] However, the truth is far more complex, and the stages of the Gentile mission were much more gradual than envisaged by De Ridder. The first tentative steps in the direction of the Gentiles were really taken from within the very heart of Judaism, in the synagogues, and from within Israel itself.

Even though the majority of the Jews of the Hellenistic synagogues were more open to new teachings than their compatriots in Palestine, they still tended to resist the Jewish Christian preaching – or, at least, some aspects of it; but the Gentile proselytes and God-fearers attached to the synagogues proved to be more curious and interested and were won over in significant numbers, thus in the longer term forming the nucleus of a Christian movement with a new identity of its own. But that development was the result of a gradual process, a very gradual one in some places.

The early Jewish Christian mission could easily be regarded from within the synagogues as a reform movement because Judaism was not a monolithic or uniform religion in the mid-first century. As Alan Le Grys writes, 'Judaism in the first half of the first century was full of energy and diversity, as well as dissent.'[10] In Jesus' lifetime, the canon of the Hebrew Bible had not yet reached a fixed form. In fact, certain later writings could well be regarded as subversive attacks on earlier passages of Scripture. For example, the book of Jonah takes it upon itself to attack the commonplace notion of the period leading up to Christ's lifetime, that Gentile nations had no respect for God, and no will to repent or to live a godly life. For most Jews, mission to the Gentiles was a waste of time; only God could one day bring about the knowledge of himself among the Gentiles. But the author of Jonah, while portraying the eponymous hero as a reluctant missionary, shows how Nineveh could hear the word of God and repent of her wicked ways. The book of Ruth can similarly be understood as an attack on Ezra's earlier purity laws forbidding Jewish intermarriage with Gentiles.

So while this fluid situation with regard to the canon of Scripture prevailed, different groups – apocalyptic and wisdom schools, Pharisees, Sadducees, Essenes, Herodians and Zealots – any of these could promote their own brand of Jewish theology. The question inevitably arose later among the rabbis, had God pronounced his final word? Did the Scriptures contain everything necessary to live by God's Law and find salvation, or was there more to come? Had the final word on the interpretation of the Law been pronounced? Or perhaps it was a feasible undertaking to collate the oral Torah and traditions of the elders so that such an interpretation could be produced. The Sadducees believed that all of God's binding Word was contained in the Five Books of Moses. The Pharisees believed that other books could profitably be added to Torah in order to understand God's will, and they also held that the *oral* law must be used to interpret the *written* Torah. The Essenes at Qumran were busy writing down the works of their 'Teacher of Righteousness' alongside other traditional 'Scriptures'.

Another great area of disagreement lay in attitudes to the Temple cultus in Jerusalem. In the first century the Herodians (political collaborators) and the Sadducees (the Temple priesthood) had a vested interest in maintaining the power and prestige of the Temple. In all probability, most Jews did look to the Temple as their spiritual home, and to its festivals as great opportunities for pilgrimage and occasions for celebration of their religion and their unity in the one God.

Yet the Temple cultus was corrupt in the eyes of many. It was compromised through its love of political power and its closeness to the Roman authorities. Perhaps one day a pure and worthy High Priest would come like a new broom or like a refiner's fire to purge the Temple and to burn the dross away. Such a vision is reflected philosophically in the works of Philo, or from a Christian standpoint in the Letter to the Hebrews. The cultus was also seen as corrupt in that it penalized the poor and created obstacles for certain groups who wished to worship in the 'House of God'. Jesus himself said that the Temple should be a 'house of prayer for all the nations' (Mark 11.17). The buying and selling of sacrificial animals was controlled by the Temple police. The lambs, goats, pigeons or doves brought along by ordinary people were deemed unacceptable. Truly unblemished animals were only available in the outer court of the Temple, and must be purchased with Tyrian coinage. Then there was a small matter of rates of exchange and commission, as well as the problem of a monopoly on the sale of sacrificial animals.

Yet another obstacle ran along social and sexual lines: the Gentiles present could only advance as far as the outer court, and could by no means enter the inner court – on pain of death! Women could enter the inner court, but only gather on the eastern side. Men only therefore could fully participate in the Temple cultus, by entering in to worship or pray. As for the Holy of Holies, only one man – the High Priest – could enter therein, and then only once a year, on the Day of Atonement.

All of this system smacked – to some – of privilege and party spirit. Supposing the Chief Priest was corrupt? Could another priest – or a teacher of righteousness – object to his sinful ways?

Mission in the Gospels

When this apparently happened, it was the teacher who was sent into exile, not the priesthood which was reformed. The teacher of righteousness then gathered his supporters around him and formed a community called Essenes who were a thorn in the side of the establishment, roundly condemning the whole Temple cultus as it existed and hoping for its destruction.

In addition to the Essenes, many Hellenist Jews of the Diaspora – people like Stephen in Acts – also found the Temple cultus objectionable. What was its function? Why should every Jew in every land pay a tax to the Temple? Where did the money go? Could not the synagogues maintain the worship of God and observance of the Law? Why should the High Priest always come from the ranks of the Sadducees? – they did not even believe in resurrection or eternal life. Why was only the High Priest allowed into the presence of God?

But the most crushing objection came from an Old Testament precedent: did God really need to live in a palace, a house made by the hands of men? (See Acts 7.48–50). Did he not prefer to live among his people? – going wherever they went, his presence always accompanying them, as in the days of the patriarchs, when God's glory, the *shekinah*, dwelt in a moveable tent like the tents the people lived in whilst crossing the wilderness. And have not the priests always been at loggerheads with the prophets, persecuting them and refusing to listen?

So the arguments ran, and they raged at the time of Jesus, setting up a potentially divisive rift between the Judaism of the Jerusalem priesthood and various other groups of Jewish believers either antagonistic towards the Sadducees (like Pharisaism), or suspicious of aspects of the Temple cultus (e.g. the Greek-speaking Jews or 'Hellenists'), or downright hostile to the priesthood and all it stood for (e.g. the Essenes and followers of John the Baptist).

The New Testament reflects aspects of this heated debate of the early to mid first century. And of course Jesus himself is portrayed as having little time for the malpractices of the Temple. He has little sympathy with those admiring the wonderful buildings of King Herod and ominously remarks, 'Do you see these great buildings? Not one stone will be left here upon another; all will be thrown down' (Mark 13.2). While visiting the Temple, he grew angry at the confusion and changing of money and selling of sacrificial animals and overturned some of the merchants' tables (Mark 11.15–18 and par. John 2.13–21). This acted parable was also intended to predict the destruction of the Temple. Even Jesus' comments about the widow's mite (Mark 12.41–4) could well, in the original situation, have reflected his anger that a poor person was expected to give to the Temple all she had to live on (Mark 12.41–4). This all leaves us in no doubt that Jesus himself not only had reservations about the Temple cultus, but believed that it was under God's judgement, because of its corrupt practices and its greedy priesthood.

Thus, all of the preceding themes constituted subjects for debate. What could be considered a scriptural theology? Which books should be part of the canon of Scripture? What was the place of the Temple cultus in Israel's religion? These momentous topics were discussed and dissected from a great variety of viewpoints and from the partisan viewpoint of different groups and sects; yet all remained under the umbrella of Second Temple Judaism. Diversity and dissent were not only permitted in Jesus' lifetime, they were the order of the day!

Judaism reformed and reformulated

It was only after the destruction of the Temple and of Jerusalem at the end of the Jewish rebellion of AD 66–70 that Judaism itself began to undergo a complete revision and reformulation. The crisis in Palestine proved to be not a moment of catastrophe for many, as can well be imagined, but a time of opportunity for some. The Pharisaic rabbis, who held a position of respect and influence in Jesus' time, but by no means a position of power or domination in Jewish religious life, were able to seize the moment. The hitherto rather obscure figure of Rabbi Johanan ben Zakkai came to the fore as a new leader of the Jewish community.

Rabbi Johanan was, in John Muddiman's words, 'in some ways Judaism's equivalent of Paul'.[11] Yet although he was a near contemporary of Paul, Johanan did not emerge as an authority figure until the 70s. He was a pupil of Hillel, a liberal-minded rabbi with an aversion to the ways of violence. From about AD 20–40 Johanan lived in semi-retirement in Galilee, supporting a wife and child, and training just one pupil, Haninah ben Dosa (who was also to make his name later). Johanan made little impression in Galilee, and thought it an area too given to sudden enthusiasms rather than considered views and dedicated observance of Torah. He returned to Jerusalem and became a leading critic of the corruption and venality of the Temple establishment – which was where true power and influence lay at the time. He then succeeded Gamaliel I as joint leader of Hillel's school after the master's death.

The Talmud (*Gittin* 56a.b) recounts that Johanan became aware that Jerusalem would fall to the Roman armies. On the advice of his nephew, he pretended to be ill, and then to have died! Two of his disciples carried him out of Jerusalem as a corpse. But once outside the city, Johanan went to meet Vespasian and hailed him as king. This did not at first please the Roman general, who saw such flattery as a slight on the majesty of Caesar. But when the Emperor died soon afterwards and the troops acclaimed Vespasian as their choice to replace him, the new emperor was then inclined to regard Johanan as a prophet! He called him back and promised to grant him a request. Johanan asked for land in Yavneh (Jamnia) near Jerusalem, for a company of wise men (including the family of Gamaliel) and for physicians to heal the sick rabbi Zadok. Thus the seeds were sown for the Academy at Yavneh where the repair and re-ordering of Jewish religious life could begin.

Rabbi Johanan is also said to have looked on the site of the demolished Temple one day (*Mishnah–Avoth* 1.2) and to have declared that the atonement once made through the sacrificial cult was still available through deeds of faithful love. He quoted Hosea 6.6: 'I desire steadfast love not sacrifice'. Johanan set about building a new foundation for Jewish religious life and practice on the basis of this conviction: that the doing of God's will and the seeking of God's guidance – found in the Torah and taught in the synagogues – could effectively replace the Temple cultus and the sacrificial system.

Yavneh was soon to become the centre and headquarters for the reorganization and restoration of Judaism after the obliteration of the Temple. The party of the Pharisees – until then influential but without real power – now saw a golden opportunity to reinforce observance of the Torah and to reinvent Judaism as a more narrowly defined and less tolerant orthodoxy, whose doctrine and legal interpretation would be in their own hands. But to reinforce their authority they in turn leaned upon the authority and precedent of earlier rabbis and ultimately of the 'oral Torah', which purportedly went back to the time of Moses. The rabbis of Javneh thus embarked upon the massive and marathon task of codifying the law and applying it to every aspect of everyday life.

Their main method of interpretation was called *halakhah* (literally, 'walking') and was intended to show people how to behave (or 'walk') in such a way as to keep Torah and to please God. Another parallel method of interpretation used was called *haggadah* (teaching) and elaborated on the scriptural texts by the use of dreams, stories, poetry and sermons devised to illustrate the principles of life discernible in God's Word.

Through the immense efforts and considerable achievements of Rabbi Johanan's Academy at Yavneh, Judaism became a religion of the Book and, more particularly, of the Law. The Academy, quoting again the words of John Muddiman, 'synthesised scribal teaching into a common stream of tradition and bridged the gap between Palestine and the Diaspora'.[12] Effectively, the rabbis now viewed the whole Jewish people as the Diaspora, for Palestine was effectively in the same position as the rest of the Jewish 'nation' – without access to Temple festivals and sacrifices and without the guidance of a Temple priesthood.

Information about the reform of Judaism after AD 70 could appear to be a long digression in a book about the early Christian mission. Yet it is necessary to understand this historical background because it directly relates to Jewish–Christian relations from the 70s onwards and it also resulted in the changing of Judaism from a broad and diverse collection of groupings and viewpoints into a much more narrowly defined and single orthodoxy. The variety of permitted views within Judaism in the mid-first century included groupings as diverse as the Christian churches, the political collaborators called Herodians, the *sicarii* (daggermen!) from among the zealots, the writers of apocalyptic literature, the followers of John the Baptist, Hellenistic philosophers like Philo of Alexandria, Roman sympathizers like the historian Josephus, writers of Wisdom literature, and so on, through a bewildering range of interest groups, political and religious parties – all holding to what seemed to them the essential faith of Judaism. But as rabbinic Judaism gradually came into its own, and as the Pharisees gradually took over the central authority previously in the hands of the Temple establishment – as this transformation gradually took place – so the variety of permitted views within Judaism was substantially narrowed and deviations from such views were not tolerated. In this way, some brands of Judaism, including Jewish Christian messianism, were rigorously excluded, wherever Pharisaic rabbis could control the life of the synagogue. Thus, from Javneh, the curse was pronounced in the liturgy of the synagogue against the 'Nazarenes and heretics', so that any remaining Jewish Christians in the synagogue could be identified and rooted out. This anathema – ironically inserted among the Twelve Benedictions – became known as the *Birkat ha-minim* and at different times and in different places caused the expulsion of Christians from the synagogues.

This new situation appears to be reflected in at least two of the Gospel communities. In Matthew's Gospel we read about a situation of violent conflict between synagogue authorities and Christian missionaries. Jesus sends out 12 disciples on mission throughout Israel. He issues a word of warning about persecution from Jewish authorities. Although this saying is attributed to Jesus, it is most probably relevant at a much later date, in the AD 80s or 90s when the Gospel was completed:

> Beware of them, for they will hand you over to councils and flog you in their synagogues; and you will be dragged before governors and kings because of me, as a testimony to them and to the Gentiles. (Matthew 10.17–18)

The import of this saying as prophecy is far more relevant to a much later situation, when there is hostility between Matthew's church (or churches) and the nearby Jewish synagogues, with whom relations had deteriorated and who now had express orders to exclude any proselytizing Jewish Christians. The references to governors and kings and to Gentiles as well as the references to a prescriptive synagogue leadership reflect a situation which has evolved and highlights Jewish–Christian relations in the Syria of the 80s and 90s.

In John's Gospel the expulsion order is even more explicit:

> They will put you out of the synagogues. Indeed, an hour is coming when those who kill you will think that by doing so they are offering worship to God. (16.2)

Again the prophetic tone is intended to strike a chord in the later experience of the Johannine churches, when the synagogues are coming under the control of a group intent on ruling Jewish Christianity out of court and on winning general favour for their own version of Jewish orthodoxy.

Even though relations between the synagogue authorities and the Johannine and Matthean Christian churches must have become seriously aggravated by the time of the publication of the Gospels, it does need to be said that the very hostile tone of the rabbinical curse and the subsequent expulsion of Jewish Christians could only have taken place in a context where there was a great deal of Christian–Jewish interaction. Right up until the AD 80s or 90s it does seem clear that Christians were actively proselytizing within the synagogues and within the Jewish communities, and this is why the reaction was so fierce. At the same time, if such proselytizing did occur, there must have been openness to the Christian message and a good deal of tolerance in many places well beyond the middle years of the first century.

Indeed, recent studies of the development of rabbinic Judaism after the destruction of the Temple go to show that the Pharisaic rabbis only very slowly and gradually gained influence and power both within Palestine and in the synagogues of the Diaspora. This process could in fact have taken several centuries. The loss of much of the national leadership in Jerusalem in AD 70 must certainly have led to new manoeuvrings for political and religious power. But local authority – even more than previously – by and large remained in the hands of village elders, local priests, wealthy families and landlords, as well as the scribes and rabbis, only a proportion of whom were Pharisees – and most of those lived in and around Palestine. So, the synagogues continued to be governed by local community leaders.[13] No early evidence points to rabbinical control – let alone Pharisaic control – over synagogues. If rabbis happened to live in a town or city, they may well have had influence or held a position of leadership in a synagogue, but they certainly did not control the life, practice or doctrine of the synagogue community before the third or fourth century.

Gentile mission: proselytes and God-fearers

The Gentiles associated with the synagogues were not sharply divided into those who accepted and those who rejected the 'true faith'. The 'God-fearers' or sympathizers – like the centurion Cornelius, 'a devout man who feared God' (Acts 10.2) were not circumcised, did not fully submit to the demands of the Law and did not undergo baptism. Yet they attended synagogue worship and were involved in the life of the synagogue. Occasionally, this involvement engendered great acts of generosity, such as the building of the synagogue at Capernaum by one who 'loves our people' (Luke 7.5). Because of such acts and because of this attitude of goodwill, God-fearers were highly respected in the Jewish community. Thus, God-fearers were believers in the one God, they celebrated and kept the Sabbath and they abstained from eating pork.

As to proselytes, they went that step further to become like Jews in every respect, although it is not clear whether in the first century all male proselytes were obliged to undergo circumcision. They became incorporated fully into the Jewish community. Tomb inscriptions in Rome give conclusive evidence of the complete integration of proselytes – for example, seven epitaphs mention two male and five female proselyte burials in the Jewish catacombs. Such a commitment could involve a high degree of sacrifice, for proselytes could face social ostracism or family rejection.

Circumcision could be an issue, and certainly was a stumbling block for many Gentiles. It was not, of course, a difficulty for women, and there were certainly more women proselytes than men in the synagogues of the Diaspora. Josephus writes, with customary exaggeration, that almost the entire female population of Damascus had joined the synagogue. He also mentions Nero's consort Poppaea Sabina as being a God-fearer.[14]

Often the ritual laws were regarded as necessary for those of Jewish race, whereas God had made incumbent upon Gentiles only the moral and spiritual directives of Judaism. Rabbis could speak of the covenant of Noah which had laid obligations on the whole human race. Obedience to this covenant could render a Gentile 'pious' and deserving of a part in the kingdom of heaven. Later, rabbis (in the *Talmud*) would argue that there were some 30 commands and 6 prohibitions applicable to all the nations. These prohibitions were idolatry, blasphemy, murder, sexual immorality, robbery and eating a live or maimed animal. And of course, these were the very sins the Gentiles were often accused of! If there were indeed reckoned to be two covenants – one for Gentiles and another (the covenant of Moses) for Jews, then it is quite understandable that the God-fearers did not feel pressurized into or criticized for holding back from full conversion. They were generally received gladly and accepted as they were.

In the light of this, it is also quite understandable how Paul who, like the rabbis, regarded Gentile sins with grave distaste, nevertheless was able to encourage Gentiles into the churches without worrying unduly about circumcision or close adherence to the ceremonial Law. Paul, though, does not revert to the covenant with Noah, but, ironically, to that with Abraham, the father of the Jewish nation, and yet regarded (by Paul and others) as the one through whom all the nations would be blessed. (Genesis 12.1–3). In addition, Luke, in Acts 15, portrays the Church Council at Jerusalem (*c.*AD 49) as laying down regulations for the Gentiles, drawing on the rules for foreigners living in Israel, as specified in Leviticus 17 and 18.

The fact that synagogue worship was free of cultic practices like sacrificial offerings, and was communicated through understandable words, prayers and songs must also have helped to attract Gentile sympathizers.

At a later stage, some Rabbis attempted to classify Gentiles into categories, but in Jesus' time the practice in the Diaspora synagogues was to accept Gentiles on an ad hoc basis, even while maintaining a rather hard-nosed and hostile attitude to the Gentile world as a whole (cf. Paul's attitude in Romans 1.18–32).

It is worth noting that there were also degrees of commitment within the Jewish community itself. The synagogue had different groups and factions in competition with one other. Some wanted everybody to learn Hebrew, the language of the Scriptures; some exhorted everyone to make regular (annual) pilgrimages to Jerusalem and to the Temple; but some disdained the Temple cultus altogether. Some agreed with the conservative Shammai, counselling strict observance of the Law and separation from 'unclean' Gentiles; others sided with liberal Hillel and preferred good relations with Gentiles, wishing to make Judaism attractive to 'outsiders'.

Just as some Jews regarded Gentiles as 'unclean' and their religions as 'idolatry' and viewed Gentile culture as 'immorality', so Gentiles also varied greatly in their attitude to the Jews. Some regarded them as anti-social, anti-Roman and subversive: such attitudes can be seen, for example, in the writings of Tacitus and Juvenal. Others regarded Jewish religion as spiritual and the worship of one single creator God as attractive. Almsgiving and the evidence of a devoted life would also have helped to give others a good impression of Judaism. The Jews of the Diaspora were in fact able to exploit the sympathy and favour with which many Gentiles viewed them, and tried to draw such people from the outside to the inside. This practice was also a model for certain early Christian communities. Where this happened, a rather passive form of mission prevailed; while elsewhere, other Christian communities saw their task as actively to reach out, first via the local synagogue, then via lecture halls and public arenas. As is clear from both Acts and Paul's Letters, the Pauline churches in particular conceived of mission as an outgoing exercise, from the inside of the community of faith to the outside world.

The Jewish approach, especially of the Diaspora synagogues, fits a model derived from the Old Testament. Israel was to be a priestly nation, a light to the Gentiles. The second section of Isaiah exemplifies this approach (see e.g. Isaiah 42.1–7 or 49.1–6). The nations would come to see Israel's God as the one true God of the entire world and would – in God's time – be drawn to God's people. The presence of God would be sensed most powerfully in the Holy Land, and more especially in Jerusalem, the Holy City, and in the Temple, with its Holy of Holies . . . This schema can be demonstrated in diagram form, as in Figure 1.1.

This all means that the nations would flock to Mount Zion (Israel) as to a beacon of light and would come to know the true God and would do homage to him. His people would of course be honoured as that holy nation, the nation of priests, who had borne witness to the truth all along. The dynamic of this model is from the outside (the world) to the inside (the promised land).

That model can be compared with another, also represented by a series of concentric circles. This is more like the Lucan conception of mission. Beginning from the Temple in Jerusalem, the mission moves outwards through Judea and Samaria into the cities of the Diaspora and from there 'to the ends of the earth' (Acts 1.8). The communities of the Diaspora come into the picture as Peter proclaims the gospel in Acts 2.5 and following. Luke shows how every community around the Mediterranean

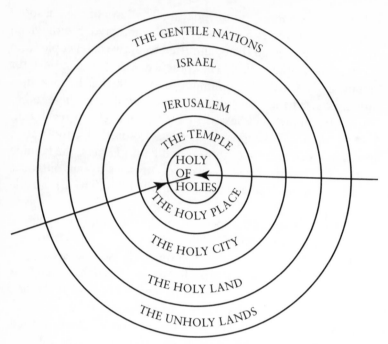

Figure 1.1

is represented, from Libya and Egypt through to Syria,
Mesopotamia and across into Galatia, Phrygia and Greece as far
as Italy, finishing up at the heart of the known world, or the
Empire, in Rome itself. The schema is represented in Figure 1.2.

When the question has been asked, was there a *Jewish* mission
in the first century? – it has sometimes resulted in a debate over
the definition of 'mission'. There are those who regard 'mission'
as the attracting of converts and adherents through *a ministry of
presence*. But there are others who understand the term 'mission'
only in a more active sense; as a conscious, organized effort to go
out and convert through evangelism or proselytizing. Regarding
the Jewish mission of the first century, an older school of thought
represented by the likes of Adolf Harnack and Joachim Jeremias[15]
tends to affirm that there certainly was a Jewish mission, for
the synagogue communities drew Gentiles into the life of faith.
A more recent school of thought, represented by such as S.

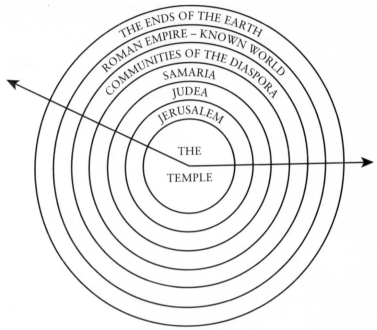

THE ENDS OF THE EARTH
ROMAN EMPIRE – KNOWN WORLD
COMMUNITIES OF THE DIASPORA
SAMARIA
JUDEA
JERUSALEM
THE
TEMPLE

Figure 1.2

McKnight, M. Goodman and I. Levinskaya,[16] understands mission in exclusively active modes, essentially as outreach. They would deny that there was any real evidence of a Jewish mission to the Gentile world in the first century.

The problem is that this is not so much a difference between 'active' and 'passive' modes of mission: it is the difference between two alternative theologies of mission. In the one case, God initiates mission by revealing himself from Zion to all the nations in an eschatological event, which leads to a process of ingathering. All people of goodwill are drawn to 'Israel' or to the people of God to experience for themselves the glory of God and his presence among his people. In the other case, the Lucan model, God sends his Son Jesus out on a mission to the world (John 3.16) and thus, wherever God's people go, Jesus is with them. They become witnesses wherever they go, for they themselves are bearers of Christ ('Christians') or 'Temples of the Holy

Spirit'. So then others are drawn to the people of God wherever God's people may be. These two alternative theologies of mission are a little like the difference between the static grandeur of the Temple, which cannot move but which draws people to itself, and, in contrast, the moving tabernacle of the presence, which leads God's people out and guides them and is able to be with them wherever they go.

Christian mission in the time of the Gospels

Assuming that the Gospels were published between about AD 65 and 95, the period of mission that they reflect in the life of the Christian Church is the period that follows on from the endeavours of the apostle Paul and the events described in the Acts of the Apostles. The Christian Church in Palestine did not participate in the armed struggle against Rome – a period of strife which lasted from AD 66 to 73. This most likely distinguished it from mainstream Judaism and made it a focus for persecution. The Gospel of Mark was almost certainly the first written and was composed during or at the end of this period. With the demise of the Temple and its cultus, not only were the ruling Council of the Sanhedrin and the aristocratic sect of the Sadducees destroyed, but also fringe groups based in Palestine, such as the Essenes, were either scattered or re-formed elsewhere. In time, the pharisaic rabbis were able to rule out of court other brands and branches of Judaism, and the diversity of the mid-first century gave way to a more monolithic faith. This time of transition and upheaval, both in the political and religious realm must also have been a time when Christian mission to the Gentiles was becoming the order of the day in many places, the time when Gentiles were becoming a sizeable proportion, if not a majority, in most Christian churches.

In Jerusalem, the birthplace of the Church, a Jewish form of Christianity, or a messianic form of Judaism, continued in dialogue with the synagogue and in relationship with the Temple, right up until the early 60s. James the Just, the 'brother of the Lord' was honoured as leader of the Jerusalem congregation, but around AD 62 was put to death at the hands of a Jewish mob, as described in Josephus' *Jewish Wars*.[17] Shortly afterwards, conflict broke out between Jews and Romans. The Jerusalem Church, like most of the Christian Church around the Empire, did not side with the Jewish cause, and the congregation most probably decamped to Pella not far away; but effectively it was a spent force, and no great personality arose in the aftermath of war to rival the Rabbis Johanan, Gamaliel II and Akiba, all of whom either established or consolidated the Pharisaic rabbis' claim to guide the Jewish people and reformulate the Jewish faith. Bishops of Jerusalem came and went, but they made little impression on the church as a whole.

Consequently, between 70 and the end of the first century, Christianity became a religion largely based on the geography and organization of the synagogues of the Diaspora, except with this great change: that there were eventually a greater number of Gentiles than Jews in the membership of Christ's Church and, even where Gentiles were in a minority, it was an ever growing minority, and caused considerable strains and tensions within a once homogeneous community. From its position as a kind of rival synagogue in many towns and cities of the Diaspora, the Church began to establish its own independent identity and to reach out into the large centres of population, both Jewish and Gentile, and from there gradually to have a greater and greater influence on the regions and the Greco-Roman world. Conversely, that same world was beginning to have an increasing influence on the life and thought of the Church, although throughout the first century the Jewish influence – both of the Scriptures and religious life of Judaism – still had by far the most fundamental impact on the Church's life and thought. As W. H. C. Frend insists, in *The Rise of Christianity*, 'The life, thought and organisation of the church can be understood only within the framework of Hellenistic Judaism.'[18]

Even at this stage, Jewish–Christian relations were close, though increasingly hostile by and large. Paul speaks of the Judaizers visiting and campaigning in his churches (e.g. Galatians 1.6–9) – and such a situation continued for a long time. Counter-

attacks by orthodox Jews and the pro-Jewish faction within the
Church left their mark on the late books of the New Testament
and on some of the sub-apostolic texts. Right up until the second
century, Jews and Christians were *rivals for proselytes* in the
Jewish and Gentile world (e.g see 2 Peter 2.1–3; 1 Timothy
1.3–7). The later New Testament letters still adopt Jewish
literary styles and forms: the letter to James (*c.*AD 80?) is so
Jewish it has been considered to be something adapted and
adopted by the Church from Judaism; although such an idea
in the late first-century context seems far fetched. The letter
addresses 'the twelve tribes (which are) in the Diaspora' and
proceeds to impart pastoral advice in a manner which any
synagogue would recognize and accept without demur. In 1 Peter
the letter is addressed to 'the exiles of the diaspora in Pontus,
Galatia, Cappadocia, Asia and Bithynia', for all the world as
though written to communities of the *Jewish* Diaspora.

Even the devotional practice of church members still resembled
those of the synagogue: Christians prayed three times a day and
fasted twice a week like the Jews; except that the fast days
were moved to Wednesday and Friday (instead of Monday and
Thursday), to commemorate Christ's arrest and crucifixion. The
Sabbath was still fairly widely observed by Christians of the first
century[19] – although Sunday became increasingly important as
the day for worship of the risen Lord – marking, as it did, the day
of resurrection. In the long run, and in the predominantly Gentile
churches, Sunday later came to replace the Jewish Sabbath
altogether.

Christians at the end of the first century still professed one God
and one only; they read and used the Jewish Scriptures as their
authority and guide to the will of God and as pointing to
fulfilment in Christ; they took into their system the thought
forms of Jewish eschatology (including angelology), the idea of
Messianism and Jewish ethical theory and practice (apart from
the ceremonial food and purity laws). Even so, some things were
being transformed, and we will come to that later. But, like the
Jews, Christians claimed to be the holy ones of God, or 'saints'
(*hagioi*), the people of God (e.g. Hebrews 4.9), a 'royal priest-

hood and a holy nation' (1 Peter 2.9). Matthew still regarded the Christian community as 'Israel' and Luke sees them as 'Israel' or 'the new Israel' (see pp. 37–9, 102–5).

Even the interpretation of the Bible followed along the lines of Jewish methodology: allegory, midrashic commentary, *pesher* (applying prophecy etc. to specific contemporary situations); and *haggadic* or *halakhic* forms of interpretation (e.g. Hebrews 11) – all of these are found frequently in the New Testament. Of course, the application of scriptural passages had a very different goal from Jewish interpretation, but the methods were similar. For example, Paul demonstrates in a midrashic passage how Abraham – like all Christians – is justified through his faith (Galatians 4.21—5.1) and Matthew – in *pesher* style – often highlights passages which are held to be prophecies of Christ's coming (e.g. 1.23; 2.6; 4.15–16).

As has been indicated, there were changes and transformations as the churches modelled on the synagogues made the transition to becoming independent Christian churches, and working out all the implications of their new dispensation. Yet it is still true to say that throughout the first century, all Christianity was heavily influenced by Jewish thought and life. Even in the second century, Jews and Christians were still debating and arguing with one another, as evidenced by Ignatius: 'If anyone interpret Judaism to you, do not listen to him, for it is better to hear Christianity from the circumcised than Judaism from the uncircumcised' (*Philadelphians* 6.1). The focus changed in the second century, however, and most Jewish–Christian disputes were over prophecy – whether the Messiahship of Jesus could be proved or not.

It was only in the course of the second century that Christians saw themselves less as 'Israel' and distanced themselves from rabbinical Judaism and set Christianity up in contradistinction to it. The Church then preferred the epithet 'universal' or 'catholic', which seemed to be a deliberate contrast with a more introverted and inward-looking Judaism. In doing this, the Church clearly and openly embraced that mission to the nations which they then argued that Judaism had failed to fulfil – forgetting of course that it was first through the Diaspora synagogues that Gentiles had started to turn to Christianity.

In the course of time, a very distorted picture began to emerge; that of a Judaism which had betrayed its calling and had set itself against Christ and had deliberately decided to persecute Christians. Such ideas are present, for instance, in the writings of Ignatius. But as I have attempted to show in this chapter, such a picture is a travesty of the truth. Deplorably, however, it has been an enduring image – the older brother resentfully setting his face against the younger brother – and it has unfortunately had wide currency in Christian thinking in the centuries ever since.

2

Matthew's Gospel – making disciples

A Jewish gospel?

Matthew's Gospel has traditionally been regarded as the most Jewish of the Gospels – with some justification. In Matthew, Jesus insists that his mission is 'only to the lost sheep of the house of Israel' (15.24), and he apparently never seeks out any Gentiles, nor does he encourage his disciples to embark upon a Gentile mission during his lifetime. In addition, the disciples are sent out with a specific injunction to 'Go nowhere among the Gentiles, and enter no town of the Samaritans.' They too have a mission to 'the lost sheep of the house of Israel' (10.5–6).

Jesus' attack on the Jewish purity laws in Mark (7.1–23) is reproduced in Matthew (15.1–20), but the sweeping conclusion, pronouncing all foods clean (Mark 7.19), is pointedly omitted by Matthew. When Jesus is approached by a Syrophoenician woman, in Mark 7.24–30, he enters her house, the house of an 'unclean' Gentile. In Matthew, however, the woman becomes a 'Canaanite' and Jesus does not set foot in her house, presumably because a Jewish rabbi had a fear of contamination (Matthew 15.21–8).

Jesus in Matthew enjoins upon his disciples a strict observance of the Law, and insists that their righteousness must exceed that of the Scribes and Pharisees (5.20). He tells them:

> whoever breaks one of the least of these commandments, and teaches others to do the same, will be called least in the kingdom of heaven; but whoever does them and teaches them will be called great in the kingdom of heaven. (5.19)

The kind of observance that this entails is a matter for discussion.[20] At this point it seems that Matthew is engaged upon an internecine Jewish debate over which group – Pharisee or Christian – has a right to claim the moral high ground of a true interpretation and observance of the Law, or, to put it another way, which group can lay claim to the allegiance of the Jewish community as a whole. Christians of Matthew's community are in competition with the Pharisees not only for God's favour but also for favour in the eyes of the Jewish people. It could well be that this was exactly the situation prevailing in Matthew's community at the time the Gospel was published, around AD 85. The Christians and the Pharisaic rabbis were rivals for the heart and soul of the religious life in the area – perhaps in and around Antioch in Syria.

This case can be made even more strongly when we look at the Sermon on the Mount in Matthew's Gospel (Chapters 5–7). Jesus there delivers a new or alternative interpretation of God's Law. As Jesus ascends the mountain, Matthew clearly wishes to remind his readers of Moses, the great prophet and lawgiver of Israel. Jesus is not a mere rabbi like the Pharisees of Yavneh or elsewhere, but is a new Moses and one greater than Moses. On the one hand, Jesus deepens or spiritualizes the commands of the Torah and, on the other hand, he appears to refuse to accept the letter of the Law in certain instances;[21] rather, he promulgates his own new understanding of the Law on his own authority. This was Jesus calling Israel to a new, simpler and more heartfelt devotion to God's Law and to a new holiness of life, where inner motives matter at least as much as external observances. It must have reminded Matthew's congregation and all who read the Gospel of the new covenant foreseen by Jeremiah (Jer. 31.31–4) and by Ezekiel (Ezek. 34.30–1), when, in the age to come, the Messiah would spell out the truth about God's Law and enable all to comprehend it and keep it. And the result would be that they would all know the Lord, 'from the least of them to the greatest' (Jeremiah 31.34). It would also have reminded them of the prophecies of Isaiah, when the voice of the Lord's servant would ask for a hearing: 'Listen to me, you that pursue righteousness, you that seek the Lord . . . the Lord will comfort Zion; he will comfort all her waste places.' Then God promises his people:

> [A] teaching will go out from me and my justice for a light to the peoples . . . Listen to me, you who know righteousness, you people who have my teaching in your hearts; do not fear the reproach of others, and do not be dismayed when they revile you. (Isaiah 51.1, 3, 4, 7)

All this would have struck a chord with Matthew's readers, and they might well have remembered that this great passage in Isaiah goes on to say; 'How beautiful upon the mountains are the feet of the messenger who announces peace, who brings good news, who announces salvation, who says to Zion, "Your God reigns"' (52.7). Whatever the original context of this passage, to Matthew's audience it meant that the Messiah had come to call Israel back to God and to teach them how to know God's will and to obey it.

Matthew and the Gentiles

Yet even though Matthew's Gospel is most evidently the gospel of 'Jewish righteousness' and of the observance of the Torah, nevertheless the evangelist does at the same time show considerable interest in the Gentiles; and at the end of the Gospel sums up the work and mission of Jesus by placing these awesome words on the lips of the risen Lord:

> All authority in heaven and on earth has been given to me. Go therefore and make disciples of all nations, baptizing them in the name of the Father and the Son and of the Holy Spirit, and teaching them to obey everything that I have commanded you. And remember, I am with you always, to the end of the age. (28.18–20)

Interestingly enough, this passage, often called the Great Commission, also connects with the latter part of Isaiah, for in Isaiah 49.6 we read:

> [The Lord] says, It is too light a thing that you should be my

servant to raise up the tribes of Jacob and to restore the survivors of Israel: I will give you as a light to the nations, that my salvation may reach to the end of the earth.

In some ways, parts of Matthew's Gospel can be viewed as a commentary (or *midrash*) on the later chapters of Isaiah and this is a theme to which we shall return, but for the moment to dwell upon the Great Commission passage, which actually begins with verse 16 of Chapter 28; it is important to note that Matthew summarizes and recapitulates in the space of these few verses many of the earlier themes of the Gospel – Jesus' authority, obedience to commandments, making disciples – and at the end echoes words from the very beginning of the Gospel: 'I am with you always' which strike a chord with 'They shall name him "Emmanuel", which means, "God is with us"' (1.23). Kostenberger and O'Brien call this 'the unifying climax of the entire gospel's teaching on mission that is anticipated in many ways throughout Matthew's narrative'.[22] So the Gospel in its entirety is somehow caught up in the overarching commission, 'Go therefore and make disciples of all nations.' How then do we reconcile this with Jesus' mission 'only to the lost sheep of the house of Israel' and his determination not to contravene or supersede the Jewish Law or lifestyle?

Any attempt at such a reconciliation must first examine carefully the references to Gentiles occurring in Matthew's Gospel and see if inferences can be drawn from them about the evangelist's attitude to the Gentile mission and to the conditions for inclusion of Gentiles in the Church.

Beginning at the beginning, we find at the very outset of Matthew's Gospel a genealogy. In keeping with a 'Jewish' gospel this begins with Abraham, the father not just of Isaac, but of the whole of Israel. Yet it should also be borne in mind – though this is not mentioned – that Abraham is the one through whom all the nations will be blessed (Genesis 12.2–3).

The genealogy first makes mention of the fact that the Messiah will be the son of David (Matthew 1.1). As we proceed and sift carefully through the names, we discover that Matthew makes a point of bringing in *non-Jews* who were among Jesus' ancestors. Tamar (1.3), a Canaanite, widow of Jacob's eldest son Er, bore Perez and Zerah by Jacob. Then there is Rahab (1.5), another Canaanite – and a prostitute – who helped Joshua's spies at Jericho (Joshua 2.6) and who was the wife of Salmon and mother of Boaz. Soon afterwards we encounter Ruth, a Moabitess (1.4), who married Boaz and whose great-grandson was King David himself. After that, we find one of David's wives, Bathsheba, who may or may not have been an Israelite (her father was Eliam and her grandfather Ahithophel, one of David's thirty chosen warriors). But the point is, she is remembered here as 'the wife of Uriah the Hittite' (see 2 Samuel 11.3). Matthew makes a point of stressing her Gentile connections (Matthew 1.6).

The recognition of these Gentiles in the genealogy undermines the Nehemiah theology that Israel must be of pure race and forbid intermarriage in order to please God (Ezra 9.1—10.17). At the least, outsiders can be included in the Holy Nation, and, put more positively, it takes more than purity of breeding to bring to birth the Messiah, the great leader of Israel. As Anthony Saldarini says, 'Though ethnic groups often imagine that their communities are separate and boundaries impermeable, all peoples and groups absorb outsiders over the course of time. This process is clearly reflected and accepted at the beginning of the gospel.'[23] But might this not also reflect the situation in Matthew's community, that of a majority Jewish Christian group but with significant (and growing) numbers of 'outsiders' being accepted and absorbed into the fellowship? Already in the genealogy is hidden a political agenda.

Other interesting points about the names in the genealogy are these: the four mentioned are all women, and yet Matthew could have chosen to mention only the father's names. In addition, all four became actively committed to the Jewish community and were thoroughly integrated. They were helpers of Israel. Does this then also reflect a contemporary situation in which Gentile women were valued as members of the Matthean community because they are committed to messianic Israel?

In the very next chapter of the Gospel, at the birth of Jesus,

Matthew, alone of all the Gospel writers, introduces the magi –
commonly, but incorrectly, called 'the wise men' (2.1–12). Right
from the outset, the Gentile world is drawn on a pilgrimage to
Israel and particularly to pay homage to the Messiah. The magi
are led by the study of astrological conjunctions of planets and
stars to conclude that a momentous event – the birth of a new
king or of the expected Jewish Messiah – is imminent. The divine
portents combine with scriptural prophecy to lead them to Israel.
They are not converts or followers of Jesus – not even proselytes
or God-fearers, but remain Gentile astrologers – yet they
acknowledge the birth of Jesus as an event of cosmic significance.

There follows a section in which the fulfilment of Old
Testament hopes is emphasized: a ruler comes from Bethlehem
'to shepherd my people Israel' (2.6 quoting Micah 5.2); the
massacre of innocent children by Herod and 'Rachel weeping
for her children' (2.18 quoting Jeremiah 31.15). Then John the
Baptist, 'the voice of one crying out in the wilderness' (3.3 quoting Isaiah 40.3). The theme of fulfilment of Scripture is a
strong one throughout this Gospel. Then in Chapter 4, after the
temptations in the wilderness, and right at the beginning of Jesus'
active ministry, the Gentiles come into view again. Jesus moves
from Nazareth to Capernaum in the land of Zebulun and
Naphtali (Matthew 4.13). Matthew quotes from Isaiah 9.1–2
and draws our attention to the phrase 'Galilee of the Gentiles'.
The implication is clear: Jesus' ministry is to be effected in the
sight of the Gentiles, as a light shining out, as a beacon for the
nations. This ministry may not be for the Gentiles or on their
behalf, but it will be made visible to them for a reason. Zebulun
and Naphtali were the first tribes to be exiled by the Assyrians,
and will now be the first to be restored. There may not have been
a large number of Gentiles in this area, which was predominantly
Jewish, but there was certainly a mixed population, and Jesus
would be living within a two-hour walk of a predominantly
Hellenistic city, Sepphoris.

The idea of a 'light to the Gentiles' fits in with the Old
Testament ideal of the nations becoming aware of Israel's God
and of the 'nation of priests', the people set apart for God. From

a mere awareness would well up a desire to come near, to approach – this is the meaning of the word 'proselyte' from the Greek verb *proserchomai*, to draw near. It would appear that in Matthew's understanding the Gentile mission over the duration of Jesus' ministry is to be a growing awareness, a recognition, a drawing near on the part of Gentiles of good will. And that is exactly what we find in the Gospel. The Gentiles – like the magi first of all – seek out Jesus on the basis of what they have seen or heard. They do not yet know him as he is, but they have heard about him: 'So his fame spread throughout all Syria, and they brought to him all the sick, those who were afflicted with various diseases and pains, demoniacs, epileptics, and paralytics; and he cured them' (4.24). Why does Matthew mention Syria of all the Gentile nations? Many scholars would see this as a veiled reference to the fact that Matthew's own community was resident in Syria, and that therefore members of the congregation were in direct descent from those who had earlier heard of Jesus' fame. The community is thus linked to Jesus' original mission, even though that was not an outgoing mission to Gentile lands.

The pattern of mission Matthew seems to envisage fits in with the schema described by (second) Isaiah. We will return to this theme in more detail shortly, but, to serve as an illustration, in Chapter 49 of Isaiah the task of the servant of the Lord is seen by the prophet as 'to bring Jacob back to [God], and to gather Israel to himself' (v. 5). Immediately afterwards in this same prophecy, however, the Lord tells his servant,

> It is too light a thing that you should be my servant, to raise up the tribes of Jacob and restore the survivors of Israel; I will give you as a light for the nations, that my salvation may reach to the end of the earth. (Isaiah 49.6)

The fact that Jesus goes up on a mountainside (Matthew 5.1) to preach and teach the people is an indication not only that this work is in the sight of the Gentiles, but also that it is a manifestation of the divine light coming to Zion to radiate out to the nations.

After the teachings of the Sermon on the Mount, we reach

Chapter 8 and the story of a centurion in Capernaum (vv. 5–13). But just before that there is a brief interlude in which a leper is healed and is instructed afterwards, '[G]o, show yourself to the priest, and offer the gift that Moses commanded, as a testimony to them' (8.4). This is inserted in all likelihood to reassure many in the Jewish section of Matthew's community – and in the Jewish community at large – that Jesus behaved impeccably as a Jewish rabbi, keeping the Law and showing respect to the religious authorities. Only with that timely proviso does Jesus deal with the Gentile centurion. In this case, it is made clear that Jesus can touch unclean people, because purity passes from him, rather than the reverse process of impurity being transmitted to him. But here in this episode, Jesus does not enter a Gentile house or sully himself. He heals the centurion's servant at a distance. In so doing, symbolically he keeps the Gentile mission at arm's length, but without ruling it out of court entirely.

The centurion is highly commended by Jesus: 'Truly I tell you, in no one in Israel have I found such faith' (8.10). The mention of *faith* is common in Jesus' dealings with the Gentiles in Matthew. Jesus marvels at the persistence of the Canaanite woman (15.22–8) and tells her, 'Woman, great is your faith! Let it be done for you as you wish.' And the story then concludes, 'her daughter was healed instantly' (v. 28).

It would appear that Matthew can accept the Gentiles into God's kingdom – or the 'Kingdom of Heaven' – on the basis of *faith*. But this does not seem to tally with the main theological thrust of the Gospel, which insists that true discipleship has to be a certain kind of 'Jewish' obedience and righteousness of life, as demonstrated in works such as almsgiving, prayer and fasting. Matthew's Christians are to produce fruit worthy of the kingdom (21.43). Yet in the same way as godfearers and perhaps even proselytes could be accepted into the synagogues (especially in some areas of the Diaspora),[24] on the basis of *faith* and a worshipful commitment to the one true God, so presumably Gentile Christians could be accepted into Matthew's community if they demonstrated *by changed behaviour* real faith in Christ as Messiah.

The crucial difference, however, was this: in the case of Matthew's community there were no stages or gradations of acceptance. In the synagogues, God-fearers could progress from worshipping to observing dietary and ceremonial rules, then to submitting to the Torah in its entirety, then to being circumcised. In Matthew's community, the stages were purely stages of discipleship, without clear distinctions. The commitment would be to the Law of Christ, to righteousness of life and to submission to the leadership. Such stages were not easily measured or numbered. To all intents and purposes then, Matthew's community could – at least in principle – accept Gentiles into full membership on the basis of their faith and good intentions alone.

The leaders of the most conservative wing of the Church we know anything about in detail – the church in Jerusalem – met with Paul and Barnabas and perhaps other radical Church leaders at the Council of Jerusalem (*c.*AD 49; see Acts 15) and, according to the Acts of the Apostles, imposed no requirement of circumcision upon Gentile members, but only the requirement of abstaining from things polluted by idols and from fornication and from whatever had been strangled and from blood (Acts 15.20). This does not even amount to a keeping of dietary laws, and Paul seems to have ignored even these strictures with impunity. According to the Letter to the Galatians Peter simply sought to maintain unity and a sense of fellowship throughout the Christian diaspora by asking Paul to remember the poor in Jerusalem through a collection (Galatians 2.10). Paul certainly did fulfil this part of the deal, even though the Corinthian church was rather reluctant to accede to his request. Now, the Matthean community may have taken its cue from Jerusalem, the most powerful and respected church in the Christian communion before the sack of Jerusalem, but, even if they had followed such regulations as those apparently imposed on Paul, this would not have amounted to much more than a few moral appeals to the Gentile conscience.

By the time the Gospel emerged, the authority of Jerusalem had largely evaporated anyway. In the course of time, the Matthean community, with an ever increasing number of Gentile converts, must have made the transition to become a fully independent and predominantly Gentile-controlled church. Of course, this was not without pain, tension, heart-searching and heated debate; but it was effected without the imposition of legalistic rules or a series of hurdles for converts to clear before they could be baptized.

So, to return to the Gentile centurion. At the end of the story, Jesus promises him salvation on terms of equality with Jews, God's children. 'I tell you, many will come from east and west and will eat with Abraham and Isaac and Jacob in the kingdom of heaven, while the heirs of the kingdom will be thrown into outer darkness' (8.11–12). A. J. Saldarini rather grudgingly comments on Matthew's attitude to the Gentiles at this point: 'They will, like the centurion, believe and be rewarded, but their reward will be at a heavenly banquet presided over by the Jewish patriarchs.'[25] But this misses the point. Surely, if there is full table fellowship between Jew and Gentile at the banqueting feast of the coming kingdom, why should there be anything less than that on earth in the Church? Matthew's Gospel may have a rather ambivalent attitude to the Gentiles, but, when all is said and done, Jesus' promise here must be taken in a positive sense, as setting up a mixed community of faith and salvation without preconditions about food or other ceremonial law. Matthew certainly believes that salvation comes through the Jews first, as Saldarini recognizes, but that is conceived as the plan of salvation, not as a guarding of privileges or imposition of laws.

Chapter 8 then has another 'interlude' which relates to what is to come, and what, paradoxically, is already now taking place. Jesus heals Peter's mother-in-law and then exorcizes many possessed by demons: 'and he cast out the spirits with a word, and cured all who were sick' (8.16). Then there is a quotation from Isaiah (8.17) – and this again seems to indicate to Matthew's Jewish readers that Jesus' primary mission is the restoration of Israel. After a couple of other incidents, during which Jesus is transported into Gentile territory, there comes a most testing exorcism.

Two maniacal demoniacs confront him: 'They were so fierce

that no one could pass' (8.28). Matthew attempts to upstage Mark in the degree of fear and horror! In Mark's account there is one demoniac living among the cave tombs. Mark depicts him as a desperate but pitiable man 'howling and bruising himself with stones' (Mark 5.5). But the man does not bar the way. Matthew even more than Mark wishes to portray Gentile territory as threatening and dangerous; the habitation of evil spirits and all manner of ungodliness. Yet Jesus is able to cleanse both the demoniacs and the land itself with a mere word, for the pigs are precipitated to their death as the demons also perish with them. At the end, though, the Gentile people beg Jesus to go away, and the demoniacs do not ask to follow him. In Mark the people are similarly fearful, but the story ends on a positive note: the man, now in his right mind and sitting quietly, asks Jesus if he might be a follower, but Jesus refuses and tells him to go back to his own people. Then follows a word about the man's mission: 'he went away and began to proclaim in the Decapolis how much Jesus had done for him; and everyone was amazed' (5.20). Not yet conversion, but a positive response. But for Matthew the Gentiles are not yet ready to accept Jesus. Perhaps this reflects something of the mixed experiences of the community again.

At the end of Chapter 9, Matthew returns to the theme of mission: 'The harvest is plentiful,' says Jesus, 'but the labourers are few; therefore ask the Lord of the harvest to send out labourers into his harvest' (9.37–8). This declaration precedes the sending or commissioning of the twelve, and Matthew evidently wishes to show that mission is an integral part of discipleship. The disciples are to be formed in imitation of their master. Just as the Son of Man 'has nowhere to lay his head' (8.20), so the disciples are not to receive any payment; nor are they to take money, nor bag, nor a change of clothes – not even food (10.10). This mission demands a response from those who hear; for those who accept the gospel word, there is peace and blessing (*shalom*); for those who reject the word, there is harsh judgement: 'It will be more tolerable for the land of Sodom and Gomorrah on the day of judgement than for that town' (10.15). The note of judgement is often sounded in Matthew's Gospel.

What is interesting is that after this mission – a mission only to Israel, ending in the possibility of blessing or judgement on Israel's towns and villages – Matthew returns to the theme of mission in Chapter 11, but this time extends it to include the Gentile response to Christ. Since the cities where Jesus had been most active had not repented they are condemned: 'Woe to you, Chorazin! Woe to you, Bethsaida!' They are then contrasted with the Gentile cities and the Gentile response: 'For if the deeds of power done in you had been done in Tyre and Sidon, they would have repented long ago in sackcloth and ashes' (11.21–2).

In this way, Matthew contrasts Israel's shocking lack of faith with the Gentiles' surprising possession of great faith. Just as the centurion's faith was greater than any seen in Israel (8.10), and just as the Canaanite woman was commended for her faith –'Woman, great is your faith' (15.28), so in the community of God's new age the Jewish people will be surprised by the presence of many Gentiles of great faith.

This theme of paradox – unexpected reward and judgement, unexpected faith – will be taken up again in Chapter 12. A long quotation from Isaiah 42.1–4 refers back to the suffering servant of Israel and includes the words: 'he will proclaim justice to the Gentiles' (Matthew 12.18), and then concludes, 'And in his name the Gentiles will hope' (12.21). A little later in this chapter we find out the significance of this prophecy: 'An evil and adulterous generation asks for a sign, but no sign will be given to it except the sign of the prophet Jonah' (12.39). It is the leaders in Israel who are envisaged in this word of judgement; they have led the people ('this adulterous generation') astray. Then Jesus in Matthew compares Jonah – the prophet who went to the Gentile city of Nineveh to preach repentance – with the 'Son of Man'. As Jonah lay in the tomb of a great fish's belly for three days and nights and then emerged alive, so the Son of Man – presumably Jesus himself – will also lie dead and buried in a cave tomb three days and nights, and then will rise again to life.

After this eschatological event – the first fruit of the resurrection of the dead – the Gentiles come into the reckoning again:

'The people of Nineveh will rise up at the judgement with this generation and condemn it, because they repented at the proclamation of Jonah, and see, something greater than Jonah is here!' (12.41).

So Jesus, in Matthew's terms, is one greater than Jonah, who was the evangelist of the Gentiles. And not only that, but the Queen of Sheba (a leading representative of the Gentiles) will rise up at the judgement to condemn 'this generation' because 'she came from the ends of the earth to listen to the wisdom of Solomon, and see, something greater than Solomon is here!' (12.42). Jesus is greater than Jonah, who went on mission to the Gentiles, and he is also greater than Solomon, who was the exemplar of the man of wisdom.

There are two conclusions arising naturally out of this. First, the day of judgement is going to produce a great surprise. Rather than Israel, God's people, being allowed to stand in judgement over the unfaithful, ungodly Gentile nations; they instead will be allowed to stand in judgement over her! Second, the ingathering of the Gentiles – in other words, the Gentile mission – will not take place until the time appointed; that is, until after the death and resurrection of Jesus, who, like Jonah, must first lie in a tomb for three days and nights.

Eschatological mission

When Matthew is considering the Gentile mission, he does so within an eschatological time frame. First comes the mission to Israel, as is fitting, for they are God's chosen people and must be gathered together as the eschatological community or flock. Then, after Jesus has achieved this mission in his earthly life and ministry, there follows the mission of God's redeemed people to the Gentiles. This is done in the power of the risen Christ. Then finally, at the day of judgement, many Gentiles who have accepted the Messiah will paradoxically be in the position of judging many Jews who rejected him.

The time scheme of this eschatological framework is re-emphasized in the great judgement parable of Chapter 25 – the parable of the sheep and the goats (25.31–46). This event takes place at the time 'when the Son of Man comes in his glory' (v. 31) and when 'all the nations will be gathered before him' (v. 32). Who is going to inherit the kingdom? Well, it is neither Jew nor Gentile as such; rather it is anyone who gave the Son of Man food when he was hungry, and drink when he was thirsty, welcomed him when he was a stranger, clothed him when he was naked and visited him when he was in prison. Those who are on the right hand of the Son of Man (the 'righteous') are surprised at this outcome: 'When was it we saw you hungry?' they ask in puzzlement (v. 37). Those on the left hand are self-righteous and query the judgement: 'When was it that we saw you hungry or thirsty [etc.] and did not take care of you?' (v. 44). The answer is, when one of 'the least of these who are members of my family' (25.40) was helped, the Son of Man himself was helped. And when one of the least was ignored or neglected, the Son of Man himself was ignored or neglected.

Once more, blessing and judgement in this Gospel do not run along the lines of ethnicity or nationality. Those living a righteous life may be Jew or Gentile, and either may find salvation – or be condemned. The outcome is determined by two factors: response to Jesus (as Son of Man) and belief in him (these are 'my brothers') and, in addition, righteousness of life ('just as you did it to the least . . . ') (25.40).

Thus, at the end of time, Matthew envisages a righteous community of those who believe in Jesus and who love one another and live according to God's will – they may be Jews or Gentiles. This community of right belief needs to ensure right behaviour: good relationships, dedication to God's law as taught by Jesus and transparently good attitudes to others. These alone are the proofs or fruits of true discipleship.

The idea that Matthew does not favour a Gentile mission, or views it as an unfortunate necessity, because he steers Jesus well clear of Gentile mission in the Gospel, is a wrongheaded approach to the question. In fact, Matthew, like Mark, has an eschatological time frame in mind, which means that he understands the time of Jesus as the time for mission to Israel (yet even then a mission enacted in the sight of the Gentiles). The Gentile mission will come alongside the continuing Jewish mission *after the resurrection,* when the conditions are in place for it to be initiated. The main responsibility for this Gentile mission will therefore fall on the disciples, who nevertheless will sense the risen Lord guiding and leading them. Then at 'the end', when all is summed up, Gentiles and Jews will be judged along with 'all the nations' on terms of equality. To imagine that Jesus restricted his mission to Israel and never envisaged a Gentile mission at all – a position Alan Le Grys[26] appears to advocate – is a misunderstanding not only of the world-view of the Gospel writers, but of Jewish and early Christian eschatology as a whole.

This means that Matthew's Gospel is not couched in the form of a dialectic between those keeping the Law and clinging to Jewish ways on the one hand and those preaching faith alone as a condition for Gentile membership of the church on the other hand. Neither are there necessarily two layers of gospel tradition representing an earlier and a later stage of development in the life of the community. Rather, the Law of Christ and of righteous living applies to all – Jew and Gentile – but it is not the same as the rabbinical interpretation of the Law or rabbinical demands placed on a Jewish lifestyle.

The mission to Jews and Gentiles has an eschatological inner logic: it is related to stages in the scheme of salvation. Such an understanding does justice to the tensions in the Gospel, but also goes a long way towards resolving these tensions. And, since Matthew's church must have become predominantly Gentile in the course of time, we must assume that these tensions were indeed finally overcome or relegated to the past. There is real tension at the time of writing the Gospel because there is a difficult transition. A predominantly Jewish community used to regarding themselves as the people through whom salvation is dispensed are now gradually seeing their power challenged and perhaps overturned by the influx of Gentiles who want an equal share of power and decision-making, as well as equal conditions for entry into the Church.

There is also tension in so far as Matthew's community is

attempting to conduct a mission on two fronts at the same time. First, it is in a fierce and sometimes bitter competition with the Pharisaic rabbis for the heart and soul of the Jewish community. This battle has taken place mainly in and around the synagogue. Then it is also coming to terms with a Gentile mission, which, while experiencing some success at one level, is also creating many problems for the inner life of the community. In modern terms, the group dynamics are being very much unbalanced and upset by the changing nature of the community. The tensions are therefore both historical and theological, but they are not tensions over whether a Gentile mission should be permitted or whether Gentiles need to be circumcised or observe food laws or anything of that order. Such questions have already been addressed and answered before – in the time of the Jerusalem Council and the missions of the Apostle Paul.

Matthew and the mission to the nations in Isaiah

One important question still remains to be answered, namely, what would the mission to the nations achieve, in Matthew's eyes; what was its purpose? From a twenty-first-century perspective, the answer might seem obvious: it could achieve church growth, it would offer people the chance of a new life, or salvation; it would bring people of different races and ethnic groups together in unity and harmony; it could create better moral standards and help people to live a life pleasing to God. But are these answers not somewhat anachronistic? Are they not couched in the abstract philosophical terms that Western thinkers are so fond of? In the *first* century what was Matthew's own vision of the eschatological reality of worldwide mission?

There are two things to say at the outset. Matthew's vision would surely be one derived primarily from the Old Testament, that is, from the Scriptures of his own day. His Gospel is largely based on the overriding idea that Jesus was the fulfilment of the hopes of the Holy Scriptures. Matthew is the Gospel writer who above all quotes texts which are specifically seen as coming to fruition in the life and work of Jesus Christ. Not only that, but he most probably sought these texts out himself and did not simply adopt them from early Christian writings or from Mark and Q.[27] The fact is that Matthew does not cite a text by just employing the familiar wording, as in the Greek Septuagint (LXX) for instance. Rather, as Davies and Allison point out, the Matthean quotations are thoroughly assimilated to their contexts and are hard to extricate as pure 'proof texts'. And, in addition, 'outside the formula quotations Matthew both conflates texts and shows knowledge of more than the LXX'.

Secondly, Matthew as a writer steeped in Old Testament thought has a vision which is Hebraic, that is concrete, visual and pictorial. Just as Jesus' own visions of the Kingdom of God are not abstract but drawn from the images of everyday life, so Matthew's idea of the mission to the nations is also couched in the imagery of the prophets of the Old Testament. In particular, Matthew is indebted to the prophecies of Isaiah. Half of all the quotations in the Gospel are taken from Isaiah, and a good proportion from Isaiah 40—62: prophecies about coming out of exile and into a new land of promise. Then Matthew also quotes twice from Zechariah, once from Hosea, once from Jeremiah and once (probably) from the Psalms. None of these quotations comes from the Pentateuch and clearly most come from the prophetic writings. Whether this reflects Jesus' own preferences is a matter of conjecture, but at the stage of the Gospel's composition, Matthew is his own *targumist*, sometimes adapting Scripture for his own purposes and quoting in his own way, sometimes glossing his quotations with words betraying commentary rather than literal accuracy.[28] The translations certainly do not always conform to the Greek of the LXX.

Now a saying of Jesus in Matthew 8.11–12 in the context of the healing of the Roman officer's servant – that is, in the context of mission to the Gentiles – highlights what has been said about the pictorial nature of Hebrew eschatology, and also gives us an insight into Matthew's understanding. Jesus says:

I tell you, many will come from east and west and will eat with Abraham and Isaac and Jacob in the kingdom of heaven, while the heirs of the kingdom will be thrown into the outer darkness, where there will be weeping and gnashing of teeth.

This clearly owes a lot to Hebrew thought-patterns – the patriarchs presiding, the banqueting feast of the kingdom, the contrasting images around 'come' (*erxesthai*) and 'cast out' (*ekballesthai*), and the expression 'from the east and the west' to denote the whole world. The gathering of the nations can only be accomplished through Israel and with the blessing of the captains of Israel's faith. There is a form of Last Judgement, but with a very provocative twist in the tail – the Gentiles will be welcomed in but many of the children of Israel – God's chosen – will be turned away.

If we now concentrate on Isaiah's vision of the Gentile mission, we find that Matthew takes up some of the motifs, without necessarily quoting the relevant passages. Of course, in considering this, we must lay aside the arguments of modern scholars about the division of Isaiah into three or more distinct periods of prophetic activity. Near the beginning of the book of Isaiah we read of a highway being constructed so that the Gentiles will be able to travel from their cities to Jerusalem (Isaiah 19.23). This theme is taken up again later in Chapter 60: 'Nations shall come to your light, and kings to the brightness of your dawn' (v. 3). The Gentiles come bearing precious gifts (vv. 5–9) and stream towards Jerusalem in an endless procession. This is of course a theme taken up indirectly in Matthew's account of the visit of the magi from the east (Isaiah 2.1–12). The story continues in Isaiah with further descriptions of this great migration: the Gentiles come 'on horses, and in chariots, and in litters, and on mules, and on dromedaries, to my [God's] holy mountain, Jerusalem' (Isaiah 66.20). In this way, the book of Isaiah ends on a note of glory and triumph: 'And I am coming to gather all nations and tongues; and they shall come and shall see my glory' (66.18).

The difficulty with this vision, from Matthew's point of view, is surely that the mission seems to be going in the wrong direction. It is the traditional biblical view of the Gentiles being drawn to admire Israel, to come on pilgrimage to Jerusalem and finally to acknowledge and worship Israel's God. But the Great Commission depicts Jesus sending the disciples out to the four corners of the earth, going out to the Gentiles, not waiting for them to come in. However, on closer examination, there is in Isaiah an indication of an outward mission *prior to* the final drawing in, or ingathering, of the nations:

> I will set a sign among them. From them I will send survivors to the nations . . . to the coastlands far away that have not heard of my fame or seen my glory; and they shall declare my glory among the nations. They shall bring all your kindred from all the nations as an offering to the Lord . . . to my holy mountain Jerusalem. (66.19–20)

The goal of this eschatological mission is not only to proclaim to the nations the coming of the Lord, and to bring them knowledge of the true God, but also to draw all people together for worship in a renewed Jerusalem and at a renewed Temple. Then, as Matthew picks up, God's house 'shall be called a house of prayer for all peoples' (56.7 cf. Matthew 21.13). Thus, the eventual blessing of the Gentile nations is conceived in two stages: first as an outward mission of witnesses from Israel announcing the good news of God's reign; then as an ingathering of the nations to Jerusalem at the very end. When the great pilgrimage to Jerusalem takes place, there will be the great messianic banquet on the mountain of the Lord. This event is in fact first envisaged early on in the Isaianic prophecies: 'On this mountain the Lord of hosts will make for all peoples a feast of rich food . . .' (Isaiah 25.6–8). This time will usher in a new age of peace and 'shalom' (66.12–13); death will be destroyed and a new heaven and a new earth will be created (66.22–3).

The goal of the Gentile mission is primarily the revelation of God on his holy mountain. But it is also a breaking down of the divisions between Jew and Gentile and a sharing in table fellowship – that is, reconciliation through friendship, trust and shared faith. From Matthew's so-called 'Jewish' point of view this means that Israel herself must be converted to make the ingathering of Gentiles possible; at the same time the Gentiles are guaranteed a share in the revelation of God and in salvation itself. They are full participants in the messianic banquet, as foreseen by Isaiah. The old strictures about 'clean and unclean' are swept aside as at the last the patriarchs of Israel share God's banquet with people from every nation. All are on an equal footing and all earthly distinctions have disappeared.

In Matthew we witness a foretaste of this time in the feeding of the five thousand and in the feeding of the four thousand. The separation in the Gospel is perhaps to show that Israel has to be renewed and fed first, and only after that can the Gentiles be received with the necessary grace and goodwill. In the beatitudes, Jesus says 'Blessed are those who hunger and thirst for righteousness, for they will be filled'(5.6). In Matthew's account of the Last Judgement in Chapter 25 we have the image of a scattered flock being gathered together by the shepherd of God so that all the sheep can be united, both Jew and Gentile: 'All the nations will be gathered before him, and he will separate people one from another as a shepherd separates the sheep from the goats' (v. 32).

The Temple of the Last Age is, for Matthew, that Temple which is Jesus' body, raised in three days after its destruction. Peter becomes its foundation stone (Matthew 16.18). Thus, in the Gospel, the Gentile mission is seen both as an outward mission, an announcement to the nations and a reaching out to all people, and also as an inward mission, a mission of ingathering, a coming to Jesus but also a coming to join the original people of God who have remained faithful – the Jewish believers in Christ. Jesus' followers are in this way both 'the light of the world' and also 'a city on a hill' (5.14). Both of these images have a resonance with Isaiah's vision of the last days. For Matthew the city is the renewed Jerusalem which is the Church; and the light is the light of Christ shining out to the nations. For this reason, the city on the hill *cannot* (*ou dunatai*) be hidden. When the bright beam of God's radiance (the *kabhodh*) shines out, it is the signal for the great eschatological gathering of the nations.[29]

The hallmark of this time is joy: 'Sing for joy, O heavens, and exult, O earth; break forth, O mountains, into singing! For the Lord has comforted his people, and will have compassion on his suffering ones' (Isaiah 49.13). Even if the present is a time of persecution and troubles, it is still the time to rejoice, because it is the time when the faithful see God's promises coming true: the Gentiles are turning to the true God and are learning from the redeemed Israel. This note of eschatological joy is maintained throughout the later chapters of Isaiah. An echo of this is found in the parable of the talents (Matthew 25.14–30). At the time of final reckoning, the faithful servants are given charge of many things and are invited to 'enter into the joy of your master' (vv. 21, 23). The story of the final judgement follows on and in verse 34 those who enter into the kingdom are described as 'you that are blessed by my father' and are invited to 'inherit the kingdom prepared for you from the foundation of the world'. The people envisaged here include the Gentiles, and so Jesus, in Matthew's Gospel, makes it clear that it was God's express intention from the beginning of time to reach out to the nations through Israel. In the heart of God was a longing for all people to know him and his salvation; in other words, God had a plan for *mission* above all things.

Other parables have a missionary flavour too. The parable of the good seed and the weeds (13.24–30) ends with an ingathering or harvest. The parable of the net thrown into the sea (13.47–50) speaks of catching 'fish of every kind' (v. 47) before the final judgement. And to take the example of the parable of the mustard seed, the kingdom is the grain of seed which grows into a great tree so that the birds of the air can nest in its branches. In later rabbinic literature the birds are taken to be an image of the Gentiles.[30]

So we see that Matthew has a clear concept of the final incorporation of the Gentiles into the kingdom of God, but *subsequent to* Israel's faithful carrying out of the mission to the nations. This takes place in the time of God's establishing of the kingdom in power, and Matthew, following Mark, understands this to be the time inaugurated in Jesus' ministry and most of all activated through his death and resurrection – events which have ushered in God's new age.

We can perhaps at this point detect *four* phases of mission,

leading up to the final ingathering: first, there is the call to
Israel (culminating in Jesus' mission to Israel); then there is the
growing light which is sensed or seen by the Gentiles, a few at
first, then an increasing number. This takes place as from the
coming of the Christ, and as the Magi coming from the east bear
witness to this new phase. Then, at a third stage, there is the
fuller and more deliberate reaching out to the Gentiles by the
remnant of Israel; that is, those who believe in Christ and who
are ready to obey his call to go and make disciples of all nations.
Finally, there is the ingathering at the time of the End and of the
Last Judgement. This time is envisaged in some of Matthew's
parables, especially the parable of the sheep and the goats
(25.31–46). All such parables of judgement envisage both
Gentiles and Jews standing before God on terms of equality.
Both sets of people are to be judged primarily on their actions; in
other words, on whether their lives have borne fruit worthy of
the kingdom of God.

These four phases all overlap, but are distinguishable in
principle. At the time of Jesus' ministry and through the events of
the end of his life, it is as though time has been compressed or
concertinaed. The time of mission is yet to come but has already
come; the time of judgement and of the last things is still to come
but is already here. The reason for this has to be because
Matthew regards the ministry and works of Jesus as indicators
of God's new age, the eschatological time predicted by the
prophets. It becomes present in Jesus, and then what follows is
the outworking and fulfilling of what has already taken place
proleptically in Jesus' own time.

For those determined to focus fixedly on the early words of
Jesus – that he has come for the lost sheep of Israel alone – it is
impossible properly to understand Jesus' dealings with Gentiles
in the Gospel and particularly in the light of the Great
Commission at the end of the Gospel. It then becomes necessary
to speak of 'contradictions' in the Gospel or of phases in the
history of the Matthean community. For those who like an
account where everything follows a clear pattern and nothing
is done 'out of order', certainly Matthew's is a confusing and

frustrating gospel. But it helps towards understanding Matthew if it is recognized that the time of Jesus' coming is for the Gospel writer an exceptional time, a time when the powers and events of the Last Times are 'beamed back' in a kind of time warp. Then, after the resurrection, nothing is the same as before. For the time of the Church stretches out once again through history and is no longer encapsulated in a moment of eternity. That *moment* of Jesus' life, death and resurrection is an *anticipation* of the later enthronement of the Son of Man. The time of the Church's mission is the time when increasingly that enthronement should be made a reality in the world and in people's lives. Then comes the time of the *Parousia* – the visible arrival of the Son of Man in glory – and the time of the Last Judgement. This is when all things are gathered together and fulfilled; when those Gentiles who have responded to God's call will see his glory on Mount Zion.

The time of the Church is a time when Matthew – quite possibly following the thoughts and teaching of Jesus before him – sees the coming to pass of the prophecies of Isaiah. In Isaiah 56.6 those who obey God and live righteous lives have a share in the great celebration, the feast of the kingdom:

> And the foreigners who join themselves to the Lord, to minister to him, to love the name of the Lord, and to be his servants, all who keep the sabbath, and do not profane it, and hold fast my covenant – these I will bring to my holy mountain, and make them joyful in my house of prayer; their burnt-offerings and their sacrifices will be accepted on my altar; for my house shall be called a house of prayer for all peoples. Thus says the Lord God, who gathers the outcasts of Israel, I will gather others to them besides those already gathered. (Isaiah 56.6–8)

The end of this passage is, of course, quoted by Jesus himself in Matthew 21.13 when he acted out the destruction of the old Temple system and the inauguration of the new. In the passage from Isaiah this is clearly a vision of how the Gentiles will come to Zion, to the Temple of God and ultimately into the kingdom.

What also seems probable is that Jesus himself meditated on this passage and saw in it the pattern for his own ministry and mission. Jesus' fascination with the prophecies and teachings of Isaiah are in all likelihood faithfully represented in Matthew's Gospel; where we see signs of meditation upon the Servant Songs (Matthew 8.17; 12.18–21; 26.67; cf. Isaiah 53.4; 42.1–4; and 50.6); upon the teaching through parables (13.14–15; cf. Isaiah 6.9–10); upon God's love for Jesus as Son (3.17; 17.5; cf. Isaiah 42.1 *Targum*); and upon making oaths and paying lip-service (5.33–7; 23.22; cf. Isaiah 50.6; and Matthew 15.8–9 cf. Isaiah 29.13). It is only Matthew of all the Gospels who gives us these insights which are not about what Jesus said and did, but in all probability about what he *thought* and how he understood his role in God's plan. That so much of this is related directly to *mission* – Jesus' own mission and God's mission to Israel and to the nations, surely demonstrates that the subject of mission is central to the preoccupations of this Gospel writer.

The Great Commission

In the light of all this, the Great Commission begins to make sense and to fit in with the schema of the Gospel as a whole. Otherwise it appears as an isolated boulder or a stumbling block. It is now time to revisit this passage in the light of our new perspective on mission in Matthew. Kostenberger and O'Brien[31] call this passage 'the unifying climax of the entire Gospel's teaching on mission, that is anticipated in many ways throughout Matthew's narrative'. In a similar vein, Davies and Allison, in their mighty commentary, give the following encomium:

> [This passage] is, from the literary point of view, perfect, in the sense that it satisfyingly completes the Gospel: we could hardly improve upon it. Nothing is superfluous, yet nothing more could be added without spoiling the effect. The grand denouement, so consonant with the spirit of the whole Gospel because so full of resonances with earlier passages, is, despite its terseness, almost a compendium of Matthean theology.[32]

High praise indeed, and justified comment, for Matthew, in these few phrases, does indeed recall and summarize many earlier themes. The passage sets a high tone and the whole world is encompassed in its purview. Some scholars see similarities with near-eastern enthronement rituals – with the themes of authority, lordship and universal acclamation. The passage is also – and perhaps more – reminiscent of Old Testament commissioning narratives, such as Numbers 22.22–35; Exodus 3.1–4; Judges 4.4–10; 1 Samuel 3.1–4; and 1 Chronicles 22.1–6. It is particularly linked to Joshua's commissioning by God (through Moses) which ends with the Lord's word to Joshua: 'You shall bring the Israelites into the land that I promised them; I will be with you' (Deuteronomy 31.23).

The very last words of the Hebrew Bible are echoed in these, the last words of the Gospel. In 2 Chronicles 36.23 King Cyrus proclaims:

> The Lord, the God of heaven, has given me all the kingdoms of the earth, and he has charged me to build him a house at Jerusalem, which is in Judah. Whoever is among you of all his people, may the Lord his God be with him! Let him go up.

In the Great Commission Jesus claims, 'All authority in heaven and on earth has been given to me', and the idea of sending the people on their way is echoed in 'Go therefore and make disciples of all nations' (Matthew 28.18–19).

The fulfilment of prophecy is subtly alluded to, because the whole setting recalls the Son of Man coming in glory in Daniel 7.13. Jesus' own prophecy about the coming of the Son of Man is also in the process of fulfilment (see Matthew 24.30 and 26.34). Galilee now becomes the launching pad for outreach into the Gentile world. This of course was hinted at in 4.15 with the reference to 'Galilee of the Nations'.

The word 'mountain' reminds Matthew's audience of other spectacular contacts between God and human beings: there is Moses on Sinai (Exodus 19.3–25) and Moses on Mount Nebo in sight of the promised land (Deuteronomy 34.1–4). These allusions are reminders that Jesus is the new Moses showing the disciples the lands they are to enter and conquer. In the Gospel itself the mountain is a place of revelation, especially the revelation of Jesus as God's agent, and especially in the transfiguration story (17.1–8).

The Great Commission also harks back to other parts of the Gospel itself: to the temptation story when Jesus resisted *Satan's* promise of the kingdoms of this world (4.8–10) and to the Sermon on the Mount, where the law is interpreted and promulgated with divine authority (5.1—8.1). The idea of the disciples as a mixed bunch of faithful workers and some 'doubters' (i.e. people of 'little faith') is also revisited here, and is foreshadowed by Peter's attempt to walk on water (14.31–3). The leading concept of Jesus' authority echoes the words of 11.27, highlighting Jesus' intimate knowledge of God. He receives from the father and does the father's will. Authority vested in a man by God is part of the Matthean understanding of the 'Son of Man' motif (e.g. 24.30; 26.64) and is essential to Matthew's idea of Jesus as king (e.g. 2.2, 6). This is authority not from a worldly source, exercised by 'lording it over others' (as of Herod), but authority to heal and to restore on God's behalf; authority to create a kingdom of righteousness and peace (11.2–6; cf. 8.8–13).

'Making disciples' is also a major theme throughout the Gospel. The noun (*mathetes*) is used no less than 73 times and the verb (*matheteuein*) some 13 times. It is encapsulated in the words, 'Every scribe who has been trained for the kingdom of heaven is like the master of a household who brings out of his treasure what is new and what is old' (13.52). This also links up with 'teaching' (28.20) which demonstrates that Jesus is passing on a vital part of his own mission to the disciples. In Matthew Jesus has a teaching ministry par excellence. 'All that I have commanded you' (v. 20) is a reminder that this teaching is not simply the imparting of information or truth but concerns understanding of and obedience to God's will. It is not yet catechism, but it is more than proclamation and preaching.

The mention of 'the nations' most probably includes Israel

as well as the Gentile nations[33] and begins to fulfil the promise made to Abraham in Genesis (12.3; 18.18; 22.18), first mentioned in Matthew 1.1 and reiterated in the quotation from Isaiah's servant song cycle (Isaiah 42.1–4) which ends 'And in his name shall the nations trust' (Matthew 12.21).

It is worth noting that the term 'nations' (*ethne*) does not have the same specific designation in the Greek as in English. It has a range of meanings and could denote an ethnic group or tribe, a social class (e.g. rural or urban), a political subdivision or a guild or association. The Hebrew term *goyim* was usually used to mean non-Jews in contrast to Israel, even though many Jews lived scattered around the Roman Empire. For Matthew the Church community itself is 'a nation' (*ethnos*), as is the whole Jewish Diaspora. But in the Great Commission passage, it is clear that 28.19 refers to all peoples, both Jews and Gentiles.

Jesus in Matthew is sometimes critical of the Gentile nations; for example they worry about material possessions instead of trusting in God (6.32); they love their own sort (5.47); they babble when they pray (6.7) and elsewhere they are associated with tax collectors (6.46–7; 18.17). He also has Jesus speak of the rulers of the nations lording it over their own people (20.25). None of this amounts to the kind of scathing attack found in many Jewish writings and in the letters of Paul, however (e.g. Romans 1.18–32). Then later, in the parable of the sheep and the goats (25.31–46), where the saved are symbolized as 'sheep' and the damned as 'goats', both groups appear to be a mixture of both Jews and Gentiles. Matthew does not condemn the Gentiles en bloc as idolaters.

In effect, just as Matthew's church – his own friends and allies – is composed of both Jews and Gentiles, so the opponents of the Christian community are both Jews (especially the Pharisees) and Gentiles (especially the Roman authorities).[34] Thus, as Saldarini puts it, 'Ethnic boundaries are transcended in order to focus on the relationship to Jesus and his group of believers, as the ultimate criterion for the judgement of all.'[35] So Matthew's usage in the Great Commission passage follows the Greek usage, and refers to a community of like-minded people rather than to a racial grouping.

The mention of baptism in the name of the Trinity in the Great Commission may seem anachronistic on the lips of Jesus. And no doubt it is. It is even unusual in the Early Church, which often baptized simply in the name of Jesus. But the formula is perhaps an echo of Jesus' own baptism. When Jesus was baptized, the Father affirmed and commissioned him and the Spirit descended upon him.

The final phrase of the Great Commission, 'I will be with you always, to the end of the age' relates back to the coming of 'Immanuel – which means, God with us' (1.23), and also recalls the promise in 18.20, 'Where two or three are gathered in my name, I am there among them.'

So these verses (28.16–20) do reiterate many of the earlier themes of the Gospel and gather different strands together. However, at the same time there is also a sense of novelty, a sense of new beginnings, in this commissioning story. The situation of the mountain brings to mind not just Galilee but now the whole world; Jesus' mission is no longer limited to Israel but encompasses all the nations.

The mention of baptism conjures up a picture of the new-born Church at work; and the passing of responsibility to the disciples makes it clear that this envisages a new departure – the mission of the Church – and not just another aspect of Jesus' mission. Evidently the implication is that mission is to be carried out corporately, in the mutually supportive structures of the Church, rather than by vulnerable individuals working alone or in pairs. It is the group of disciples now representing the Church as a body who respond to Jesus' instructions.

The statement 'I am with you always' not only looks back to Jesus' physical presence in the world, but now looks forward to his continuing *spiritual* presence guiding and encouraging a new generation of followers. Matthew says little about the Holy Spirit and omits the ascension story perhaps in order the more to stress this fact – that it is the presence of Jesus, directly mediated, which persists and which places the Church in the same position as the first disciples – that of knowing his presence among them in the midst of all their activities and prayers.

This commissioning story is, as Davies and Allison point out, 'open-ended', inviting the reader to become a participant in the ongoing story. 'The result is that the believing audience and the ever-living Son of God become intimate.'[36] The *reader* is among the disciples receiving the commission to 'go, make disciples of all nations'. And indeed it is well known that this passage has spoken to many people in modern times, and has provided a tremendous impetus for the Church's mission. It has in fact become the commanding passage for the call to the wide-ranging missions of the nineteenth and twentieth centuries. It spoke to men like William Carey and women like Gladys Aylward who pictured *themselves* among the disciples around Jesus being sent out and succoured by the divine presence.

The significance of Jesus' resurrection for Matthew is not purely that words of prophecy have come true, nor even that Jesus' work and mission had been vindicated. It is far more that the humble and suffering servant of Isaiah had been exalted: 'All authority in heaven and on earth has been given to me' (Matthew 28.18). This forms a contrast with the quotations from Isaiah's servant songs, which Matthew alone among the evangelists seems to regard as messianic prophecies. In 8.17 Matthew states explicitly – in regard to Jesus' healings and exorcisms – 'This was to fulfil what had been spoken through the prophet Isaiah, "He took our infirmities and bore our diseases".' Matthew is here quoting from the passage so important to the Early Church fathers – Isaiah 53.1–12 – in which the redemptive and vicarious sufferings of God's servant are described in terms resembling crucifixion. This can also be compared with Matthew 12.18–21 quoting from Isaiah 42.1–4.

Because of Jesus' new status, the resurrection also marks the start of a new era. The king is now enthroned; he has power and authority bestowed upon him. He is the rightful ruler of all the nations as the anointed of God. The disciples' task is now to ensure that this awesome new situation is made a visible reality; that the nations do indeed bow the knee, not to the emperor but to the Christ; that worldly kingdoms worshipping the emperor as a god do indeed become godly kingdoms worshipping Christ as king. There is nevertheless at the same time continuity between the Jesus who gathers the weary and the overburdened and says, 'Take my yoke upon you, and learn from me; for I am gentle and humble in heart' (11.29), and the kingly figure who is invested with God's power and who is ruler of the entire world, the one who is eternally alive and whose life has eternal significance.

This passage also makes it clear that the mission of the disciples is not something they engage in as, when and where they like, or do because it seems a good idea to recruit new followers. Rather, this mission – or commission – is at the behest of the risen Lord. It is at his instigation and direction. It is the *missio dei* – God's own mission – which is accepted and carried forward by those who are prepared to co-operate in doing God's work in God's way. The final promise, 'I am with you always, to the end of the age', is not simply a word of comfort or encouragement, but a sign that this mission is to be directed, carried out and brought to completion by Jesus himself. It is his responsibility; he will lead it and will provide it with the power it needs to enable it to succeed. Whether the disciples are part of the process in breaking up stony ground, in ploughing the soil, in sowing the seed, or in actually reaping the harvest is entirely dependent upon the one who initiates and oversees the mission. The disciples' role is simply to preach and teach, to welcome and baptize, to be faithful in living a righteous life, in setting an example and in helping others to live life for God. They are now to be servants as Jesus himself was a servant; they are to carry in the weakness and frailty of the flesh the presence of the divine; they are the light of the world (5.14) and the light of Christ shines in them.

Thus the Great Commission at the end of Matthew's Gospel is the key to the Gospel as a whole. All the teaching of Jesus is now to be passed on to the Gentiles; the king is now coming into his kingdom; healing and justice – hitherto hallmarks of Jesus' ministry in Israel – will now spread into the world at large. The presence of the Lord – restricted to those around him in his lifetime – will now be available to all who follow him.

We are in a position to assert that the injunctions of Matthew 10.5–6 and 15.24, that the disciples are not to go beyond Israel in their mission and that Jesus' own mission is restricted 'to the lost sheep of the house of Israel', are now well and truly super-seded. It could be that Matthew is merely stating a historical fact, but the whole movement of thought in the Gospel, culminating in the Great Commission, makes it clear that these injunctions have no permanent relevance. With the resurrection and exalta-tion of Jesus a new situation prevails and new conditions of life apply. The resurrection is a time of eschatological *fulfilment* for Matthew and takes over from the time of eschatological *promise* of Jesus' life and ministry. Because of that new time frame, new considerations must now come into play. The time for the mis-sion to the nations has at length come around. In other words, the earlier injunctions and the final commissioning story do not stand in flat contradiction to one another. They belong to differ-ent periods of time, different conditions of life and where dif-ferent factors apply. If the powers of God's new age were enter-ing the world through the words and works of Jesus during his lifetime on earth, now finally they have become available to all who are his disciples, even to those 'of little faith' (the 'doubters' of 28.17); and the great change is that the words and works of Jesus are now to become the words and works of his disciples – if they remain faithful to their calling. The limiting word 'only' earlier in the Gospel ('only to Israel') now changes into the 'all' of the Great Commission: 'all authority', 'all nations', 'teaching all', 'observing all' and finally, 'I am with you always'. The mission is now all-inclusive and all-embracing.

So in this brief conclusion to the Gospel, Matthew looks both backwards and forwards. A contrast is drawn between the mission of Jesus and of his disciples *to Israel* – a tough and some-times fruitless mission in the weakness of the flesh – and the mission of the risen Lord and his disciples *to the entire world* – a mission which seems full of promise and potential, acted out in the power of the resurrection and with the strengthening presence of the Christ. The work which was limited and severely restricted

– by lack of faith as well as by geography – is now to be expanded and universalized. The teaching and promulgation of God's Law now becomes the principle for the new life of the Church. Jesus' titles, bestowed during his lifetime – Son of Man, Lord, Teacher, Son of Abraham, Immanuel, *now take on new meaning*. The 'Son of Man' is no longer the suffering servant figure, but the one who is given 'authority, glory and sovereign power', as in Daniel's vision (7.13). 'Lord' no longer has the commonplace Aramaic sense of 'sir' or 'master', but indicates someone with the status of God himself as ruler of all the nations. 'Teacher' is now not merely 'rabbi', as of a Jewish scribe or elder, but is the exponent of the will of God, the 'Torah'. 'Son of Abraham' means no longer simply a member of the Jewish race, but the one who fulfils the prophecy that through Abraham all the nations of the world will be blessed. And, finally, 'Immanuel' is no longer the child of promise lying in a manger, bringing hope but not assurance. Rather, this is the Son of God who will be with his people always, even to the end of the Age.

Thus the Great Commission not only recapitulates the themes of the Gospel as a whole, but it transforms them and imbues them with new depths of meaning and significance. In the same way that the human Jesus now becomes the Christ of power, without any radical discontinuity, so likewise the disciples move from a parochial engagement with members of their own family – that is, Israel – to being brothers and sisters of people from every tribe and race, every language and nation.

Matthew's commissioning story is a clarion call to his community – and perhaps to the whole Christian Church – to take courage, to be bold, to have faith. Some of Jesus' disciples – and particularly in the Matthean community itself – may well have been 'doubters'; they may well have been only half-heartedly committed to the new way of righteousness; they may not have witnessed the miracles and successes of Jesus' own ministry. But Matthew tries to galvanize their faith by providing a new *raison d'être* for the Church, and that is *mission to the nations*. The Church is to find its faith, its hope and its very life in reaching out beyond itself. It must continue to engage with 'Israel' – those

Jews who have not already gone over to the way of rabbinical Pharisaism – and, to an ever greater degree, must now engage with the Gentile world.

Jesus' commission is therefore, in Matthew's eyes, the new and powerful motive force driving the life of the Church. As the Church goes out into the world at large it will find that the presence of the Lord is there in the midst of its mission – preparing the way, encouraging the witness, ensuring the fruit. The Jesus who lived and acted in the past comes to life as the risen Lord as and when the Church fulfils its calling – to go and make disciples of all nations. Far from being a puzzling afterthought, or a stand-alone boulder, the Great Commission is the very heart and soul of Matthew's Gospel and is the section that best relates to the Church's life today. This means in effect that mission in general – and the mission to all the nations – is central to the Gospel's preoccupations. Although this fact has been under-recognized and underplayed, it is nevertheless vital to a proper understanding of the Gospel and to a clear perception of its message.

3

Mark's Gospel – the kingdom revealed

A brief survey of the literature on Mark in recent years reveals that almost every conceivable aspect of the Gospel has received extensive treatment – except mission. It is difficult to locate a single text on Mark as a missionary document, or on Mark's attitude to the Gentile mission. And yet even a cursory look at Mark shows that mission is a primary concern of the author. The announcement in the very first verse, 'The beginning of the good news of Jesus Christ, the Son of God', however we interpret it, sets the tone: it is the proclamation, the spreading abroad of news about an auspicious event or arrival. This announcement is linked with the only Marcan quotation from Scripture as editorial comment. All the other quotations in the Gospel are on the lips of characters in the story (mainly Jesus).[37] The other Gospels use quotations differently, mainly to indicate points in the narrative where the Old Testament is being fulfilled in Jesus' life.

Mark begins his quotation with 'As it is written in the prophet Isaiah'. First of all, this highlights the importance to the Early Church as a whole of the prophecies of Isaiah, but more than that, it demonstrates that these very prophecies are understood as shedding light on the mission of the Church, as we shall see. But secondly, there is a problem with the quotation in Mark's Gospel in that it is not simply taken from Isaiah, but is a composite quotation. It is in fact a combination of Malachi 3.1, Exodus 23.20 and Isaiah 40.3 – 'See, I am sending my messenger ahead of you, who will prepare your way; the voice of one crying in the wilderness: "Prepare the way of the Lord, make his paths straight".' In many manuscripts the copyists dealt with this problem by changing the opening ascription to 'As it is written in the prophets'.

If we assume that the attribution to Isaiah is original, then either Mark made a mistake, or he perhaps wanted to impress upon his readers the fact that the beginning of the good news is foretold and anticipated in that particular prophet. But Isaiah 40.3 is not primarily cited as a text about John the Baptist – his authentic pedigree as a 'wilderness prophet', his role as the forerunner to the Messiah – rather, the text is cited because the restoration of Israel promised in Isaiah was being fulfilled. Isaiah – for Mark and his readers – was precisely the prophet who forecast the time when the heavens would be opened (Isaiah 64.1), the Spirit poured out in a new way (61.1), good news from God would be proclaimed (40.9–10) and God himself would come in power (40.10). To bear all this out, Mark goes on to describe just these things: the heavens are torn asunder (Mark 1.10), the Spirit comes down upon Jesus (1.10), good news is proclaimed (1.14) and the kingdom of God is ushered in (1.15). All of this has clear implications for mission: it is the time for the spreading of a new message; it is the time when God will intervene in the world in a new way; it is the time for a response from all who hear the good news.

Mark also returns to Isaiah in Mark 4.12 when he quotes from Isaiah 6.9–10:

> Go and say to this people: 'Keep listening, but do not comprehend; keep looking, but do not understand.' Make the mind of this people dull, and stop their ears, and shut their eyes, so that they may not look with their eyes, and listen with their ears, and comprehend with their minds, and turn and be healed.

Why does Mark make use of this passage, which can only be interpreted as negative, as a reason for the failure of Jesus' mission in some quarters? The answer is surely that Mark sees in Isaiah not only the announcement of the mission but also the fate of that same mission. It will be accepted with joy in some places and by some people, but elsewhere and among other people it will be rejected. The proclamation will meet with great success (as described in Mark 1.22, 28, 33, 45), but there will also be obdurate resistance (as described, e.g., in 2.7, 16, 18, 24). The opposition of some – those who are spiritually blind – is therefore within the overall will of God. It is something prophesied in Scripture; therefore it is to be expected. So Mark's is a form of apocalyptic theology, which stresses the sovereignty of God and which emphasizes that those things which God has willed are bound to come to pass.

Thus, at the very outset of the Gospel the whole mission of Jesus is described in a nutshell, and, very significantly, it is the prophet Isaiah who is seen as the prophet of God's future mission par excellence. As we have already seen, Matthew also regards Isaiah as the prophet of latter-day mission, although he describes this in a very different way. The importance of Isaiah in the self-understanding of the Early Church and its mission has been too little noticed or has been neglected up until the present time.

The mission of Jesus will, according to Mark, be seen primarily through the actions of Jesus – and his disciples, for, early on, he recruits helpers for the task of mission (1.14–20). Thereafter, signs of the kingdom of God accompany everything that is said: a man has a demon expelled from him (1.21–8); many people are healed of diseases (1.29–34). Wherever the message is delivered, there are signs following: 'And he went throughout Galilee, proclaiming the message in their syagogues and casting out demons' (1.39). If there is one thing we can be sure of about Mark's Gospel, it is that Jesus is a man with a mission. He is depicted as constantly appearing here and there, going backwards and forwards across Lake Galilee; and, in the wider sphere, moving gradually but inexorably towards his destiny – on a symbolic and then a real journey to Jerusalem, there to confront his detractors and there to fulfil the purposes of God for his life.

Jesus' mission encounters opposition right from the outset: he is obstructed in his mission by the religious authorities as well as by sceptical people of little faith. In Chapter 6 he is rejected in his own home town of Nazareth, and there he ruefully reflects, 'Prophets are not without honour, except in their home town, and among their own kin, and in their own house' (6.4). Then Mark adds an editorial comment which shocked later evangelists and the Church fathers: 'He could do no deed of power there . . . he was amazed at their unbelief' (6.5–6). This cul de sac then leads Jesus to take the mission off in a new direction: he sends out the twelve disciples on a campaign of their own, to the villages in the surrounding region and he gives them instructions as to how to conduct themselves on a mission.

After the death of John the Baptist, the theme of mission resumes. Jesus feeds five thousand men (6.30–44) and Mark deliberately and pointedly gives this story missionary overtones: 'he had compassion for them, because they were like sheep without a shepherd' (6.34). Shortly afterwards Mark provides his readers with a second feeding miracle: the feeding of the four thousand (8.1–10). Most commentators fail to see the significance of this second recounting of a feeding story and often merely regard it as a doublet, as though Mark has two traditions of the same story and rather haplessly and unnecessarily put them both into his short Gospel. Even the recent and largely excellent commentary on Mark by Joel Marcus follows the traditional line:

> The 'knot' in the narrative [i.e. the disciples' question], together with the striking parallels between the two passages, suggests to many commentators that 6.30–44 and 8.1–10 are variant accounts of the same event, both of which Mark has inherited from tradition.[38]

That may well be the case, but can that really be the reason Mark makes himself look foolish by telling the same story twice within the space of two chapters? Are there not real *differences* as well as similarities between these two stories? We will shortly return to this theme.

The Gospel narrative next comes to a period of preparation – an interlude during which the disciples are asked to reflect on who Jesus is, and on the purpose of his mission (8.27–38). The

Transfiguration account makes some of the answers clear to the disciples – and to the hearers and readers of the Gospel (9.2–13). Jesus speaks about the necessity of his suffering and death as an integral part of his mission – even the central ingredient of his mission (8.31–3; 9.30–2; and 10.32–4). After other healings and teachings, Jesus then enters Jerusalem in humility and in triumph (11.1–11). Clearly, the story of this mission is moving towards its denouement. Jesus curses a fruitless fig tree and then overturns the tables in the Temple. These acted parables are also coded messages to Mark's Christian audience: Jesus' mission will create a new Israel, one capable of bearing good fruit; and there will be no more need for a corrupt Temple with its sacrifices and rituals. The worshipping community will focus on a temple not made by human hands but fashioned by God himself – the Body of Christ. We will also be revisiting this theme.

The parable of the tenants in the vineyard drives home the earlier points (12.1–12). In the way he tells the story, and through his comment at the end, Mark spells it out: 'When they realized that he had told this parable against them, they wanted to arrest him' (12.12). A good deal of the subject matter around this section of the Gospel concerns Jesus' authority and the meaning of his coming. It concludes with a prophecy of the destruction of the Temple (13.1–2).

The rest of Chapter 13 speaks in apocalyptic language of the troubles and tribulations to come. More than likely, the churches of Mark's own region would have recognized these trials as the flipside of mission. Those who dared to challenge the powers and the established order through the preaching of the resurrection of Christ must expect a backlash of antagonism and even persecution (13.3–23). A word of encouragement follows the many words of warning:

> Then they will see 'the Son of Man coming in clouds' with great power and glory. Then he will send out the angels, and gather his elect from the four winds, from the ends of the world to the ends of heaven. (13. 26–7)

So the mission of the followers of the Son of Man will triumph in the end and will reach into the whole world. They will all be gathered in to celebrate at the heavenly banquet in the kingdom of God.

However, before all this happens, Jesus' own earthly ministry must come to its time of fulfilment at the cross. And so Mark moves forward to the Passion narrative, which takes up a third of the entire Gospel: the anointing at Bethany (presaging his death and burial); the betrayal by Judas; the Last Supper; prayer in Gethsemane; the arrest; the trial before the Sanhedrin, then before Pilate; the sentencing; the mockery and torture by the soldiers; then the crucifixion. The Gospel culminates in this death, and the resurrection is like a new door opening, a transformation of reality, the dawn of a new day, or even of a new age. The story might end on a note of anticipation and trepidation (16.8), but, even so, the reader is left in suspense, on the edge of a new departure. The disciples are called to follow Jesus who goes before them into Galilee (16.7), which hints that the mission of the Church is about to be inaugurated.

A brief overview of Mark's Gospel in the manner described makes clear the pattern of events and the dynamic motive force of the Gospel: it is the mission of Jesus and of his disciples. Yet it is very easy to lose sight of this in a welter of detail or to focus on only one particular aspect of the story. The movement from place to place, event to event – and, particularly, the general movement from Galilee to Jerusalem – is of Mark's own creation and is designed to give an impression of an urgent mission which must be fulfilled with single-minded purpose. The schema of Mark is not really based closely on any early chronology or historical reconstruction – John's Gospel with its very different chronology makes that clear. The layout of Mark shows that the evangelist conceived his Gospel from the outset as a mission document.

The pattern and progression of Jesus' ministry and work in Mark reveals not only that there is an overall mission theme in Mark, but that there is also a gradual opening up of the mission.

It has its beginnings in the local setting around Nazareth and its immediate neighbourhood, to the region of Lake Galilee: then there is an oscillation to and fro, criss-crossing the lake, going from Jewish to more mixed population areas and back again. This is how it happens: the Galilean mission begins in 1.14–20 and follows through until 4.41. Then there is an excursion into the region of Gerasa; this serves as a premonition of the mission to the Gentiles (5.1–20). Then the Galilean mission resumes (5.20—7.23) and after this Jesus' work takes him beyond the confines of Galilee and leads to encounters with the Gentiles (7.24—8.10). That marks the end of this pattern. Thereafter, the conflict with the authorities and the journey to Jerusalem take precedence. Before examining this matter in further detail, it is worth pausing for a moment to ask the preliminary question, 'What is the content of Jesus' mission?' For Mark, the answer is perhaps simple and yet enigmatic; it is 'the kingdom of God'. But what exactly is the kingdom?

God's kingdom and Jesus

The kingdom of God is first mentioned explicitly in the four-teenth verse of the first chapter of Mark: 'Jesus came to Galilee, proclaiming the good news of God, and saying, "The time is fulfilled, and the kingdom of God has come near; repent, and believe in the good news".' These words seem meaningful, but they are mysterious.

As in apocalyptic literature the good news has to be disclosed. The mind needs a revelation from God to understand the message, and the message itself needs to be clothed with content. And, as Mark himself indicates elsewhere, to those without spiritual discernment the kingdom will always remain a mystery, while to those to whom God unveils the secret all starts to become clear. When asked about the purpose of his teaching in parables, Jesus tells his disciples:

> To you has been given the secret of the kingdom of God, but for those outside, everything comes in parables; in order that

'they may indeed look, but not perceive, and may indeed listen, but not understand; so that they may not turn again and be forgiven'. (4.11–12)

The passage may be puzzling, especially in the light of the need for a response of faith in order to understand, but Mark does not in any way alleviate the harshness of the quotation for his readers.

The Gospel begins with the main subject: 'The beginning of the good news of Jesus Christ, the Son of God' (1.1). As the events unfold it is clear that everything focuses on Jesus, and everyone is judged in the light of their response or relationship to him. Jesus becomes both the subject and the object of faith. He is indeed the subject of one quarter of the verbs in the Gospel, with a further fifth spoken by him in his teaching and parables. Through his healings, exorcisms and miraculous works of power (*dunameis*) as well as through his teaching, he becomes the object of faith; and all who put their trust in him or seek his blessing are commended, whatever background they come from.

The action and teaching of the Gospel discloses that the kingdom itself is revealed by Jesus, through whom the powers of the Age to Come are already present. At the same time, the kingdom is revealed actually *to be* the presence and person of Jesus. The works of power of the gospel and the authority in the teaching of Jesus are in fact signs that God is active in a new way. For those with eyes to see, the charismatic presence of Jesus in Mark reveals the indwelling Holy Spirit, or better, the radiance and power (*shekinah*) of God himself. So it is Mark's intention to demonstrate that the kingdom is both revealed by Jesus and revealed *to be Jesus*.

Yet despite the fact that the key to the kingdom in Mark is *christological* – that is, how Jesus is understood, or who he is understood to be; nevertheless the disciples (and others) are consistently unable to perceive the truth or to fathom the meaning of Jesus' mission. They have the secret (*musterion*) of the kingdom, yet repeatedly fail to grasp its significance. This is evident in the three boat scenes (4.40–1; 6.50–2; 8.14–21). The disciples also display complete misunderstanding by wanting the best places in the kingdom for themselves (10.35–45); they set their minds against Jesus' suffering (8.32–3; 9.32; 10.32–41); they fall asleep in Gethsemane and desert Jesus, and, to cap it all, Judas betrays him and Peter denies him (14.37–50, 66–72). Matthew tries to soften this unflattering picture of the disciples' obtuseness. Where, in Mark (4.40), they are completely lacking in faith, in Matthew (8.26) they become 'men of little faith', while Luke allows the disciples to plead with Jesus to 'increase our faith' (Luke 17.5). Some see this as reflecting the fact that Mark's own community has leaders who are dull-witted and who mislead the flock – people with a wrongheaded theology.[39] In fact, it is truer to say that the disciples find Jesus extremely difficult to comprehend fully. To grasp that a mere man is the embodiment of the kingdom of God is not easy! Jesus does not give up on them, even though he does become frustrated with them. He continues to teach them more than he teaches the crowds (see 7.17–23; 8.34–8; 10.23–31; 11.20–5; 13.5–37). And of course at the end his mission is entrusted to their safe-keeping (14.28; 16.7).

Thus, it is important to interpret the kingdom in the light of Mark's Christology – that is, in terms of Jesus' actions, teachings and the revelation of his nature. It is also equally important to understand Jesus' mission and the mission of the Church in the Gospel by making use of this christological key again – how does Jesus present the message of the kingdom and how do we see it in action through his ministry?

In the authority of Jesus (*exousia*), one encounters the authority of God and of his Word. But Mark also shows that the kingdom is a place of compassion, gentleness and mercy. Jesus associates himself boldly and deliberately with outcasts and marginalized people. This theme will be taken up and greatly developed by Luke later on, but it is already present in Mark's remarkable stories of table fellowship with tax collectors and sinners (2.14–17), his friendship with women (1.30–1; 5.25–34, 35–43; 12.41–4; 14.3–9; 15.40–1, 47; 16.1–8); with children (10.13–16) and with lepers (1.40–5). He speaks on behalf of the 'little ones' of the world and takes up their cause (9.42; 10.24–30). Mark also treats the Gentiles as a marginalized group, because they are considered to be ritually unclean in Jewish eyes. Jesus' willingness to engage with Gentiles (without actually seeking them out) is part of his willingness to engage with all 'outcasts' (see e.g. 7.24–30).

The kingdom has been the eschatological hope of Israel and of her prophets, but is now present or at hand, for 'the time is fulfilled' (1.15); the wedding feast prepared (2.19); the seed is already growing secretly (4.3–9, 26, 30); the Elijah figure has already come (9.13). The signs of God's power in action are signs that God is establishing the kingdom upon the earth. This is something that was expected in the end times.

Jesus in Mark exudes a sense of assurance that nothing can prevent the final triumph of God, not even his own suffering and demise. In fact, paradoxically, Mark manages to convey forcefully the idea that it is precisely through Jesus' victimization and crucifixion that the kingdom is ushered in.

Signs of a universal mission

As has already been intimated, Mark imposes a geographical pattern upon his material. That is not to say that he invents the historical record, but rather that he makes it much more clear-cut and symbolic than it might have been in reality. He focuses his account of Jesus' ministry upon Galilee (1.2–8, 21); uses a central section to mark the transition to a new phase (8.22—10.52) and completes Jesus' mission as a whole in Jerusalem (11.1—16.8). Most of Jesus' proclamation and demonstration of the coming kingdom takes place in Galilee, while the enemy offensive – plotting, verbal attacks, trial, torture, putting to death – largely takes place in Jerusalem. Much of this probably does reflect historical tradition, although John's Gospel has it that Jesus went up to Jerusalem several times at least to participate in the major Jewish festivals. This sounds eminently possible if Jesus observed normal Jewish protocol, so Mark is probably simplifying the real situation, to say the least. Why does he do this?

It is most likely that he wishes to create a polarization between Galilee – the place of religious enthusiasm, messianic hopes, charismatic healers – and Jerusalem – the centre of power, vested interests and of a corrupt political and religious establishment. He also wishes to highlight Galilee as an area of mixed population where Jesus' own mission began a movement which culminated in the Gentile mission of the Church. For it was from the Galilean base that the Church began to expand eastwards and northwards into Syria – into Gentile territory. There is, in all likelihood, a link to be established between Christianity's beginnings in Galilee and later developments in Syria. Commentators are now arguing over whether Mark's Gospel itself might have had a Syrian provenance.[40] Thus, Jesus' promise to his disciples near the end of the Gospel: 'But after I am raised up, I will go before you into Galilee' (14.28). The word 'go before' (*proagein*) relates back to 10.32 where Jesus is depicted as leading his disciples towards Jerusalem. After the terrible events which took place there – in Jerusalem – Jesus now expresses a wish to return to the place of mission and outreach, in order to renew his work, but in a new way: in the power of the resurrection and in an unrestricted embracing of the Gentiles. This return to Galilee is a signal that a new mission is about to be inaugurated. The community will be gathered and commissioned and given a share in spreading the kingdom in word and power to all the surrounding regions.

The symbolism of Galilee as a mission base is hinted at even in the earlier parts of the Gospel. Jesus' journeyings around and across the Sea of Galilee are not motiveless movements, but are rather demonstrations that, starting from mission to Israel, Jesus will reach out to the Gentiles with tentative, anticipatory steps towards a mission which will burst into full life later on. Up until 4.35 Jesus' ministry is located exclusively in Jewish settings. But then Jesus embarks for 'the other side'. Then follows the storm story during which Jesus shows beyond doubt that, like God himself, he is able to control the forces of chaos. Quite possibly, one aspect of the account of the storm is that Jesus is able to face and master the demonic powers which defend and protect the Gentile areas on the other side of the lake.

Upon reaching the far side of the lake, Jesus comes into contact with the Gerasene demoniac (5.1–20) – a Gentile in Gentile territory. Gerasa was one of the towns of the Decapolis originally founded by Alexander the Great as a group of ten free Hellenistic cities. Now Jesus has to master the forces of chaos in a different way, this time the forces of chaos within human life. The demoniac is described as having superhuman strength to break his chains and to smash the irons on his feet. 'No one had the strength to subdue him' (5.4). The impression of evil and chaos is very powerfully conveyed in Mark's account: 'Night and day among the tombs and on the mountains he was always howling and bruising himself with stones' (5.5). The man is at the mercy of external destructive forces and has no power to save himself. A greater power is needed. Jesus is able to pacify the man, just as he was able to calm the storm at sea. So he liberates the man from the unclean powers controlling him and turning him against his own nature. These spirits 'screamed in a loud voice'; not now to intimidate but through a fear of Jesus 'the Son of the Most High God'. Jesus then sends the unclean spirits into a herd of pigs, as they begged him to, but then the pigs destroy themselves by rushing over the side of a cliff and into the lake.

The presence of pigs shows beyond doubt that this is Gentile territory. And the fact that the pigs are destroyed as well as the evil spirits banished is a sign to Mark's Jewish readers that not only is the Gentile madman cleansed but also the land is being cleansed too. Mark manages in a few words to convey an overwhelming sense of *impurity* and *danger*: evil spirits, screaming, nakedness, burial tombs, a herd of pigs – all of these things would have induced a sense of horror and revulsion among Jews. Yet at the end of the story the man is drawn away from the tombs, he is 'clothed and in his right mind' (5.15). The pigs have gone, the spirits are exorcized. The man then wants to leave the territory and follow Jesus into the boat, but Jesus refused and ordered him home to his family to 'tell them how much the Lord has done for you, and what mercy he has shown you' (5.19). The incipient Gentile mission has begun: 'And he went away and began to proclaim in the Decapolis how much Jesus had done for him' (5.20). Although Mark the evangelist stops short at speaking of conversions of the Gentiles, for the time presumably was not yet ripe, he simply adds: 'and everyone was amazed' (5.20).

In Matthew's account the story ends when the people of Gerasa went out to Jesus to beg him to leave their territory (Matthew 8.34). The testimony of the demoniac to the Ten Cities is omitted. The symbolism is altered. The Jewish and the Gentile missions are, in Matthew, to be kept very much apart for the duration of Jesus' ministry. Jesus' mission during his ministry is only to the lost sheep of the house of Israel. But Mark is happy to leave the story open-ended. From the time of Jesus' ministry, the first-fruits of the Gentile mission are already in evidence. The spread of Jesus' fame – and the widening of his mission – are both irresistible and inevitable. When Jesus tells the demoniac to tell his family 'how much the Lord has done for you'(5.19), the man then tells everyone what *Jesus* has done for him. The acts of Jesus are thus equated with the mighty acts of God, another sign that Jesus is the embodiment of the kingdom.

The whole story, in its Marcan form, is reminiscent of Isaiah 65.1–7, where God reaches out to a people who had not sought him; a people who sit in tombs, consult the spirits of the dead, who eat pork and drink broth made from meat offered in sacrifices; who speak evil of God at their pagan hill shrines.[41] But the difference is startling: in Isaiah God's anger flares up against such people like a fire (Isaiah 65.5), but in Mark's account Jesus' mercy reaches out to such people, not like a consuming fire, but more like a refining, purifying fire.

The link between this passage and the stilling of the storm incident (4.35–41) as well as with the debate about 'binding the strong man' and driving out Satan (3.22–30) provides a context in which this exorcism story can be seen as a further – even a new – demonstration of God's coming kingdom, when even the souls of the Gentiles will be cleansed and their land purged of idols and spirits. The full horror of the scale of evil in the Gentile territories is brilliantly communicated through the imagery of the story: the madman with superhuman strength terrorizing the area, the location with graves and unclean spirits, the multiple possession by a legion of spirits, the stampede of the pigs over a cliff-side, the fear of the cowed population.

Embarking upon the Gentile mission is obviously regarded by Mark as not something to be embarked upon lightly or without forethought. It requires great courage and spiritual strength. It will draw frightening opposition on many fronts, and those who confront the spirits of such places will face persecution. The demonic unclean Gentiles, like the oppressive power of a Roman legion, will not willingly be dislodged from the lands they have occupied. There will be opposition and counter-attacks wherever there is such mission. Yet, Mark is wanting to reassure his audience that the power of God will ensure victory. The kingdom can and will be established. The liberation of the possessed man thus becomes a symbol for the anticipated redemption of the world.

The very next story takes Jesus back across the lake to the western side, into Jewish territory and to the local synagogue, to a pure and sacred space. Jesus continues to display the awesome power of the new age of the kingdom by raising the synagogue official's daughter from death to life. As Joel Marcus says: 'It will become clear just how discontinuous with the sad, predictable course of affairs in the dying old world is the eschatological power of the rejected Jesus – a power still coursing through the Marcan community.'[42] Jesus also heals a woman who had been losing blood for 12 years and whom nobody could help or cure (5.21–43). After these seemingly impossible healings, Jesus is astonishingly rejected by his own people in Nazareth (6.1–6). Even this is a signal from the evangelist that Jesus' mission will soon begin to turn away from an unbelieving Judaism to a more receptive paganism, from Jewish mission to Gentile mission.

Immediately after this episode, Mark returns to the theme of mission with the sending out of the twelve disciples. The number twelve hints at the restoration of the twelve tribes of Israel, as does the very phrase 'among the villages' (6.6). They are sent out in pairs and are forbidden from taking any money or luggage with them, apart from a walking staff and sandals. They must travel light and depend on the hospitality of others. In fact, hospitality – the response to the work of the twelve – becomes the touchstone for salvation or judgement: 'If any place will not welcome you and they refuse to hear you, as you leave, shake off the dust that is on your feet as a testimony against them' (6.11–12). The disciples go out proclaiming repentance, casting out demons and healing the sick (6.12–13). They are over-joyed at their own success (6.12–13, 30), a fact which actually betrays their lack of faith and understanding more than their achievements!

Jesus' mission instructions in Mark are terse and cryptic, as in the parallel from Luke 9.1–6, but the Lucan mission instructions based on another source ('Q'?) in Luke 10.4–7 soften the rigour and make the lifestyle more positive – 'Whatever house you enter, first say, "Peace to this house!"'(Luke 10.5). Mark concentrates more on the ascetic living and on the possibility of rejection and antagonism – this is a theme of Mark's Gospel of course, and perhaps reflects difficulties encountered by missionaries in the Marcan church(es). Yet Mark's theology implies that the greater the opposition the greater God's power and the manifestation of the kingdom. Persecution and opposition should not deter those on mission: it should encourage them to act even more boldly and to proclaim the gospel even more forcefully (see 13.9–13). Jesus does not give up on any region, but keeps extending his mission. The mission instructions show that the important ingredient for mission is *faith* – and this means not only faith in God's power to save and to heal but also faith that he will provide for the physical needs of his servants and for their well-being. They do not need bread or money, nor even a change of clothes.

These instructions would have reminded Jewish readers of the sustaining power of God when the Israelites were wandering in the desert for 40 years. They received 'bread from heaven' in the form of manna and they did not need to replace their clothes. The staff is reminiscent of the 'staffs of power' carried by Moses and Aaron (Exodus 4.7–8): Mark may wish to imply that this departure on mission is like a new exodus, a 'way out' which leads to the promised land of God's kingdom. They will be sustained on 'the way' by God's grace alone. The Greek of 6.7

says that Jesus *began* (*erxato*) to send the twelve on mission; and we can infer that this was the inception of a missionary activity which would continue into the time of the Church and its subsequent missions. There is a foreshadowing of the post-Easter activity of the apostles and later disciples. And once more Mark – through subtle suggestions and hints – manages to link together the Jewish and Gentile missions. Ben Witherington notes that:

> The Twelve are clearly seen as an extension of Jesus' own ministry. They are his authorized agents. As it stands, the text reads as though we are to see in this commissioning a fore-shadowing of the eventual post-Easter roles of the disciples, but this commission during the ministry was apparently unique and limited in scope. Thus the provisions about clothing and eating were never taken in the Early Church to be generally applicable to all missionary ventures.[43]

The death of John the Baptist (6.14–29) forms an interlude which metaphorically gives time for the disciples' mission to run its course, but which also forms a contrast with what follows. Witherington calls the beheading 'a gruesome banquet' (p. 212) and what follows 'a grand feast' (p. 217): 'One foreshadows the demise of Jesus, the other the rise of the eschatological feast in the dominion of God' (p. 217).

Jesus remains in Jewish territory for the feeding of the five thousand. The connection of this episode with mission is made explicit from the outset: 'The apostles gathered around Jesus, and told him all that they had done and taught' (6.30). The disciples are now recruited by Jesus to be full helpers in his mission, despite their foibles and failings. On the whole, Mark shows that the disciples are well capable of doing Jesus' bidding, even if they do not always understand the full implications of what they are doing!

The feeding theme recalls the Exodus motif once more, reminding readers how Israel was fed in the desert from God's own hand (Exodus 16). Feeding also has connotations with teaching and instruction and with spiritual nourishment. Bread was a traditional Jewish symbol of the Torah – the teaching and guidance of God. The first feeding miracle begins a chain of miracles illustrating the drawing of both Jew and Gentile into the kingdom.

If we take the two feeding miracles together, it becomes clear that Mark has a purpose behind the duplication, as we intimated earlier. The first episode (6.30–44) takes place on the Jewish (western) side of the lake, while the second (8.1–10) takes place on the more Gentile (eastern) side, and follows on from the encounter with the Syrophoenician woman (7.24–30) and the healing of the deaf mute (7.31–7). The crowd in the first feeding miracle is described as being 'like sheep without a shepherd' (6.34), a traditional image for Israel and her leaders. They came from all the towns in the region (6.33) and ran to meet Jesus, showing great enthusiasm. The locality is also mentioned in 6.36: 'Send them away so that they may go into the surrounding country and villages and buy something for themselves to eat'. In Israel surely they will find something to sustain them! And there it is the disciples' responsibility to feed them. So they are cast in the role of apostles, leading and feeding the people who have been let down by their own leaders. The people are grouped in companies of 50 and 100, reminiscent of the grouping of Israel in the desert – an echo of Exodus 18.25 and of Numbers 35.14. After the feeding, the disciples gather in 12 baskets of leftover bread and fish, as though each Israelite tribe had a little to spare.

In the second story (8.1–10), Jesus is in the vicinity of the Decapolis once again (7.31). The number of disciples is not mentioned. Jesus is sorry for the crowd, not because they are like sheep without a shepherd, but because 'they have been with me now for three days and have nothing to eat' (8.2). They are in a desert place with no nearby villages or houses. This time Jesus has seven loaves at his disposal, as well as 'a few small fish' (8.5, 7). There were also seven baskets of pieces left over. These numbers are surely significant. And particularly given that the numbers in the second narrative are all different from those in the first. The number 5,000 could relate to the five books of Moses (the Torah or Pentateuch). The number 4,000, however, is puzzling. Could it refer to the four corners of the earth?[44] The waiting period of three days in the second narrative could be an indeterminate length of time, but traditionally was understood as the time God waits before coming to the aid of his people (see e.g. Hosea 6.2). Here, of course, it might foreshadow the eschatological power of God in raising Jesus and thereby coming to help his people. The seven loaves and seven baskets would denote fullness or completeness. With the inclusion of the Gentiles, Jesus' mission therefore becomes complete. It was also thought that the Gentile nations numbered 70 in all. Not only that, but the Gentiles come under the decrees of the Covenant of Noah, which traditionally has seven commandments.

These stories have many connotations, especially with the feeding miracles of Elijah and Elisha (1 Kings 17.8–16; 2 Kings 4.1–7, 42–4) and the banqueting feast of the coming kingdom of God (e.g. Isaiah 25.6–9). Looking forward, there is also surely an allusion to the Eucharist or Lord's Supper, with the teaching and spiritual food of a service of worship. But strangely, the connection with *mission* is often overlooked.

Very clearly, the *first* feeding miracle shows Jesus manifesting himself to Israel as the new Moses, but in the second story, there is no allusion or reference to Moses (or Elisha) at all. Some of the *second* crowd come 'from far off' (8.3) – a way of referring to the Gentiles in the first century. Because Mark has composed each story so carefully, with such deliberate use of different vocabulary and different numbers, there can be no doubt that he means to tell his audience that the banqueting feast in the kingdom of God is going to be for both Jews and Gentiles. But they are treated separately in the Gospel because the two missions are conceived in different terms: one is a restoration, a coming out of Egypt into the Land of Promise; whilst the other is conceived as a new departure, a generous and gracious reaching out of redeemed Israel (that is, Jesus and his disciples) to a lost and forlorn people who are hungry both physically and spiritually, who are leaderless and far from God. The two stories are therefore separated in time deliberately in order to indicate that Jesus' mission to the Jews will come first, and then his mission to the Gentiles in its own due time.

Clearly, to understand why Mark allows two similar feeding miracles into his Gospel, it is necessary to look at the stories from the point of view of mission.

Between the two feeding miracles we have several further stories which take the form of a transition between what went before and what comes afterwards. Jesus' disciples head for Bethsaida, once again crossing the lake (6.45). Jesus appears walking on the water when the boat was in the middle of the lake (6.47). This recalls the earlier stilling of the storm (4.35–41) and a comment also reminds the reader of the first feeding story: '[The disciples] did not understand about the loaves, but their hearts were hardened' (6.52). This comment is enigmatic, especially away from the context of the feeding miracle, but it probably means that the disciples' hardness of heart is like that of the Israelites in the desert. Jesus' disciples have seen him feed a vast crowd with no resources to speak of, in the same way that God himself fed the Israelite multitude with manna from heaven. He had thereby manifested himself as one greater than Moses, one with God-like powers. Now the walking on the water confirms this aspect of God-like control over natural phenomena.

The confrontation with the Pharisees in 7.1–23 looks both back and forward. Jesus explains that ritual external cleansing is pointless and unnecessary: 'But the things that come out are what defile' (7.16). The need is for inner purity and holiness of life. This is not dependent upon ritual washing or purification rites. The importance of this can hardly be overemphasized. Jesus in this way gives short shrift to the notion that ritual purity is a necessary part of the observance of God's Law. He effectively declares all foods clean, as the evangelist himself declares in an editorial note in verse 19. This then paves the way for table fellowship with the Gentiles, something inconceivable to Jews intent on keeping the Law strictly. In addition, he makes it possible for Gentiles to come to God on the same terms as Jews.

The prerequisite is a cleansed heart, a clear conscience and a pure faith.

This point about Gentile access to table fellowship comes across in the story immediately following, when Jesus meets with the Syrophoenician woman (7.24–30) and then with a deaf mute (7.31–7) – and it is confirmed in the story we have already examined, the feeding of the four thousand (8.1–10). First of all, Jesus moves on and enters the Gentile areas once again, 'to the region of Tyre' (7.24) and enters the unclean environment of a Gentile house. Once again, uncleanness is signalled by the presence of an evil spirit: the woman's daughter 'had an unclean spirit' (7.25). Mark states baldly that the woman was a 'Greek' – shorthand for a Gentile (7.26). The exorcism is understood in terms of *feeding* and Jesus resists the woman's request with harsh words: 'It is not fair to take the children's food and throw it to the dogs' (7.27). The word 'dog' (*kunarios*) was used at the time as a term of abuse for Gentiles (e.g. 1 Enoch 89.47, 49). Yet the woman remains undaunted by this: 'Even the dogs under the table eat the children's crumbs' (Mark 7.28). Jesus relents, praises the woman's wit as well as her faith and heals the daughter (7.29–30).

The severity of Jesus' rebuke might well reflect tension between Galileans and Tyrians. Much of the agricultural produce of Jewish Galilee ended up in Gentile Tyre at this time. This meant that Jewish peasants often had to endure hunger.[45] It might also show Mark's readers that Jesus did not readily abandon his mission to Israel as his first priority. Nor did he regard Gentiles in exactly the same light as God's children, the Jewish people. The specific designation of the woman as Syrophoenician, meaning a Phoenician living in the Roman province of Syria as opposed to Carthage (Libya), could easily be a clue to the origin of Mark's own Gospel, for his readership might well have understood the precise location indicated, because they themselves lived in the same part of Syria, or nearby.

The word 'first' (*proton*) in 'Let the children be fed first' (7.27) is important, since it confirms that Jesus saw his mission as to Jews *first*. 'First' is not the same as 'only'. The expansion of the gospel mission will occur in its due time; that is, after events have taken place which make it possible, in the divine scheme of things. This is an eschatological timescale which views outreach to the Gentile nations as a sign of the last times, a harvest which is a final ingathering prior to the last judgement: 'first the stalk, then the head, then the full grain in the head' (4.28).

The Syrophoenician woman resembles other wise women of the Bible who overcome dismissive male attitudes by the use of wit, cunning and intelligence – qualities much admired in the Middle East in Jesus' time. The woman from Tekoa in 2 Samuel 14 manoeuvres King David into changing his mind about the banishment of Absolom. Elsewhere, Esther is able to persuade the king to kill Haman for plotting to destroy the Jews in Persia, and by further cunning diplomacy she enables her people to protect themselves: a role they accepted rather too enthusiastically (Esther 7 and 8)!

Because Jesus has already overruled the dietary laws which separated Jew and Gentile socially, he is now able to respond favourably to the Gentile woman's petition. Perhaps he would have preferred to 'hide' in Gentile territory – he does attempt to keep his 'secret' in other Gentile contexts (Mark 5.19–20; 7.24, 36–7). Yet the one who is a light to the Gentiles cannot keep his light hidden; for, as Mark is aware, God's purpose is that the Messiah in particular, and Israel in general, will be a light for all nations. Jesus' reluctance to help the Gentile woman probably therefore has more to do with a sense that the time is not yet right, rather than any racial or ethnic prejudice. This is surely correct in the light of Jesus' other contacts with Gentiles. Once again, it is necessary to look at a Marcan passage from the point of view of the evangelist's understanding of mission.

Modern indignation at Jesus' 'offensive' reply is perhaps anachronistic, just as Martin Luther's notion that Jesus is intent on testing the woman's faith is more applicable to his own preoccupations than being in the mind of the evangelist. The reaching out to the Gentiles – the great opportunity and challenge of the Early Church – is surely a response to Jesus' own openness and encouragement of such a mission. It is vital to see

Jesus' one-off response to this Gentile woman in the light of that general understanding. His approach in other situations provides something of a counterbalance to his apparent reluctance in one instance (e.g. 7.31; 13.10; 15.39). And in the final analysis, Jesus does go out of his way to help the Syrophoenician woman.

The story of the Gentile woman is remarkable in several ways. It is the only example in Mark of Jesus entering a Gentile house, and it is also the only example of a person changing Jesus' mind. It portrays a very Jewish Jesus who is fastidious about mixing with Gentiles, despite his strong theological convictions. He clearly sees his own people as God's children. The new wine of the gospel (see 2.21–2) is already breaking the boundaries of Judaism and of the old dispensation. Yet Mark uses this passage to insist upon the precedence of the Jews in God's plan of salvation. The help afforded to this woman nevertheless gives a foretaste of the universal mission which is bound to come, and which will preoccupy the thoughts and actions of the church in the days to come.

The healing of the deaf mute (7.31–7) is not often seen as having anything to do with the Gentile mission – but then nor are various other passages, such as the feeding of the four thousand or the old and the new wine. It is only when Mark as a whole is viewed as a mission document that many of the parables and stories relate to that theme in new ways. It is important to note in this context that for this healing miracle, Jesus has remained in mainly Gentile territory – still the Decapolis region (7.31): Jesus' itinerary is certainly complicated.

Superficially this is a physical healing, but at a deeper level it speaks of the dire spiritual condition of the Gentiles. They cannot hear God's voice, do not know his Word, and are unable to speak of his grace. Jesus' behaviour in this instance shows great sensitivity. He takes the man aside, uses a kind of sign language to communicate what he is about to do, and says the Aramaic word '*Ephphatha*' ('Open up') which could easily be lip-read. Jesus' actions enable the Gentile's ears to be opened to hear his word and his tongue to be loosened so he can spread the good news of God's grace. In this way, we witness here something far more than just another healing miracle (or exorcism). Rather, it serves as a paradigm. It is a symbolic opening of ears and loosening of tongues by God's power. Where beforehand the deaf mute – and those like him – had lived in ignorance and darkness with regard to God, now he is made whole in more senses than just the physical.

Jesus enjoins secrecy upon the people who witnessed this event, perhaps once again because the time was not yet right for the Gentile mission. Nevertheless, the power and the light of God cannot be contained or hidden: 'the more he ordered them, the more zealously they proclaimed it' (7.36). The Gentiles are now becoming more responsive than most Jews: 'They were astounded beyond measure, saying, "He has done everything well"' (7.37). Not yet Gentile conversion, but an openness, a time for preparation.

In this story of the deaf mute there are also echoes of Isaiah 35.5–6, which is about that eschatological time when God will heal the blind and the deaf. The difficulty with the Old Testament passage is that the prophecy contains words about God's judgement falling on Israel's enemies (35.4, 8). These enemies are not specified as Gentiles; neither does Mark apply any words of judgement when Jesus has dealings with the Gentiles. In this he is similar to Luke, who reports Jesus reading in the synagogue a lesson from Isaiah 61.1–2. In that case – to be found in Luke 4.18–19 – Jesus is shown as deliberately omitting or passing over in silence the words of judgement at the end of Isaiah 61.2. The gospel tradition – very likely passing on a tradition about Jesus' own attitude, sees God's eschatological purpose as an intention *to bless* the Gentile nations with good news of salvation, rather than to condemn and punish them as Israel's enemies.

Mark's pattern of taking Jesus back and forth between 'Jewish' and 'Gentile' regions now begins to come to an end, and the completion of the whole first section of the Gospel culminates with Peter's confession of Jesus as 'the Christ' at Caesarea Philippi (8.27–30). It is worth pointing out that this takes the form of a testimony in the sight of both Jews and Gentiles.

Caesarea Philippi was a major Hellenistic city built in honour of the Emperor Augustus. So in a city dedicated to a false god the identity of the true God is revealed. Going a little further, but without stretching the point too far, we could say that Jesus' intention, if not to embark upon a Gentile mission, is nevertheless *to unite Jews and Gentiles through their faith in him*. The confession at Caesarea Philippi seems designed to demonstrate this, by focusing on Jesus as the saviour of Jew and Gentile alike. Once again, Mark makes the most of this coded information about geographical locations.

The bringing together of Jew and Gentile in unity surely reflects the hope of the evangelist himself. Mark is showing the unifying work of Jesus as a pattern for the ongoing mission of his own community and of the Church in general. As Senior and Stuhlmueller rightly suggest, in more general terms: 'The community is asked to consider Jesus' embrace of Jew and Gentile – even through rejection and death – as the pattern of the proclamation of the Gospel that now "begins".'[46]

After Caesarea Philippi the focus shifts – to the time of preparation for Jesus' suffering and death. The theology of the cross – of Jesus' suffering paradoxically revealing God's glory – dominates the rest of the Gospel. But even in all this there is significance for the Gentile mission, because it is the very rejection of Jesus in his own homeland which is seen by Mark as the way by which the route to the Gentile mission is opened up. It becomes crystal clear that Jesus' ministry is going to meet with hostility and rejection from the religious and political leaders in Israel and even from members of his own family and those closest to him. But that same ministry will be accepted and welcomed with various degrees of openness and faith on the part of the disciples and the Gentiles.

There was little or no expectation in early Judaism that the Messiah would come to suffer, and that despite the Servant Songs of Isaiah. The likelihood is that they were not understood as messianic prophecies in Jewish circles in Jesus' time. Mark has a difficult task trying to convince both Jews and Gentiles that the suffering of the Messiah was necessary and that his death had a universal significance and a bearing on the salvation of the world.

The stages in the scheme of salvation

The first half of Mark's Gospel (1.14—8.21) is taken up with Jesus' ministry and mission; the second half with rejection, end-time prophecies and then the passion narrative, leading up to crucifixion and resurrection. However, the two sections are not completely separate. The first half contains some premonitions or anticipations of what is to come in its conflict stories, in which Jesus encounters irrational hostility. He is accused of blasphemy (2.6–12), of eating with unclean people (2.16–17), of refusing to fast or observe the Sabbath (2.18–20; 2.24–7; 3.2–3) and of being in league with the devil (3.20–30). His own family accuse him of being mad and attempt to abduct him (3.31–5) and a plot is hatched to murder him (3.6). All of this takes place within the first three chapters of the Gospel. In the same way, the second half is not only about conflict and rejection or what is to come in the future; it contains further elements of straightforward teaching and ministry (e.g. 9.14–29; 10.13–16, 17–31, 46–52).

However, it is noticeable that much of the teaching and ministry in the second half has an edge to it and often relates directly to the events of the end of Jesus' life. The Transfiguration scene points forward to Jesus' glorification (9.2–13). The disciples' argument about who is greatest (9.33–7) and request for the best places in the kingdom (10.35–45) give rise to talk about suffering and also point to the disintegration of fellowship among the disciples. The triumphal entry into Jerusalem also has a shadow side; it is clearly a provocative act in the eyes of many. Was it a rallying of the troops in preparation for rebellion? The acted parable of the cursing of the fig tree (11.12–14) has a confrontational element – is this the cursing of Israel? And the parable of the tenants in the vineyard (12.1–12) reinforces the impression: Israel's leaders have betrayed the prophets and the son of the owner of the vineyard. No wonder the parable ends with the Jewish leaders wanting to arrest Jesus. And so it goes on:

everything that Jesus says or does in this section takes on a prophetic aspect.

Matters come to an early crisis when Jesus attacks the very power-base of Israel's leaders – the Temple. By overturning the tables of the moneychangers in the entrance area, he condemns the exploitation of the poor and simultaneously blocks the smooth running of the sacrificial cult (11.15–19). All of Chapters 11–13 of the Gospel take place in the setting of the Temple and, before leaving, Jesus condemns the Temple to destruction: 'Do you see these great buildings? Not one stone will be left here upon another; all will be thrown down' (13.2). Mark in this way focuses on the Temple, which has become the central symbol for Israel's corrupt established religion, and is seen as the base for an opposition whose power, prestige and authority Jesus threatens to undermine. Jesus' prophetic words about the Temple have the effect of a curse oracle. However, one of his sentences is given a special significance by Mark, namely, the quotation from Isaiah 56.7, 'My house shall be called a house of prayer for all the nations' (Mark 11.17). By this Mark wishes to indicated that Jesus conceived of a new temple in the age to come, which would be a universal place of worship for all peoples. This will be what J. Donahue calls 'the eschatological house of prayer for all nations'[47] which will replace the Temple made by human hands.

Another quotation, from Psalm 118 (a favourite Psalm of the Early Church), gives a clue as to how this will come about: 'The stone that the builders rejected has become the chief cornerstone. This is the Lord's doing: it is marvellous in our eyes'(vv. 22–3). The rejection of Jesus allows God to open up true spiritual worship to the Gentiles through the creation of a 'spiritual' edifice; a new community of worship who themselves become living stones built upon the foundation stone of Christ's body.

At the moment of Jesus' death, there is the sign of the curtain in the Temple torn from top to bottom (Mark 15.38). The Holy of Holies, 'containing' the glory of God's presence, now becomes accessible. There is no bar on direct access to the very heart of God and to the Holy Place. In this way, Mark confirms what

Jesus has in effect prophesied, that all those searching for God – whether Jew or Gentile – will now find him, because the death of Christ is effective for all people. This point is further reinforced immediately after the curtain incident, when a Roman centurion, representing the Gentile races, seeing how Jesus died, exclaims, 'Truly this man was God's Son' (15.39). This moment of revelation is also a prefiguring of the response of many other Gentiles to Jesus and marks the real beginning of the mission to the nations.

The Gospel of Mark is thus split into two sections. The first climaxes with Peter's confession of the Christ at Caesarea Philippi and this has its counterpart in the second section when Jesus is asked *by his enemies* – and the High Priest in particular, 'Are you the Messiah, the Son of the Blessed One?' To this Jesus replies unequivocally in Mark: 'I am; and "you will see the Son of Man seated at the right hand of the Power", and "coming with the clouds of heaven"' (14.61–2). The first recognition, by Peter, is tentative, hesitant and is made at the end of a few other suggestions. Yet this is the response of faith. In the second instance, Jesus answers the High Priest with a firm certainty, but the response is unbelief and a sanctimonious piety. The High Priest tears his clothes and cries, 'Blasphemy!' (14.63–4). There is a progression from Peter's dim perception with the eye of faith (as through a glass darkly) to the open certainty of the second confession, on the lips of Jesus himself; but this fulfilment is accompanied by fear and loathing and murderous hostility.

In another pattern of contrast, there is in the first half of Mark the yearning of the Gentiles who are searching for God. The demoniac, the Syrophoenician woman, the deaf mute, all represent different types. Jesus' mission is, however, still directed towards Israel. Even so, the Gentiles are given signs of hope. The declaration at Caesarea Philippi is made in the sight of the Gentiles as well as the Jews. By the end of the second section, it is clear that hope is being fulfilled in reality. The Jewish Temple, with all the power structures of Judaism, is to be destroyed and a new 'house of prayer for all nations' will take its place, in which the Gentiles are included. At the death of Jesus, the Temple curtain is rent in two. All searching for God can now end in coming to know God through Jesus Christ. And the *Gentile centurion* is accordingly given a clear vision of this truth – a vision which comes to him as a spiritual insight and not from any human reasoning: 'Now when the centurion, who stood facing him, saw that in this way he breathed his last, he said, "Truly this man was God's Son"' (15.39).

Then, after the resurrection, the young man in white at the empty tomb instructs the women: 'But go, tell his disciples and Peter that he is going ahead of you to Galilee: there you will see him, just as he told you' (16.7). The mission of Jesus is about to recommence, but with this great difference; it will be a new departure. Beginning from Galilee, the disciples will move out into the world at large.

Very unfortunately, this last fact is not made absolutely explicit in Mark, because the Gospel ends abruptly at 16.8. We do not have clear evidence of the move from the earlier adumbration of the Gentile mission to the full-scale outreach and harvest. Matthew ends with a commissioning story (28.16–20) but Mark ends instead on a note of fear, flight from the tomb and silence from the witnesses to the resurrection. The logical and necessary conclusion to Mark's Gospel is surely missing, presumed lost. Arguments have raged among scholars in the latter half of the twentieth century over the ending of Mark. Is an ending such as 'they said nothing to anyone, for they were afraid' (16.8) possibly a final conclusion to this Gospel?

Some have reasoned that it is not only a possible ending but a logical and likely ending. Professor Morna Hooker is one who came to this view after reflecting on the various arguments, which she summarizes lucidly at the end of her commentary. She holds that the ending is a grammatical possibility (it actually ends with the Greek word *gar* meaning 'for' or 'because'). She also holds that Mark intended the Gospel to be open-ended, and that the note of awe, mystery and new revelation is in line with Mark's theology throughout:

If we are unhappy with the ending of Mark's gospel as he has left it, it is perhaps because we expect him to 'round it off' with an appearance of the risen Lord; we want assurance that Jesus has met the disciples, pronounced forgiveness and recommissioned them. Instead we have the 'evidence' of the women, who are invited to inspect the empty tomb and told, 'He is not here; he has been raised', and we have the message to the disciples to return to Galilee, where they had seen Jesus before, and where they will see him again. Though they have denied Jesus and been ashamed of him, they are nevertheless offered a second chance of learning, once again, what it means to be disciples – disciples, this time, of the crucified and risen Lord. We are offered nothing more. But is this, perhaps, because Mark is inviting us to make our own response? Is it because this was a starting-point for Mark's own readers? They could not go and inspect the tomb for themselves: they had to rely on the evidence of others that it was indeed empty. As for seeing the risen Lord, that was a possibility for them all . . . [48]

These comments are in all likelihood quite true. Mark has left the text open, in order to address his readers and to appeal to them to have faith in the resurrection. However, there is more to it than that. Surely the argument must hinge on the answer to another question; namely, does the present ending (at 16.8) effectively tie up the loose ends and give the impression of completeness? In other words, has Mark finished the task he set out to achieve? The answer to this would appear to be 'no'. The appropriate ending, or new beginning – whichever is preferable – must surely be the imparting of faith to a group of disciples who have hitherto been vacillating and unprepared, who have last been seen scattered and left in disarray. Further, the *significance* of the resurrection needs to be clarified by a sending out on mission; in order to indicate that the believers now have new work to undertake, namely, the mission to all the nations. Surely Mark's ending requires something more similar to the commissioning story in Matthew. The disciples would then be reunited, restored, and equipped for the work ahead of them.

Robert Gundry[49] takes a very different view from Morna

Hooker. He examines in detail the ending not only of Mark, but of the other Gospels too, and comes to the conclusion that there are fragments of Mark's original ending in Luke 24 and in Matthew 28 and in particular in Matthew's commissioning narrative (28.16–20). This seems to be in many ways a reasonable assumption. After all, the other Synoptic Gospel writers have followed the Marcan Gospel chronology and in many sections of the Gospel have reproduced Mark's material almost unchanged. Why should they depart from their normal pattern of writing when they encounter the resurrection narratives?

There is a further argument, that Mark has been indicating all along that the death and resurrection of Jesus is to introduce a new phase of the salvific work of God. What is prefigured in the early section should now have a visible fulfilment in the final section. A deliberate silence about the next and greater stage of Jesus' mission – carried out in the power of the resurrection – can surely not be the order of the day. Rather, the new beginning needs to receive the seal of Jesus' own authority. The followers of Jesus – the women and the men, the first disciples as well as those following on – need to know what they should be doing next. The later additions to Mark – both the shorter and longer ending (laid out clearly in the NRSV in English) seem to be bolted onto the original Gospel without much thought as to logic or style. They are merely a summary of the resurrection appearances given in the other Gospels. They do not do justice to Mark's original plan for his Gospel nor to his theology. The eschatological time frame visible in the Gospel as a whole does not reach its proper conclusion. Neither is the more personal dilemma raised by the fear and flight of the women brought to resolution. Nor does the present ending of Mark explain how the men came to hear the news about the empty tomb and the resurrection.

Morna Hooker's suggestion that the author, by leaving the Gospel open-ended, is inviting the audience (or reader) to go with him to a Galilee of the imagination in order to embark upon a new mission with the risen Lord 'going before' is an attractive and creative idea, but it does not answer any of the difficulties raised above, not does it take account of the fact that the instruction of the young man in white (16.7) is a specific message to the disciples alone. Apart from that, both Matthew (28.16–20) and John (21) bear witness to a tradition of Jesus' appearing to the disciples in Galilee. And Matthew's commissioning narrative, considered in detail in the last chapter, looks suspiciously like a theological embellishment and enlargement of a simpler Marcan account.

Robert Gundry rightly emphasises that Mark is at pains to show the Passion narrative as the fulfilment of earlier predictions and prophecies. It is reasonable to expect the same pattern of fulfilment of earlier promises in the resurrection account as well. So as Mark begins his Gospel with the announcement that this is the beginning of the gospel of Jesus Christ, he should logically conclude it with a corresponding announcement of a new phase of the gospel story beginning from the time of the resurrection.

Whatever may be the case about the true ending of Mark, it is possible to say that all the preceding narrative and commentary in the Gospel anticipates the fact that the resurrection marks the end of the beginning and the beginning of the end: for at last with Jesus' death and resurrection the time has come for the fulfilment of God's promise to the nations. They will be included in his mission and in his plans for the salvation and blessing of the whole world through faith in Jesus Christ.

4

Luke–Acts – the fulfilment of God's mission

The traditional view of Luke–Acts has it that the author, Luke, was a Gentile, writing for a Gentile audience. This view was confidently expressed by F. C. Overbeck in his German commentary from 1870: 'Nothing could be clearer than that Acts has abandoned Jewish Christianity as such and is written from the point of view which recognises Gentile Christianity as the absolutely dominant element in the Church.'[50] In more recent times, too, a similar view has tended to prevail. S. G. Wilson, in *The Gentiles and the Gentile Mission in Luke–Acts*, wrote that Luke's church 'was almost certainly a predominantly Gentile Church. The influx of Jews had ceased long before, and the enmity between the Church and Judaism had grown more bitter and the gulf wider after AD 70.'[51] Ernst Haenchen, in his influential commentary on Acts, argued that throughout Acts from the first page to the last, Luke was engaged 'with the problem of the mission to the Gentiles without the Law. His entire presentation is influenced by this.'[52]

Even at the end of the twentieth century this view still enjoyed wide popularity. David Bosch in *Transforming Mission* wrote: 'Luke . . . was perhaps the only Gentile author of a New Testament book and wrote for Christians who were predominantly of Gentile origin.'[53]

One of the few scholars to take issue with the general consensus, Jacob Jervell, has had to battle long and hard to promote a Jewish Luke writing for a predominantly Jewish Church. In his *Theology of the Acts of the Apostles* he laments the fact that 'for years the scholars were nearly unanimous in viewing Acts as a Gentile-Christian document, written by a Gentile Christian for Gentile Christians.' Then he continues, 'This is not tenable any longer, as it is based to a great extent upon the idea that after AD 70 Jewish Christianity had disappeared, was of no importance, existing only as a marginal feature outside the church.'[54] Jervell's contention is that virtually all the churches throughout the first century consisted of mixed congregations of Jews and Gentiles, in which the Jews were often the predominant or leading group. He attempts to demonstrate that Luke–Acts is written from a conspicuously Jewish point of view, and even argues that Paul is presented by Luke as the Apostle to the Jews and not the Apostle to the Gentiles.

There are in truth many aspects of Luke–Acts which highlight the Jewish nature of the writing. First of all, Luke is eager to write the first part of his Gospel in the style of the Septuagint (LXX), the Jewish translation of the Scriptures into Greek. His aim is to present an account which sounds and reads like a continuation of the Scriptures, one which is, in effect, a continuation of and completion of the Old Testament. Luke's style does change, especially when the disciples encounter Gentiles in the book of Acts, and a more secular, Hellenistic form is adopted (see e.g. Paul at Athens – Acts 17.16–34 and the shipwreck in Acts 27). However, the point here is that Luke makes a serious attempt to write his Gospel in continuity with and in the style of The Hebrew Bible.

Both Luke and Acts also begin with the clearly expressed need for the *restoration of Israel* (Luke 1.68; 2.25; Acts 1.6). There is the hope for a king of David's line to return to the throne and to rule over Israel (Luke 1.32–3; and Acts 2.30). The first part of Luke is firmly set in the context of Israel and the yearning for a Messiah who will be the consolation of Israel. John the Baptist is a forerunner in the mould of Elijah, to prepare the way for the Lord's coming. The birth promises to Elizabeth and Mary recall the promises to Sarah and Hannah in Israel of old. The songs of Mary and Zechariah are couched in the language of the Psalms and the prayers of the Old Testament. Jesus is presented at the

Temple and is circumcised at eight days old. Simeon and Anna, representatives of the faithful of the Old Covenant, herald the fulfilment of the promises of the Scriptures in the coming of Jesus. Jesus returns to the Temple as a boy to debate the Law of God with the elders. Only briefly, at the beginning of Chapters 2 and 3 does Luke set his history in the context of the Gentile world. A little later on, Jesus teaches in the synagogues (Luke 4.15), announces his mission in the synagogue and bases it on a quotation from Isaiah (Luke 4.16–21).

At the beginning of Acts, in a somewhat similar way, Luke sets the scene firmly in Israel and in her history. The disciples are told to remain in Jerusalem; they gather at the Temple and worship there; a successor is chosen to Judas, so that the twelve can again represent the twelve tribes of Israel. The Holy Spirit comes upon the believers in fulfilment of Old Testament prophecy and those who receive the gospel message are the Jews living in Jerusalem and those from the Jewish Diaspora (2.5). The early sermons of Peter and Stephen are full of the history of Israel and of God's dealings with his chosen people.

The Christology of Luke–Acts is also Jewish, in the sense that it is never framed in the form of philosophical titles or exact definitions, but is constructed from Old Testament names such as 'king of the Jews' (Luke 19.38; 23.2, 3, 37, 38; Acts 17.7), 'Son of David' (Luke 18.38–9; 20.41) and Messiah, translated into Greek as 'Christ' or 'the Christ' and often used as an absolute title (e.g. Luke 4.18; Acts 4.27; 10.38). Other titles have a Jewish flavour, such as 'the holy one' (Acts 2.27), 'the righteous one' (3.14; 7.52), the Lord (*kurios*) (Luke 2.11, 26; Acts 2.36; 4.26; 11.17; 15.26) and 'servant of God' (Acts 3.13, 26; 4.25, 27, 30). The nature and person of Jesus as Messiah is expressed and illustrated through the stories, especially in the Gospel itself. This is very much a biblical way of drawing out meaning, using concrete imagery rather than abstract language.

In addition, in Luke–Acts the law of God is accorded great respect. Luke pointedly omits from his Gospel Jesus' attack on the Pharisees' teaching about ritual purity to be found in Mark 7; but the reason often given for this – that Luke's Gentile readers are not interested in such Jewish practices – may not be the correct reason for the omission. It could just as easily be the converse – that Luke wishes to uphold and retain the customs of ritual purification for the Christian Jews. He does not wish to give the impression that any part of the Law has been abrogated. The fact that Paul is a Pharisee has been seen as the reason why he bitterly persecuted the Church; but Luke is eager to demonstrate that Paul is *a Jew* of the first order, as good as any, and eminently qualified to take on those Jews who reject the gospel and mount arguments against the resurrection (see Acts 24.10–23). When Paul defends himself against Jewish accusations he specifically says in his defence before Felix:

> But this I admit to you, that according to the Way, which they call a sect, I worship the God of our ancestors, believing everything laid down according to the law or written in the prophets. I have a hope in God – a hope that they themselves also accept – that there will be a resurrection of both the righteous and the unrighteous. (24.14–15)

Even the admission of the Gentiles into the Church is permitted on the grounds that it is according to the Law and is the will of God in the Scriptures. When the question arises with the conversion of Cornelius, an appeal is made to Jerusalem, and the Council constituted to rule on the question decides that the Gentiles need only comply with God's rules for foreigners living in Israel – rules outlined in Leviticus 17–18. That means the Gentiles of Luke's church and of the Church in general do not need to be circumcised, because God never demanded such a thing; but rather, in order to live in harmony with the rest of Israel, it is incumbent upon them to observe a few simple regulations. In this instance – namely, the decree of the Apostolic Council of Jerusalem – Jewish Law is discussed and promulgated without any explanation. Not just Paul, but the Church as a whole, is portrayed as believing in the Law, the prophets and the messianic prophecies. Even belief in the resurrection spells, for Luke, fidelity to Israel's God and to the Scriptures (Acts 24.14–15; 26.22–3).

Apart from all these things, the setting of the Gospel and of the Acts of the Apostles is either firmly within Israel or among the Jewish communities of the Diaspora. Preaching, with rare exceptions, takes place in the synagogues, and Luke *never countenances a mission to the Gentiles in separation from a mission to the Jews.*

Even at the end of Acts, when Paul is in Rome under house arrest, Luke describes how he calls the local Jewish leaders to a meeting (28.17). Even at this late stage, the so-called Apostle to the Gentiles is concerned to tell his fellow countrymen: 'Brothers, though I had done nothing against our people or the customs of our ancestors, yet I was arrested in Jerusalem and handed over to the Romans' (28.17). Paul then goes on to discuss with a large number of the Jews the nature of the kingdom of God, and Luke insists that he tried 'to convince them about Jesus both from the Law of Moses and from the prophets' (28.23). It is only to those who refuse to listen that he says later, 'Let it be known to you then that this salvation of God has been sent to the Gentiles; they will listen' (28.28; cf. 18.6). Luke is at great pains to demonstrate everywhere in the Gospel and in Acts that Jesus' work and the Christian message is a fulfilment of the Scriptures, is in line with God's will and is the true obedience to the Law of God. Those who reject the Way are those who break the Law and are not the true Israel.

Thus, Luke clearly regards the Church as the true Israel. As Paul says: 'it is for the sake of the hope of Israel that I am bound with this chain' (Acts 28.20). Even Luke's introduction of the Holy Spirit as the prime mover in his narrative is no mere novelty, but is again the fulfilment of the promises of the Old Testament Scriptures. The Holy Spirit is the Spirit which inspired prophecy and was also promised for the Last Days, the Spirit to be poured out on all flesh (Joel 2.28–32).

In the light of all this, it seems hard to understand how the idea that Luke was a Jew writing for a largely Jewish audience has hardly ever even been put up for consideration. The assumption of a Gentile origin for Luke's Gospel and Acts has distorted scholars' understanding of mission in this two-volume work, and has also distorted scholarly views of the purpose of Luke's writing. The motivation for his historical narrative has been variously regarded as a justification of Paul and the Church's turning to the Gentile mission; as a defence of Christianity in the Roman Empire; as an attempt to gain for the Church the status of a permitted cult – a status enjoyed by Judaism in the Roman Empire. Other ideas about Luke's purpose have include the notion that Acts was written as a response to gnostic and docetic heresies circulating among Gentile 'Christians', or that Luke was keen to stir up new fervour for evangelism in a Church which had become lukewarm or introverted.

A particularly influential argument about the purpose of Luke–Acts was proposed by Hans Conzelmann in *Die Mitte der Zeit*.[55] Conzelmann argued that Luke had created the idea of 'salvation history' (*Heilgeschichte*) and had accordingly separated time into three eras: the period of the Old Covenant, up to and including John the Baptist; the special time of Jesus' mission (including the whole 'Christ-event' of Jesus' life, death, resurrection and ascension), which makes up the 'middle time' of the schema; and then the period of the Church and its continuing mission to the ends of the earth. This separation into three epochs gives the church a *raison d'être* for its life: it has to complete the mission begun by Jesus and reach the Gentile nations with the gospel. The Church in this way forgets its disappointment over the delay of the *Parousia* or second coming of Christ. For this reason, Luke has to bring in the Holy Spirit not as 'the eschatological gift, but as the substitute in the meantime for the possession of ultimate salvation'.[56]

The persuasive nature of Conzelmann's argument has given it the appearance of fact virtually up to the present day. The Conzelmann scheme may not be too far away from Luke's own understanding of the prophecies about mission in the Old Testament; but it is inaccurate enough to confuse and to mislead. This scheme of salvation history is based on one single very debatable premise, namely, that Jesus and the Early Church envisaged the Time of the End as being imminent and the lapse before Christ's return as very short. If that premise can be shown to be dubious and if it can be demonstrated that Luke – along with many other Christians of the Early Church – had a rather different perspective, then the whole scheme has to be re-evaluated and revised.

Conzelmann's case is perhaps not to be dismissed outright, however, for Luke does appear to have a clear view of salvation history and indeed writes his own history to outline the way in which the story of salvation is unfolding. However, what is not apparent in Luke's writing is that he is contesting a notion that Jesus' return has been delayed. He expends no energy on addressing the matter, and passes it over in silence. This would appear to suggest that such a strong conviction was either not expressed in the churches Luke knew, or that it had given way to a more moderate understanding of the end times.

An overview of Luke–Acts reveals that the epochs Conzelmann envisages are not to be so easily separated out. The time of Jesus seems to fulfil and complete the hopes of the time of the Old Covenant; yet some of Jesus' mission also seems to anticipate the following period, the time of the Church's mission. The book of Acts also seems to make it clear that the apostles and the Church are acting very much in continuity with what has gone before, and all through Acts the mission to the Jews runs alongside the mission to the Gentiles. It is advisable to lay to one side Conzelmann's thesis and to adopt a new template altogether and to say that the author of Luke–Acts is primarily concerned with God's mission – the *missio dei* – conceived from the beginning of time, started in earnest from the time of the creation of Israel as a holy nation, continued and in some sense brought to fulfilment (but not to completion) in Jesus' own ministry and work, and then expanded and opened out to all by the apostles and the Church.

The fact that this is indeed one and the same mission throughout is conveyed in at least two different ways by Luke. First, he demonstrates that Jesus' mission and the subsequent mission of the Church are stages in the overall mission of God as foreseen by the prophets of the Old Testament and (as in Matthew and Mark), in particular, by the prophet Isaiah.

Secondly, Luke shows the Gospel and Acts as running in parallel with each other, or mirroring one another, as they progress.
This is in effect another way of showing that here we are witnessing two aspects of the same mission, the second being simply a
logical extension of the first.

Luke–Acts and the fulfilment of Scripture

Now, let us take a closer look at these two points one by one. As
we consider the relationship of Luke–Acts to the Old Testament,
the first thing we notice is that Luke is very concerned to depict
his two-volume work as being in continuity with all that has
gone before. As already mentioned, the birth and infancy narratives set the scene firmly in the context of the semitized Greek of
the Septuagint translation of the Hebrew Bible (LXX). Jesus'
family are portrayed as devout and practising Jews, doing all that
the Law required and attending the Jewish festivals (2.39–41).
Joseph comes from the family line of King David (1.27). All the
characters surrounding the holy family are also devout believers:
Zechariah, a priest in the Temple (1.8); his wife Elizabeth;
Simeon, praying for Israel's salvation (2.25); the prophetess
Anna, who spent all her time in the Temple (2.37); and finally
John the Baptist.

There is something else which links several of these characters
with the Old Testament Scriptures; they all bear witness to
Isaiah's prophecies about God's mission to Israel. Zechariah
quotes from Isaiah 9.2: 'By the tender mercy of our God, the
dawn from on high will break upon us, to give light to those
who sit in darkness and in the shadow of death' (Luke 1.78–9).
Simeon, in his prophetic word, also makes reference or allusion
to Isaiah's prophecies (Isaiah 42.6; 49.6; 52.10) to the effect that
salvation is at hand, prepared 'in the presence of all peoples, a
light for revelation to the Gentiles and for glory to your people
Israel' (Luke 2.30–2). Then when John makes his dramatic
appearance, Luke makes it clear that John's mission is to fulfil
the greater mission of God, to prepare the way for the Messiah.
Once again, the quotation comes from the book of Isaiah, and

Luke 3.6 states 'all flesh shall see the salvation of God' (Isaiah 40.3–5). These verses, like those quoted by Simeon, were originally written in the context of Israel's exile and captivity in Babylon, at a time when the people were longing for deliverance and a return to the promised land.

The concept of God's mission, begun in ancient times and brought to fulfilment in the days of the Messiah, is a continuing theme throughout Luke and Acts. The regal anointing prophecy of Isaiah 40.3–5: 'This is my beloved son in whom I am well pleased,' is quoted at critical points in Jesus' ministry – namely, at his baptism and transfiguration (3.22; 9.35). In the setting of the mission to Capernaum, Chorazin and Bethsaida (10.13–16), Jesus himself alludes to Isaiah's prophecies (from Isaiah 23.1–18 and 14.13–15) in order to highlight the fact that the Gentile towns of Tyre and Sidon are more ready to receive God's word and to repent than the towns of Israel.

The most crucial passage in this regard is the one which announces Jesus' mission in the synagogue at Nazareth. Jesus reads from the Isaiah scroll and quotes from 61.1–2. We return to this passage shortly, but suffice it to say at this point that Jesus describes his mission in terms of God's plans for the new age of the Messiah, when wrongs will be righted, the sick healed, the oppressed freed and the Day of Jubilee proclaimed. This 'good news' is not a new departure as such: it is the fulfilment of a long-cherished hope in Israel. Once again, it is seen in the context of the book of Isaiah – in the eyes of the Early Church the prophecy of God's mission par excellence.

At the end of the Gospel we read of the two disciples on the road to Emmaus. They are depressed and downcast, but the risen Lord, travelling with them, is able to lift their spirits and to set their hearts on fire by opening up the Scriptures to them and thereby demonstrating that everything that was happening was according to God's will (24.13–35). 'Beginning with Moses and all the prophets' Jesus 'interpreted to them the things about himself in all the Scriptures' (24.27). This also compares with Jesus' later words in 24.44: 'everything written about me in the law of Moses, the prophets, and the psalms must be fulfilled'.

This theme – the fulfilment of God's mission – continues into the Acts of the Apostles. Luke is most concerned to show that the day of the Messiah has now arrived (see Acts 2.25–8, 30, 34–5; 4.11, 25–6; 13.33, 34). He makes most use of the Psalms, as though they were prophecies rather than prayers. A leading theme picked up by Luke is that the Son of David was to restore David's kingdom in righteousness and peace.

Another aspect of this fulfilment motif is that of bearing witness to the Gentile nations. This is mentioned in Jesus' final speech of the Gospel (Luke 24.47), and Peter, in his sermon in Acts 3 reminds the crowd that through Abraham all peoples on the earth will be blessed (3.25 referring to Genesis 22.18). Then, before the Jewish Council, Peter reminds his audience that the Messiah has come for all people: 'for there is no other name under heaven given among mortals by which we must be saved' (4.12).

Later on, in the course of Paul's mission, when the Apostle addresses both Jews and Gentiles in Pisidian Antioch, Paul applies to himself the words of Isaiah 42.6 and 49.6, in order to indicate that his mission has been sanctioned by God from time immemorial: 'For so the Lord has commanded us, saying, "I have set you to be a light for the Gentiles, so that you may bring salvation to the ends of the earth"' (Acts 13.47). In Lystra and Derbe he speaks of a God who created all things (14.15), once again alluding to the Old Testament (Exodus 20.11; Psalm 146.6).

At the Council of Jerusalem Paul finds an unexpected ally in James, head of the Jerusalem Church. James confirms the ongoing mission of the Church to both Jews and Gentiles by agreeing that 'This agrees with the words of the prophets' (15.15); and he goes on to quote – unusually – from Amos 9.11–12. God's plan was apparently understood as an intention to rebuild and restore David's kingdom 'so that all other peoples may seek the Lord – even all the Gentiles over whom my name has been called (15.17). The whole mission is given the seal of approval because it is seen as God's own mission. He 'has been making these things known from long ago' (15.17–18).

Both aspects of the Church's mission – acceptance and rejection by Jews and Gentiles alike – are therefore seen to be predicted and foreseen in the Scriptures. At the very end of Acts, this is made crystal clear when Paul, on trial before Agrippa, states his purpose as being to announce the light of salvation to the Jews and the Gentiles (Acts 26.23 alluding to Isaiah 42.6 and 49.6). The Paul of Acts is neither apostle to the Gentiles (as S. G. Wilson) nor apostle to the Jews (as J. Jervell): rather, he has been commissioned to go first to the Jews, then to the Gentiles. This is God's programme for mission ordained from long ago and revealed personally to Paul on the road to Damascus.

The rejection and opposition occasioned by that mission is to be expected – from both Jews and Gentiles alike. The closing words of Acts confirm what has been seen in action all through. God has hardened the heart of some and they will never understand nor accept the Christ (28.26–7 quoting Isaiah 6.9–10). The use of a quotation again shows that even this has been prophesied from long ago. The Messiah was persecuted, the apostles and disciples will be persecuted – but, after all, were not the prophets of the Old Covenant themselves persecuted by the leaders of Israel?

It is remarkable that so many writers on Luke–Acts come to their conclusions about mission without examining the fulfilment motif, which is so important to Luke, and without examining carefully the quotations from Scripture, which give insight into Luke's understanding of the eschatological time frame for the mission of the Messiah and for the mission of the Church. When attention is drawn to these things the jigsaw begins to form a pattern or a picture and it is possible to make sense of Luke's writings.

In this respect, Luke is startlingly similar to Matthew, because both stress the fulfilment motif and both make extensive use of Isaiah's prophecies to outline the programme of God's mission. All this demonstrates the fact that the Gospel writers conceive mission in terms of a design. It takes place in the eschatological last times beginning first with the mission to restore Israel as a holy nation and to reach out to the lost sheep of the House of Israel. God's intentions in this respect are fulfilled through the

Messiah. Next, the disciples or apostles (those sent out) extend and complete God's mission to the whole of Israel, including communities of the Diaspora all over the known world. This phase makes the renewed messianic Israel a light to all the nations, and leads naturally on to Gentile mission. God-fearers and proselytes attached to the synagogues are first drawn to God's Messiah, and then the witness finally takes the form of a more positive outreach to the nations. At the very end of the age, it is conceived that the Gentile nations will go on pilgrimage to Zion and will pay homage to Israel's God.

These phases are not strictly separated out and compartmental-ized, and should not be seen too much in terms of sequential events. They overlap, and are all aspects of the one single mission of God; a mission which ultimately envisages the salvation of the whole world.

Parallels between Luke and Acts

The other way in which Luke demonstrates that God's mission is one and the same mission, with different phases or aspects, is by writing Luke and Acts as to some extent running in parallel with one another. Both the Gospel and Acts have a *journey motif*; Luke takes the reader from Galilee to Jerusalem in three phases (Luke 4.14—9.50; 9.51—19.40; and 19.41–end); while Acts takes the reader from Jerusalem to Rome via Samaria, Antioch and throughout the whole Diaspora, finally arriving at the capital of the Empire. In this way, as D. Bosch succinctly put it, 'geography simply becomes the vehicle for conveying theological (or missiological) meaning'.[57] We see an example of this in Acts 9.15, where Luke describes a prophecy about Paul: 'The Lord said to [Ananias] "Go, for he is an instrument whom I have chosen to bring my name before Gentiles and kings and before the people of Israel."' It is crucial to notice the combination of both Gentiles and 'the people of Israel' in this context.

There are various other motifs running in tandem too. Early on in Luke's Gospel (3.21–2), the Holy Spirit is featured commissioning Jesus for his life's work; early in Acts the Holy

Spirit falls upon the gathered congregation in Jerusalem (2.1–4). When Jesus begins his ministry, in a 'manifesto' statement of intent, he outlines his programme (Luke 4.16–30). In Acts (2.14–39[42]), Peter addresses the Diaspora communities and then in 3.12–26 he addresses the Jews of Jerusalem, outlining the rationale for the Church's mission.

The theme of rejection also features frequently in both Luke and Acts. After his sermon in the Nazareth synagogue, Jesus faces anger and hostility (4.28–30). Later, in Acts, after his address on the Day of Pentecost, Peter is also opposed and vilified (4.1–4). As the two missions – of Jesus and of the Church – get under way, there are miracles and signs following, confirming God's approval (Luke 4.31–41; Acts 2.43—3.10). Jesus chooses 12 disciples in Luke 5.1–11 (also vv. 27–8); in Acts the apostles restore their number to 12 after Judas's defection (Acts 1.21–6). The conversion of a Gentile God-fearer has a key position in both the Gospel (Luke 7.1–10) and in Acts (10.1–48). The unnamed Roman centurion of the Gospel and the Roman centurion Cornelius of Acts are both exemplars or archetypes of the Gentile who will gladly follow Jesus – as disciples or as members of the Church.

A threefold sending out of disciples or apostles to go on mission is described in Luke 9.1–6 (for Israel); 9.51–5 (for Samaria); and 10.1–20 (for Gentile areas). The same kind of pattern holds for Acts too: a first phase occurs in 2.1–42 (Peter) – primarily to Jews in Jerusalem; then 8.4–25 (centred on Philip – see 8.26–40) for Samaria and all Judea; and finally 9.19b–25 (Paul and Barnabas – see esp. 11.22–30) for the Gentile territories. We shall return to a further consideration of this pattern of mission.

There are many other parallels, but perhaps we can drive home the point by mentioning two other aspects worthy of attention. The arrest and trial of Jesus is described in Luke 22.47–23.25, whilst the arrest and trial of the apostle Paul is described in Acts 21.27—26.32. The apostle's life is conformed to that of his master. Then, at the very end of the Gospel, the significance of Jesus' work is summed up and there is a personal commissioning of the disciples – in Luke 24.44–9. In Acts 28.17–31 Paul's life-work is summed up and the Church members are encouraged to go on continuing and completing his work. Both times, the mission is firmly rooted in the Scriptures (Luke 24.44–5; Acts 28.23) and the mission to the Gentiles is justified (Luke 24.47; Acts 28.28). There is more to be said on this.

By drawing parallels between the Gospel and Acts, Luke, the author, is able to show that the Church's mission is no novelty. Rather, it is the continuation and partial completion of the mission of Jesus. Jesus' own mission is in its turn a partial fulfilment of the scriptural promises concerning God's mission. Both the mission to Israel and the mission to the Gentiles are justified as God's plan for salvation and the 'stones of stumbling' – the opposition to these missions – are seen as the inevitable consequences, the dark side, of the work of God. There will always be those opposed to God's will; but they cannot thwart or prevent that will from prevailing.

The Holy Spirit

The mission of Jesus and that of the Church is part of the one mission of God. Luke emphasizes this fact by rooting his idea of mission in the authority of the Scriptures, and he draws many parallels between the mission in the Gospel and in Acts, in order to demonstrate that the same principles apply in both cases.

Now we have considered these things, is it then true to say that there is really *nothing new* about the mission of the Church? Surely the mission beginning on the day of Pentecost in Acts 2 gives the appearance of a spectacular new start. After the despair of the disciples at the time of the crucifixion and after their long wait in Jerusalem, surely the day of Pentecost highlights a new departure in terms of mission.

Certainly everything does point to the fact that Luke regards the coming of the Holy Spirit as a *turning point* in the dispensation of God's work. Even though the Spirit has been actively working through the prophets of the Old Covenant and through Jesus in the time of his ministry, nevertheless in an important sense the pouring out of the Spirit *'upon all flesh'* in Acts 2 represents such an explosion of new life that the Church's mission thereafter has the appearance of a new type of mission or mission in a new way. Even though the work of Jesus is for Luke the sign of God's new age, the coming of the Spirit at Pentecost brings the powers of that new age into the world at large. So, for Luke, it is at Pentecost that a new day has arrived (Acts 2.17). As the Church takes on and continues Jesus' mission, that mission veers in a new direction and has a new perspective. The limited and restricted mission of Jesus becomes a dynamic unlimited force radiating out in every direction from Jerusalem, and reaching for the far corners of the earth.

However, the new beginnings of the Church's mission ought not to be overplayed. They do still have their roots in God's mission inaugurated long before and brought to full (but geographically limited) expression in Jesus' mission. Jesus ushered in the eschatological new age, and with this vision Luke stays firmly in line with Mark's Gospel.

Right at the very beginning of Jesus' life, Luke shows that the Holy Spirit is once again active in the revival of prophecy. Mary, Elizabeth, Zechariah and Simeon all prophesy under the influence of the Holy Spirit, and the Spirit is specifically acknowledged in each case (1.35, 41, 67; 2.25). Then Anna is described as a 'prophetess' (2.36). The entire ministry of Jesus which follows is conducted under the aegis of the Holy Spirit. The Spirit leads Jesus into the desert and strengthens him to outwit and to overcome Satan (4.1–13). When he returns to Galilee, he is 'filled with the power of the Spirit' (4.14). The announcement of his mission begins with the words 'The Spirit of the Lord is upon me'(4.18). The Spirit in Jesus is greater than the evil spirits who confront him – for they also fear him (e.g. 4.33–5). Jesus' healings and teachings are carried out in the power of the Spirit (10.21). The authority Jesus communicates to those he sends on mission (9.1) is clearly the authority of the Holy Spirit.

It is also pre-eminently through the Spirit that the risen Jesus is able to continue his ministry in the church and through the mission of the church. Luke's theology of the Spirit is far more developed than Mark's or Matthew's, and, moreover, Luke makes a strong link between the Holy Spirit and mission. This link is hardly noticeable at all in the other Synoptic Gospels. The Spirit in the Church is thus in Luke the equivalent of the presence of the risen Lord in Matthew. Whereas the risen Jesus says in Matthew, 'I am with you always, even to the end of the Age', in Luke Jesus assures the disciples with the words, 'I am sending upon you what my Father promised' (24.49). In Luke's eyes, the fact that Jesus will send the Spirit is the setting of the seal on his messianic work (see also Acts 1.4–5, 8; 2.33).

So the Spirit is the golden thread joining together the gospel mission and that of the apostolic Church. Yet Luke manages to make the Spirit an even more personal presence than the risen presence of Jesus himself; for the Spirit is the inner voice, the initiator, guide, strengthener and encourager of the Church's mission. As David Bosch sums up, 'The Spirit becomes the catalyst, the guiding and driving force of mission.'[58] At every stage the Church's mission is inspired and confirmed by manifestations of the Spirit. Right from the outset the disciples' work receives the seal of the Spirit and they become 'witnesses' to all the Spirit is doing (Luke 24.49b; Acts 1.8).

In Acts 2 the Spirit comes as promised, and Luke sees this as the fulfilment of Joel 2. 28–32 (Acts 2.16–21). Once again, mission is conceived as being in the very heart of God from the beginning. The fact that the prophecy is that God will pour out his Spirit upon all flesh (Acts 2.17) also gives scriptural justification to the world-wide mission of the Church. Yet at this stage, those gathered who receive the Spirit and speak in other languages (2.4) are 'devout Jews from every nation under heaven living in Jerusalem' (2.5). In other words, the work of God in world-wide mission first reaches out to the Jews of the Diaspora. It is through them that the Gentiles will be reached, in fulfilment of the divine pattern, which is 'Israel first, then the Gentiles'.

This gift is the eschatological promise for the last age, but it had a quieter, though no less significant beginning, at Jesus' baptism – a baptism in the Spirit (3.22) prefiguring this new baptism in the Spirit at Pentecost.

The gift of 'tongues' or other languages allows the Galilean disciples present to speak of or 'prophesy' what is happening in a way everyone else can hear in their own language. This represents a reversal of what happened at the Tower of Babel or 'Babylon' in Genesis 11, when the people who had one language originally found they now all spoke different languages and could no longer understand one another (11.7). The new situation in Acts unites people together, and enables the gospel message to reach into every land and nation because it will now be understood.

The coming of representatives of all nations to Jerusalem is also a prefiguring of the eschatological pilgrimage of the peoples of every nation to Israel and to Mount Zion. This is prophesied in various of the prophetic writings of the Old Testament, but Luke once again pays special attention to the writings of Isaiah, notably 2.2–4; 18.7; 45.18–25, 60. The theme is also reiterated elsewhere, in such places as Jeremiah 3.17; 16.19; Zephaniah 3.8–11; Haggai 2.6–9; Zechariah 2.10–13, 14–16.

The Spirit's role in widening the horizons of mission is emphasized throughout the book of Acts. Philip miraculously encounters the Ethiopian chamberlain through the agency of the Spirit (Acts 8.29, 39); Peter's acceptance of the centurion Cornelius is made possible because the Spirit is poured out upon the Gentiles at this juncture (10.44–8; 11.12–18). When Peter reports the incident, he justifies his own actions by appealing to the evidence of the Spirit in the lives of Cornelius and his family (11.12). The Apostolic Council at Jerusalem also ratifies the Gentile mission – with minimum conditions and with 'no distinctions' – under the direction of the Spirit (15.28). Paul and Barnabas are set aside by the Spirit for the work to which God has called them (13.2, 4), and the Spirit indicates where Paul should go. Europe then benefits while Asia has to wait, for Paul makes his way to Macedonia and not to Bithynia as first planned (Acts 16.6–10). It is the Spirit who insists that Paul go to Jerusalem (against human advice) (19.20–2). In this way the Spirit enables the Christian mission to reach Rome itself (19.21; 21.11).

The Spirit is not only responsible for the guiding and directing of the mission of Jesus and that of the Church, but the Spirit also empowers those involved in the work. Miracles and exorcisms and other 'signs' are evidence of the Spirit's activity and support. In Acts another evidence of empowerment is that previously tongue-tied and timid followers are emboldened and given freedom to speak out – sometimes at great length (see e.g. 4.13, 29, 31; 9.27; 13.46; 14.3; 18.26; 19.8).

The Spirit also enables the disciples to face opposition, harassment and persecution (see 4.5–13; 7.54–60; 13.50–2; 16.19–26). Peter confronts the Sanhedrin 'filled with the Spirit' (4.8) and the church in Jerusalem speaks out even under threat of reprisals (4.31).

The Spirit is especially active in persuading Peter to agree to visit Cornelius, and then to accept the Gentiles into table fellowship with Jews (10.19–20, 44–8; 11.12, 15). In this way, the Spirit initiates another widening of the mission of God. And it is Peter who is 'the one through whom the Gentiles will hear the message of the good news and become believers' (15.7). In the renewed Israel, Gentile converts and especially God-fearers and proselytes previously attached to the synagogues, would be fully incorporated into the Church on an equal footing with those who were Israel by race and blood.

The content of God's mission – Luke 4.16–30

Luke has a detailed and considered view of what constitutes the message of salvation, or, to put it another way, what is the content of God's mission. This is first outlined as a prologue to Jesus' entire life's work, laid out programmatically at the beginning of Jesus' public ministry. Luke expands on a few brief verses of Mark (Mark 6.1–3) and fills out the details of what Jesus said and what happened when he visited the synagogue at Nazareth in order to read the Scriptures and to preach. He has Jesus read from the scroll a passage from Isaiah – 61.1–2 – 'The Spirit of the Lord is upon me, because he has anointed me to bring good news to the poor' (Luke 4.18). There is added a verse inserted from Isaiah 58.6: 'to let the oppressed go free' (Luke 4.18b).

Jesus' mission is seen as commissioned by God himself and

undertaken in the power of the Holy Spirit. This fits in with all the rest of Luke's theology throughout the Gospel and Acts. Jesus relates the passage to himself by stating at the end of the reading: 'Today this Scripture has been fulfilled in your hearing' (4.21). The second point is that Jesus is identified as the Servant of God in Isaiah. The third thing is that there is a connection made between this passage and the Gentile mission predicted in Isaiah; for words about that mission occur in many places in the same section of the prophetic work (see especially Isaiah 49 and 51.4–6; 56.6–8; 60.1–14; 62.10–12; 66.18–23). It is almost certain that Jesus had an awareness of this fact when he followed up the reading by talking about the outreach to the Gentiles in the time of Elijah and Elisha (Luke 4.25–8).

The centrepiece of the 'manifesto' highlights the purpose of Jesus' mission: it is to preach good news to the poor, to proclaim freedom for prisoners, recovery of sight for the blind and to let the oppressed go free. Then Jesus announces the year of Jubilee (4.18–19). The preaching of good news is clearly seen as mainly to benefit those who are at present downtrodden or marginalized. There is obviously a political and social thrust to this mission. Preaching is part of it – and even then the message will challenge the privileged and the proud and cause fury in some circles – but the rest concerns action on behalf of those who can't help themselves. The sick are envisaged ('the blind'), those who are in debt ('the oppressed') and those who are in prison. Luke does not 'spiritualize' the message in the way Matthew sometimes does (e.g. Matthew 5.3 – 'the poor in spirit'). And those needing release could well refer to the exploited and abused. However, having said that, judging from the rest of Luke–Acts there is always a spiritual dimension to the mission as well. This involves the forgiveness of sins and the deliverance from bondage to Satan (Luke 4.31–7). Both of these aspects are emphasized in many other places.

In the context of Isaiah 61 as a whole, 'the poor' and 'the oppressed' are those in exile, who have been dispossessed, who have lost their rights and their land. They are literally 'in prison' because they are in captivity and are subject to foreign rule and

domination. The promises of Isaiah 61 include promises to take
vengeance on the enemies of Israel – on those who have caused
Israel's downfall – to overthrow their despotic control and to liberate Israel from their yoke. In the wider context of the Old
Testament – and especially the Psalms – 'the poor' refers to the
deprived, those in need and those who are literally afflicted or
persecuted. (see e.g. Psalms 22.24; 34.6; 35.10; 86.1; 88.15).

At the same time, Isaiah is concerned to show that liberation
and release are *spiritual gifts* as well as gifts of material freedom
and well-being. Joy and gladness are promised; a song of praise
instead of a spirit of sorrow (61.3). The ultimate salvation lies in
living a righteous life before God and in praising God for all he
has done (61.3). Thus, a *literal* release from exile is envisaged at
a time when cities will be rebuilt and when farms, flocks and
vineyards will be given back to their rightful owners (61.45),
and when Israel will enjoy the wealth of the nations (61.6).
But salvation is much more than material well-being. Isaiah
also says 'You shall be called priests of the Lord, you shall be
named ministers of our God' (61.6). Everyone will know that
the liberated people 'are a people whom the Lord has blessed'
(61.9).

Following this double tradition of material and spiritual blessing, Luke therefore has Jesus promise a salvation which is comprehensive – material, social, political and spiritual. Those who
stand to benefit most are those who are in most need, who have
lost the most, those who long for restitution.

The quotation ends with the announcement of a Jubilee: 'to
proclaim the year of the Lord's favour' (4.19 cf. Leviticus 25.8–
10). This envisages a time when debts would be remitted and
land restored to its original owners. But once again, there is a
spiritual dimension; it is also a time when people will be forgiven
past sins and will enjoy God's favour and blessing and when 'joy
will last for ever' (Isaiah 61.7).

Once Jesus has sat down, he appears to enjoy the acclamation
of all the congregation: 'All spoke well of him and were amazed
at the gracious words that came from his mouth' (4.22). Yet very
soon afterwards, the same people are enraged and 'filled with

anger' (4.28) and they try to drag Jesus away and to throw him over a cliff. What occasioned this change of heart?

First of all, Jesus appears to have deliberately omitted the ending of the Isaiah reading. If he had continued, it would have been clear that the Day of Jubilee was also to be 'a day of vengeance' when God would defeat and overthrow Israel's enemies (Isaiah 61.2b). Jesus' listeners of the first century were, like Isaiah's original audience, in a state of exile – but this time in exile in their own land. They were suffering under a harsh military regime, they were oppressed by absentee landlords; they were crippled by high taxation and they did hard labour for little reward. Galilee at the time of Jesus was a cauldron of seething discontent, rife with rumours of uprisings and talk of rebellion. There apocalyptic hopes ran high and charismatic preachers promised a new liberation and the overthrow of the oppressive power of Rome.

The fact that Jesus did not countenance violent revolution or the 'day of God's vengeance' might have caused puzzlement at first, but then he continued with his sermon, in which the Gentiles were portrayed in a very favourable light, and Israel in a bad light. As he went on to point out, Elijah was not asked by God to help any of the many widows in Israel during a time of drought, but he was sent only to a widow from Zarephath in the region of Sidon. And Elisha did not cure any lepers in Israel, although there were many, but only cured Naaman the Syrian (Luke 4.25–7).

Having heard this surprising biblical exegesis about God's favour towards the Gentiles – even placing their needs above those of Israel – the crowd rose up and tried to assassinate Jesus. He had had the audacity to suggest that the Year of Jubilee would be a year of blessing and salvation for the Gentiles, rather than a year when Israel would see her oppression avenged.

The logic of this passage at one time led Joachim Jeremias[59] to suggest that verse 22 of this chapter of Luke, which speaks of the congregation's admiration of Jesus' gracious words, could bear a very different interpretation and should be re-translated to give a completely different effect. Jeremias advocates a translation along these lines: 'They protested with one voice and were astonished at his words about mercy.' Strangely enough, the Greek original could bear such a changed interpretation, even though it seems rather forced, and the outcome would then be that the congregation was astonished because Jesus only spoke about God's mercy and not about vengeance. Jeremias's translation has the merit of fitting in logically and naturally with what follows immediately afterwards. Even so, to translate the phrase negatively does seem to go beyond what appears to be the natural translation, and Luke has certainly not put enough emphasis on this phrase to explain the sudden explosion of anger and hostility among the people a little later on.

Another point Jeremias makes about the passage – and this perhaps holds more weight – is that Jesus refuses to include words of vengeance in another quotation; made in Luke 7.22–3. In his reply to John the Baptist, Jesus highlights the signs of messianic activity by quoting again a composite passage from Isaiah, this time from Chapters 35.5–6; 29.18–19 and 61.1. In the whole quotation he avoids any words of divine judgement, which could easily have been included.

In discussing Luke's theology, David Bosch is at pains to point out[60] that Jesus' attitude shows a consistent opposition to violence and retribution. For example, when a Samaritan town refused the disciples hospitality, James and John were incensed, but Jesus refused their request to call down fire from heaven and he would not even condemn the town (Luke 9.52–6). Again, in Luke 13.1–5 Jesus is told about a revolutionary group of Galileans whose blood the Roman soldiers mixed with their sacrifices. Yet, rather than condemning the Romans or Pilate in particular, Jesus calls the people to repentance rather than to revenge. As Bosch says, Jesus displays 'an unwavering commitment to non-violence'.[61]

Thus, the first and commanding words of Jesus' mission (in Luke 4.16–30) show support for all who are suffering or are troubled in spirit, and an attitude of forgiveness and reconciliation towards Israel's traditional enemies. This means that Jesus in Luke has an exceptional openness towards the Gentiles and a preparedness to offer them salvation on the same terms as the

Jews. It should be borne in mind too that Luke was writing his Gospel in the wake of the Jewish wars against Rome and in the wake of the destruction of Jerusalem and its Temple. The hopes of the zealots and other political activists had been well and truly crushed. But Luke, in the light of these events, is eager to promote Jesus as a man who turns his back on all talk of armed conflict and retribution. His message is presented as one of forgiveness and healing rather than of anger and resentment. And in this way the Gospel can reach out even to the Gentiles, who had, in some cases, perpetrated atrocities against Israel's people, her cherished institutions and her God.

The archetypal Gentile convert

The encounter with a Roman centurion in Luke 7.1–10 is given a central and pivotal position in the Gospel – at the end of the first phase of Jesus' mission. His healing of the centurion's servant brings to completion his activities in Galilee and occurs just before John the Baptist's request for confirmation that the Messiah has indeed come.

The centurion is portrayed as a compassionate man; after all, his appeal to Jesus is not on his own behalf, but on behalf of his dearly-loved servant. He is also portrayed as a devout and godly man. He sent some of the Jewish elders to plead his case with Jesus, and they insist that this man deserves help, because 'he loves our people, and it is he who built our synagogue for us' (7.5). This part of the story only appears in Luke. In other words, the Roman is a God-fearer, already worshipping the one true God and already attached to the synagogue and following its teaching. In a sense, he is already part of 'Israel' by adoption. Other commendations include the fact that the centurion is humble and respectful towards Jesus and is also full of faith. He understands the nature of Jesus' authority and power as delegated from God himself (7.7–8).

All of these things build up a picture of a Gentile who has come to know Israel's God and who believes that salvation comes through the servant of that God, Jesus himself. This picture reflects Jewish thinking on the eschatological mission to the Gentiles: it will be a recognition by the Gentiles of Israel's God as the one true God and it will be a coming to that God in Israel in the time of the Messiah. Both of these factors are present in this simple story. Metaphorically, the centurion is making the pilgrimage of the Gentiles to Mount Zion. He recognizes God, seeks God's help and approaches Jesus as Messiah. Interestingly enough however, in this episode there is no direct contact between Jesus and the centurion, which reinforces the impression that the time is not yet right for Gentile mission.

The same conditions are to be seen at work in the case of Cornelius's conversion in Acts 10. The episode again commands an important position in the narrative. Cornelius is also a Roman centurion; he and his whole family are already worshippers of Israel's God – in other words, are already God-fearers. Cornelius, like the other centurion, is again generous and helpful to the Jewish people. He proves his credentials both by right faith and by righteous actions. 'He gave alms in abundance to the people [of Israel]' (Acts 10.2b). He is godly and charitable (10.4) and is described as pious and God-fearing (10.22). In this story, messengers are again sent to plead the cause of the centurion, and it is the Apostle Peter who is called to the house.

Peter, however, is more reluctant and recalcitrant than Jesus. He needs to be converted himself; for he will not consider eating with a Gentile nor even entering the house of one, for fear of contaminating himself. When Peter has a dream and is told to kill and eat a selection of animals, reptiles and birds, his response is sharp: 'By no means, Lord; for I have never eaten anything that is profane or unclean' (10.14). But the answer comes swiftly: 'What God has made clean, you must not call profane' (10.15).

The question in this case is not whether a Gentile can be helped or met on his or her own ground, but rather whether an observant Jew and a Gentile can possibly share table fellowship on equal terms. Much is made of Peter's preparation to enter the Gentile's house – he is 'summoned into his house' (*metapempsasthai se eis to oikon autou* v. 22). Then, when Peter actually crosses the threshold, Cornelius prostrates himself, worshipping at Peter's feet (*peson epi tous podas prosekunesen* v. 25). He acts as though this is an unheard-of event, like the visit of a king. Clearly, Luke wants his readers to see that this is a great step of faith and a new departure.

What seemed reasonable to Jesus – the possibility of entering a Gentile's house – seems to inspire horror and revulsion in Peter and other law-abiding Jews. And actually eating and enjoying fellowship with a Gentile – sharing the same food – is another huge obstacle to overcome, and represents a giant leap forward in Peter's understanding.

If the *Gentiles* are expected – by Luke – to fulfil certain conditions for entry into the Church, in other words, if they had to qualify in some way to become part of Israel, God's chosen people, then the *Jews*, for their part, are also being asked to make concessions. The main one would be to lay aside their natural revulsion towards the supposed impurity and idolatry of the Gentiles, and to do as Jesus did – to enter the Gentiles' houses and to show full acceptance and friendship by eating with them. Then of course it follows that the Church as a whole must follow suit and do likewise: all Jewish Christians must engage in table fellowship with Gentiles on terms of equality.

Philip Esler, in his *Community and Gospel in Luke–Acts*, engages in a long discussion about the importance of Jewish–Gentile table fellowship.[62] He contends that 'an almost universal failure to appreciate the centrality of this phenomenon . . . is one of the most outstanding deficiencies of Lucan scholarship' (p. 71). Esler points out that once the principle of table fellowship has been established – in the Cornelius conversion story especially – Luke takes the discussion forward in his report on the Apostolic Council of Jerusalem (Acts 15); and thereafter makes a point of showing how Paul enjoyed the hospitality of Gentiles during his missions (Acts 16.14–15, 25–34; and 18.7–11).

This Jewish antipathy towards sharing a meal with Gentiles was very deeply ingrained. The purity laws meant first that Jews could not be sure that Gentile food was *kosher*, or clean for them to eat. It could have blood in it; the animal might have been killed wrongly; the meat might have previously been offered as a religious sacrifice. Secondly, the Gentile home and the Gentiles as people were considered to be defiled. Their idolatrous religious practices meant that they could be contaminated by contact with evil spirits. Thirdly, the Jewish purity laws guarded the integrity of the Jewish individual and the race – as set apart, holy unto God.[63]

The Pharisees in particular were especially concerned with the avoidance of anything polluting or contaminating. They always ate in conditions of strict ritual purity. The Essenes of Qumran also had strict prohibitions on eating with outsiders – even of Jewish race – and kept themselves physically intact by living apart from other people. They also had daily baths and cleansing rites.

On the one hand, ritual purity not only protected the integrity of God's Law in the eyes of devout Jews but also preserved the separate and distinct identity of God's chosen people. On the other hand, table fellowship was an expression of the closest intimacy, respect and friendship. It was the sign of a life shared in common, of mutual approval and acceptance.

It is possible that there was some diversity of practice among Jews in the first century – particularly in the Diaspora – but by and large it would have been almost unthinkable for Jews to enter into full table fellowship with Gentiles in their own homes and on terms of equality. The only exception to this would have been the Gentile proselyte, who, to all intents and purposes had become a Jew, and who, through the new religious practice and worship was effectively purified.[64] Philip Esler insists that 'as a general rule Jews did refrain from eating with Gentiles'.[65] In fact, many Gentiles remarked on the aloofness and disdainful attitude of the Jews. Tacitus, for example, said that 'they take their meals apart, and, although as a race they are much given to lust, they abstain from intercourse with foreign women'.[66]

It would appear that the Jewish people were not only concerned to maintain *spiritual* purity, but were also concerned for the complete integrity of the *physical* body. The rules of ritual purity and kosher food went far beyond fastidiousness about foreigners. They were in fact a very fundamental conviction on the part of most Jews, and the early Christian Jews must have had the greatest difficulty in persuading their fellow believers to overcome their scruples about this. For further evidence of the problem, we only need to read Paul's account of his own difficulties with Peter and the leaders of the Church in Galatians 2.11–14. In the light of this, the words attributed to Peter in Acts 10.34–5 at a very early stage in this transition are surely the thoughts of the author, Luke: 'I truly understand that God shows no partiality, but in every nation anyone who fears him and does what is right is acceptable to him.'

This is also the conclusion which arises naturally from the passage in the Gospel where *Jesus* speaks of God's dealings with the Gentiles through Elijah and Elisha (Luke 4.25–7). It also seems that Jesus himself acted on the principle outlined by Peter above in his dealings with Gentiles such as the Roman centurion. However, Luke's great difficulty is to provide adequate grounds on which the Gentiles can be accepted as equal partners with the Jews *in the church*, and to convince his fellow Jews that the Gentiles had qualified for salvation without first becoming part of 'Israel' through circumcision.

To this end, Luke conceives a three-stage incorporation into the Church. First, a Gentile must show evidence of true faith in Israel's God, and there must also be evidence of piety and right living in that person's conduct. The ideal Gentile is therefore the God-fearer or the proselyte whose faith can easily be proved. Secondly, the Gentile must have the humility to acknowledge that salvation is offered to Israel first and then comes through Israel to the other nations. The Gentile's approach to Jesus (in the Gospel) or to the church leaders (in Acts) must therefore be both humble and respectful. Thirdly, any Gentile seeking salvation must be prepared to submit to the Law of God – even though this does not necessarily mean circumcision or observance of the laws of ritual purity after the manner of a Jewish believer. In that case, what exactly did it mean for a Gentile to observe the Law of God? This question is broached in Luke's account of the debate over Gentile membership of the Church at the Apostolic Council of Jerusalem in Acts 15.

The Apostolic Council of Jerusalem

The matter of Jewish–Gentile relations in the Church was not only put to the test through reservations about table fellowship with Gentiles on the part of the Jewish Christian leadership: it also came to a head over the subject of circumcision (Acts 15.1). If Luke may not be entirely clear about the detail of the events, he is surely correct in surmising that these were the two big issues to resolve in the Church of the AD 30s to the 50s and beyond. That there was a major dispute in the Church we also know for sure from Paul's Letter to the Galatians (written around AD 51). The matter certainly came to the Jerusalem church, whose leadership appeared to exercise oversight of the developing Christian mission up to AD 70. Paul and Barnabas and others went as official representatives from Antioch.

Some of the Jerusalem Christians who followed the Pharisees' teaching still (Acts 15.5) insisted on Gentile circumcision. Peter, according to Luke, then explained how his experiences had led him to a change of heart. The seal of God's approval on Gentile inclusion in the Church was the baptism in the Holy Spirit, given to Gentiles in the same way as to Jews (15.8–9). The acceptance by Gentiles of the message of salvation meant that they had also received forgiveness for past sins (15.9). In other words, they had been purified and cleansed by the Spirit of past impurity and contamination. Paul and Barnabas then explained that God had confirmed the rightness of the Gentile mission with 'signs and wonders' (15.12).

At this point the Jerusalem church leader, James, interpreted these events. He understood that just as a righteous remnant from among the Jews had remained faithful to God by recognizing Jesus as Messiah and by forming the Christian Church, so a redeemed remnant – a people (*laos*) – from among the Gentiles had turned to the true and living God. This term *laos* was normally only applied to the Jewish people, but Luke now uses it to designate the Church as the new people of God. James then sees this as part of God's original intention and plan of salvation, and quotes from Amos 9.11–12 to prove it (Acts 15.16–18). God will restore the kingdom of David so that the Gentiles will also see the light of God's presence.

Next, the argument takes a new turn. James concentrates on ritual purity and the food laws. In other words, he is preoccupied with the business of table fellowship. But instead of insisting on the enforcement of the Law of Moses as it stands effective for the Jewish people – even Jewish Christians – he enjoins upon the Gentile Christians only the rules pertaining to foreigners living in Israel – as outlined in Leviticus 17 and 18. In other words, Gentiles must obey God's Law only as it applies to *them*. This allows James to insist on a minimal observance of the Law for Gentiles. They must only keep clear of any meat offered to idols, refrain from sexual malpractice and must not eat blood or meat from an animal that was strangled.

These injunctions might in fact go back to God's Covenant with Noah; in other words, with all the peoples of the earth. In his *Jewish Law in Gentile Churches*,[67] Markus Bockmuehl argues that in the first century there was a general understanding among the Jewish people, based on Genesis 2.16, that Gentiles were able to be righteous in the sight of God if they kept commands against idolatry and blasphemy, had courts to establish justice, and avoided homicide, illicit sex and theft. Often, suggests Bockmuehl, these commands could be reduced to just three: those banning fornication, the shedding of blood and blasphemy against God. In the commands mentioned by James at Jerusalem, we have reference to these three, although the shedding of blood is seen in the context of the killing of animals, not humans – in other words, in the context of enabling table fellowship.

It is likely that James put these particular sanctions upon Gentile believers partly because they fit the conditions of the Noachide Covenant – applicable to all Gentiles – and also because they derive from the Law of Moses, making them perhaps more authoritative with Jewish believers in his church. Whatever our conclusion, it is true to say that these relatively minor constraints opened the way for Gentiles not only to enter the Church without being circumcised, but also to enjoy table fellowship with Jews without many restrictions. The fact that the injunctions were part of the Law of Moses – in a section applicable to Gentiles only – was made clear by James when he said: 'For in every city, for generations past, Moses has had those who proclaim him, for he has been read aloud every sabbath in the synagogues' (Acts 15.21). In other words, all God-fearing Gentiles and all proselytes would be aware that these regulations applied to them.

Of course the report on the Apostolic Council in Acts represents Luke's own understanding or interpretation of the situation, and represents a solution which he could persuade his own church or group of churches to accept. When Paul reports the deliberations of the council in Galatians 2.1–10, he does not say that he was party to the agreement, nor does he see things in quite the same light as Luke. He makes no mention of the legal requirements for the Gentile believers (see 2.6); and if there were any such Paul seems to have ignored them; although it could be argued that Paul took for granted the generally accepted injunctions within the Old Testament applying to all peoples – for instance those implied throughout the whole of Genesis. This is, unfortunately, an argument from silence. Even so, when Paul elsewhere discusses the eating of food offered to idols, he advises tolerance and forbearance and suggests that refusing such meat is a way of keeping the more conservative 'weaker' members happy (2 Corinthians 8.9–13).

At the time Luke was writing, the whole council must have been a distant memory, and the Jerusalem church – then in exile – would have lost its commanding position of influence. Yet the fact is that Luke is still wrestling with this question of Jewish–Gentile table fellowship and the acceptance of Gentile Christians on equal terms with Jews. This does seem to indicate that the Christian Church – in his region at least – was still a Church with a Jewish leadership and with many conservative Jewish members who had reservations about full fellowship with converted Gentiles.

The missions of the Gospel and of Acts

In Mark's Gospel, there are two miracles about feeding great crowds of people: the feeding of the five thousand (6.30–44) and the feeding of the four thousand (8.1–10). It was suggested earlier that the repetition could well be a literary device to distinguish the mission to Israel first from the later, broader mission to Israel and the Gentiles together. But in Mark, there is only one commissioning of disciples to go out on mission, in Mark 6.6b–13. At that point the 12 disciples are sent to all the surrounding villages.

In Luke, however, we now find that things have changed. The situation is reversed. There is only one feeding miracle (9.10–17), but there are no less than three stories about sending disciples out on mission (9.1–6; 9.52–6; 10.1–12 and 17–20). The first of these more or less parallels the account in Mark 6.6b–13, although Luke does change the ending and does not mention the driving out of demons. This aspect he brings in later instead, after the mission of the 70 or 72 (10.1–12, 17–20), when the disciples rejoice that even demons submit to their authority. This then gives Jesus the opportunity to speak of the eschatological event of Satan's downfall, which is even then already foreshadowed in his own ministry: 'I watched Satan fall from heaven like a flash of lightning' (10.18). This then becomes an object lesson in authority: the followers of Jesus, through their access to the power of God's Spirit, will have the same authority as Jesus himself. And, because of the close link between the Holy Spirit and mission, this will be especially evident when they are sent out to preach and to heal.

The three commissioning stories in Luke are all different in this respect: in each case they have a different target group. The first, which, as mentioned, follows Mark, is a mission to Israel, symbolized by the sending of the 12 disciples. The second – and this is hardly ever noticed by preachers or writers – is a mission to Samaria (9.52–6). Again, the form of the pericope is that of a commissioning narrative, beginning, 'And he sent messengers ahead of him. On their way they entered a village of the

Samaritans to make ready for him' (9.52). But then the story has a strange twist: 'they did not receive him, because his face was set towards Jerusalem' (9.53). In this instance, Jesus and the disciples are rejected, but that is not entirely unusual. What is strange is the reason given, that he had set his face towards Jerusalem. Does it mean that he did not have time to turn events around and gain some success from the work? Or is it that this is another literary device, to show that Jesus is now travelling and nothing will distract him from carrying out God's will to go to Jerusalem? It is hard to say, but the passage does occur at the beginning of a new section of the Gospel; the part considered as a transition, a pilgrimage.

Whatever the case, Luke is able to turn this account into an object lesson. For the disciples James and John want to bring down the curse of 'fire from heaven to consume them' (i.e. the Samaritans) (9.54). But Jesus rebukes them. He has not come to exact retribution, but to bring salvation (9.56). The Samaritans are not to be written off. And elsewhere in Luke, Jesus is concerned to reach out to the Samaritans, and of course tells a famous parable which shows a Samaritan in a good light and the religious leaders in Israel in a bad light (9.25–37). The Samaritans must be considered from now on as potentially good neighbours (9.36–7) especially if they are in fellowship with other Christian believers.

The third commissioning story occurs in 10.1–12 and 17–20, when Jesus sends out 70 or 72 (there is uncertainty over the numbers in the earliest manuscripts). The number – whichever it is – indicates a mission to the Gentiles. It is a mission of completeness or a mission to all the nations including Israel (for the number 72 see Genesis 10). Luke adds an editorial comment, that the disciples are to go ahead of him 'to every town and place where *he himself intended to go*' (*emellen autos erchesthai* 10.1b (my italics)). The emphasis this time is on the vastness and extent of the harvest, as well as on the paucity of workers to carry out such a mission (10.2). The disciples are also described as lambs among wolves. This is surely a reference to the wild world at large – in other words, the Gentile world. And the fact that this mission

envisages the Gentiles is made plain at the end of the passage
(vv. 12–16), when Jesus compares Jewish and Gentile towns and
warns that on the Day of Judgement the Gentiles might well
receive more mercy than the Jews. The crux of the matter is
whether there are signs of repentance in evidence (10.13–15).

Now the importance to Luke of this three-stage plan for mission is made even more clear when we turn to Acts and examine
the pattern there. The author again seems deliberately to parallel
the scheme in the Gospel with a similar scheme in the Church's
mission in Acts. Returning to Acts 2 first of all, the whole of the
Jewish 'nation' seems to be envisaged: the Jews from Jerusalem
are mentioned along with the Jews of the Diaspora. Peter
addresses them as 'fellow Jews and all who live in Jerusalem'
(2.14). On that day many came to believe and were baptized:
three thousand were added to the group of original disciples
(2.41). The leadership of this initial work falls on Peter and John.
Then, after the stoning of Stephen (7.54–9) there ensues a time
of persecution, and the Greek-speaking Jewish Christians (the
Hellenists) are scattered. This setback, however, makes possible
the next advance, this time into Samaria and Judea (8.1–25). In
his commentary,[68] J. Fitzmyer sees this purely as a travel narrative
and not as a mission in its own right at all. He speaks of Samaria
as 'the land that symbolizes opposition'(p. 824). In reality, this is
a mission which envisages the whole of ancient Israel, both north
and south kingdoms – and as such it would certainly include
Samaria. But the fact that Luke specifies 'the province of Samaria
and Judea makes his intention clear' (Acts 8.16 – my italics).

Despite the fact that the Samaritans were despised by Jews
as of mixed race and holding heretical beliefs, they were still
half-Jewish by blood and shared much of their religious faith in
common with the Jews. Samaria formed part of the southern
kingdom of Judea and Jesus chose to pass through it since it was
the direct route to Jerusalem. For this second stage of mission,
Philip is assigned a leading role. Peter and John only reappear in
order to visit and to place the seal of approval on the work that
is going forward apace (8.14). Once again Luke understands the
Holy Spirit to be the sign and seal uniting Christians together and

showing God's approval of the work undertaken. In this case, the Spirit joins new Christians from Samaritan or Judean origin to those from Galilee and Jerusalem. Samaria is thus the bridge uniting the two communities of the earliest Church. This mission even provides a premonition of the Gentile outreach; for an Ethiopian eunuch – a God-fearer or proselyte – is helped by Philip to find the Messiah (8.26–40). However, the Gentile mission proper does not begin until the conversion of Cornelius.

The Gentile mission – better, the Gentile/Jewish mission – is in fact the third phase of mission in Acts, and consequently the Apostle Paul comes into the limelight. He was first introduced through a cameo appearance at the stoning of Stephen (7.58). Paul is thus at first Saul the persecutor; but then his conversion on the road to Damascus is described (9.3–9). Immediately after this incident, the centurion Cornelius and his household are introduced (Chapter 10) and Cornelius becomes the exemplar for the third wave of mission – which is both to Jews (in a continuing outreach mainly through the synagogues) and to Gentiles (usually, but not always, through the agency of the synagogues). Many of the Gentile converts in Acts are already God-fearers or proselytes worshipping the one true God of Israel.

Luke writes of those who are preaching to the Jews in Antioch (11.19), but also of others – men from Cyprus and Cyrene – who 'spoke to the Hellenists also, proclaiming the Lord Jesus' (11.20). Once again, the new phase of mission has to be vetted and approved by the Jerusalem leadership (11.22), and in due course Paul and Barnabas are sent to assist with this Jewish–Gentile mission, which begins in Antioch but radiates out from there, leading Paul into his journeys and his life's work (see 13.2). If the rest is not quite 'history' – because Acts, like the Gospel of Luke, is a somewhat artificially schematized literary work – nevertheless the historical pattern has been set and the Pauline missions fit into a context similar to what we find in the letters of Paul. They are to be missions to the Jews of the Diaspora first, reached through the synagogues; and from there to the Gentiles, most of whom are already attached to the synagogue's life and who are already favourable to Israel's faith.

One important point to grasp about all this is that Luke links together the missions of Jesus' own lifetime (in the Gospel) and the mission as it unfolds later in the Acts of the Apostles. The Holy Spirit is seen as the initiator and inspiration behind all the phases of mission activity. In Acts Luke makes this very clear. At each new stage the Holy Spirit prompts a new opening and at each new stage *a new evangelist comes into view*. By such devices, Luke is able to highlight the fact that in God's dispensation there is an overall plan, strategy or programme for mission. The beginning of the eschatological age is the time for the initial outreach to Israel to offer her salvation first. Then the whole of greater Israel must be restored, and this includes Samaria and Judea. Through these missions a righteous remnant responds and a minority of the total population receives redemption. Then, finally, the mission reaching out to the ends of the earth will be a mission both to Jews and Gentiles simultaneously. This is a long period of preparation for the end of the age. Luke makes no mention of a final gathering in Jerusalem and the banqueting feast on Mount Zion. Perhaps this is because the Jerusalem church now has little or no role in the universal mission – it has been effectively sidelined by the Roman invasion of AD 70.

It is also important to note that Paul is not, for Luke, the Apostle to the Gentiles only (although admittedly this is how he sees himself in Galatians 2.7 and elsewhere); but he is regarded by Luke as the Apostle to the Jews and the Gentiles together. Even when he warns the recalcitrant Jews of the synagogues that he will 'turn to the Gentiles' (e.g. Acts 13.46), he nevertheless continues to visit the synagogues and always goes to his fellow Jews first, right up until the end of the Acts of the Apostles (see 13.14; 14.1; 16.13; 17.1–3, 10–12, 17; 18.4, 26, etc.). It seems strange to say it, but Luke could well be representing Paul's actual practice better than he represents it himself in the Epistles.

Finally, the other vitally important point to note is that Luke makes it possible for the Gentiles to be included in the Church on equal terms with the Jews. They can be full participants in the

Christian communities without any insuperable barriers. As a consequence, in due course, not only God-fearers and proselytes will be reached – both groups acceptable by and large to Jewish believers – but even pagans will be reached too. This forms part of Luke's understanding in Acts, for, to take one example, when Paul reaches Athens he preaches at the Areopagus, the centre of pagan philosophical thought (Acts 17.16–33). The Greeks there are considered as archetypal pagans who do not know God. The city is full of idols (17.16) and the God Paul proclaims is to them 'the unknown God' (17.22). Far from being a clever missionary ploy – as so many interpreters seem to imagine – this is rather the author's way of warning his readers that such a place might be stony ground. And so it proves, because Paul has little success there. Many scoffed at the idea of resurrection from the dead (17.32), but nevertheless inroads were made into the darkness of the pagan mind – according to Acts, the first inroads into pagan society.

The messianic banquet

In a section dealing with Jesus' parables (13.6–14.35), Luke shows in two instances that he is very much preoccupied with the expanding Christian mission. In 13.28–30 (the parable of the closed door), after Jesus has stressed the need to enter the kingdom by the narrow door (13.24), there is an ending which looks like a gloss or an additional logion of tradition from another context. It is a word of judgement for some, but a word of hope for others:

> There will be weeping and gnashing of teeth when you see Abraham and Isaac and Jacob and all the prophets in the kingdom of God, and you yourselves thrown out. Then people will come from east and west, from north and south, and will eat in the kingdom of God. (13.28–9)

This word comes from the source in common between Matthew and Luke ('Q'), but Luke extends Matthew's 'from east and west' to 'from east and west and north and south', so that the fortunate ones come from the four corners of the earth. The implication is clear: at the eschatological banquet over which the patriarchs and prophets of Israel preside, people from all nations will be present. Luke also adds a telling moral to the story: 'Indeed, some are last who will be first, and some are first who will be last'(13.30). The first are surely those leaders of Israel who would naturally assume that they have priority or pride of place in God's kingdom. The last are the Gentiles who have least to expect and nothing of their own righteousness to offer.

The point is driven home in the parable of the great banquet of Luke 14.15–24. The Lucan parable again departs from Matthew's version (Matthew 22.1–14) and describes *two* groups of new guests invited to the banquet after the original guests had declined. Those who have first refusal are the 'friends, brothers, relatives and rich neighbours' (Luke 14.12); in other words, the privileged, the chosen ones. Evidently, law-keeping, righteous Israel is envisaged here. Yet in the parable these are the ones who give lame excuses and do not make an appearance at the banquet. So the next group to be invited is 'the poor, the crippled, the blind, and the lame' (14.21). No doubt these are the marginalized of Jewish society, the religious underclass who have no rights and no power or influence. Then Luke adds a third group: 'Go out into the roads and lanes, and compel people to come in' (14.23). This latter group are presumably those outside the city. Surely these are the Gentiles – those not within the boundaries of Israel, not fenced around by the Law (Torah) and having no claim on the eschatological rewards of the kingdom.[69]

It is important to notice that in the parable Jesus does not want to exclude anyone. The self-important religious leaders are seen as having the prior invitation. It is, however, their own attitude which debars them from the feast. They are not excluded, but they do need to repent or they risk forfeiting all their privileges. This is made very clear in the parables of losing and finding in Chapter 15 (the lost sheep 15.1–7; the lost coin 15.8–10; the lost son 15.11–32). In the first story the 'moral' is a warning to the respectable people who do not repent: 'There will be more joy in heaven over one sinner who repents than over ninety-nine righteous people who need no repentance' (v. 7). The other two parables also highlight the need for repentance. In the last (the lost son) the prodigal son represents the sinner who comes to repentance, and the elder brother represents the 'righteous' law keeper who refuses to take part in the banquet at the end (vv. 28–32).

The next group envisaged in the parable of the great banquet are the lower classes of Israel who are duly given an invitation to the banquet, and finally, at the last stage, the Gentiles receive an invitation. Once more we glimpse stages in salvation history or in the scheme of salvation. Those who would least have expected God's favour are surprised to find themselves sharing in the messianic feast. For them, the kingdom of God becomes a reality all the more because it is such a welcome surprise.

The same kind of message comes over loud and clear in a parable Luke places after the triumphant entry into Jerusalem and after the overturning of tables in the Temple. When Jesus is facing the greatest hostility and danger from 'the righteous' law keepers – the religious authorities in Jerusalem – Luke has Jesus tell the parable of the tenants in the vineyard (Luke 20.9–18). The parable is based loosely on Isaiah 5.1–7, where the vineyard is a symbol of Israel. The Matthean and Marcan versions of this parable follow the LXX translation of Isaiah 5.2 at the beginning of the parable – Matthew 21.33–46; Mark 12.1–12. In Isaiah's version, the prophet condemns Israel for producing bitter and sour grapes when the vine planted was capable of producing good fruit.

In the Lucan parable the owner of the vineyard sends three servants one after the other to collect his share of the harvest, but the servants are all beaten in turn and return empty-handed. Then the owner sends his 'beloved son' (20.13) The tenants throw the son out of the vineyard and kill him. Verses 15b and 16 are the most crucial of the parable: 'What then will the owner of the vineyard do to them? He will come and destroy those tenants and give the vineyard to others.' Both Matthew and Mark have a similar conclusion. The implication is clear; the leaders of Israel's life and worship have not produced the fruits of repentance and faith. The ordinary people exclaim 'God forbid' (*me genoito*) in reply to the idea of killing the son (v. 16), but as Christopher Evans says,[70] 'the people are in danger of sharing the attitude of their leaders'. Yet they can be separated from their leaders in principle – and so Jesus warns them; beware, the kingdom will be offered to others more worthy of it (v. 16).

In Luke's Gospel as a whole the 'others more worthy of it' are invariably the poor, the sick, those without power or possessions, women and children, those who do not see themselves as righteous (e.g. Galileans), those who are regarded as unrighteous (e.g. Samaritans) and, last but not least, those completely without the Law of Moses or the knowledge of God – the Gentiles. This parable also obviously has a mission dimension to it.

The Lucan Great Commission

Luke's account of Jesus' meeting with his disciples and commissioning them for their future work (Luke 24.44–9) takes a very different form from the Great Commission in Matthew's Gospel, but there are a few features in common. The authoritative, compelling tone is similar: furthermore, in both cases, the commissioning takes place after the crucifixion and resurrection. The risen Lord initiates, authorizes and accompanies the mission of the Church. This means that everything is now ready and the time is ripe for the work to spread into the entire world.

In both Gospels it is a mission 'to all nations' (Luke 24.47 cf. Matthew 28.19). Luke makes it clear that the necessary conditions are indeed in place: the scriptural prophecies about the Messiah have been fulfilled (Luke 24.46) and so have the prophecies about world-wide mission (24.47). In Matthew, a different reason is given as justification for world-wide mission; it is because Jesus has received 'all authority in heaven and on earth' (Matthew 28.18) that this mission can proceed. Luke speaks instead of preaching the message about 'repentance and forgiveness of sins' (Luke 24.47). This is a powerful theme throughout the Gospel. Matthew does not give the content of the message, but instead speaks of making disciples – through baptism, teaching and the inculcation of obedience to the Law of Christ (Matthew 28.19). These are themes which recur throughout *his* Gospel. Matthew's mission is oriented towards incorporation into the Church's life, while Luke is more concerned with individual conversion.

In Matthew, Jesus promises that his invisible presence will accompany the disciples: 'I am with you always' (28.20). Luke characteristically speaks instead of the Holy Spirit as initiator and guide of the disciples' mission: 'I am sending upon you what my Father promised' (24.49). The Spirit is not mentioned by name, but is simply the 'power from on high' (v. 49). Luke also takes up the theme of being a witness: 'You are witnesses of these things' (24.48).

The commissioning story in Luke is therefore very different from the one in Matthew; so much so that it is hard to say whether or not they are using a common source. What we can say, however, is that there was a tradition of a commissioning of the disciples by Jesus after his resurrection. Matthew has adapted the tradition so that he reiterates many of his own gospel themes and preoccupations in his account. Luke has done likewise. That is why Jesus states at the beginning of the Lucan account: 'These are the very things I told you about while I was still with you' (24.44). The commissioning story is in this way – for both Matthew and Luke – the logical conclusion of the salvation prepared by God from long before; predicted and foreseen in Scripture and then enacted and made a reality in the ministry and work of Jesus.

The commissioning theme is taken up again at the beginning of the Acts of the Apostles (1.6–11). Just before the ascension, Jesus appears to the apostles. They ask if the conditions are now in place for the restoration of Israel: 'Lord, is this the time when you will restore the kingdom to Israel?' (1.6). This is not a foolish question. Part of the ongoing mission of the Church is indeed to complete the restoration of Israel. And 'Israel' can even be understood to mean the redeemed from among both the Jews and the Gentiles. This is the sense in which Luke often understands the term. So Jesus answers without correcting the apostles. He will not say how long the period of mission will last, but he reiterates what is said at the end of the Gospel; that this mission can only be carried forward in the power of and under the guidance of the Holy Spirit: 'But you will receive power when the Holy Spirit has come upon you' (1.8). Then Jesus confirms the eschatological timescale of the mission. It is to be first to the heart of Israel – starting with Jerusalem. Then it will spread to take in the whole of Israel, including Samaria and Judea; and finally, it will reach to the ends of the earth (1.8).

Much of the material of Acts 1.6–11 recapitulates the commissioning narrative of Luke 24.44–9, but certain aspects are emphasized and clarified: the absolute need to wait for the coming of the Spirit; the ordering of the mission along the lines of salvation history; the importance of bearing witness to the gospel and to Christ; the fulfilment of God's mission before the end of the age.

However, there is a particular difference of function between the two accounts, as pointed out in Ben Witherington's *Commentary on Acts*: 'In Luke 24 the account serves as a means of closing the first volume, but in Acts 1 the story of the ascension and final instructions serves to initiate what follows.'[71] Both accounts are therefore reminders: the one recalls the themes of the Gospel; the other shows the continuity between the Gospel and all that follows in Acts. Both accounts serve to demonstrate that it is because Jesus is alive, risen again, that the Spirit can be sent, the Church can be created, the mission to all nations can proceed. Jesus' risen presence is moreover not that of a mere spirit, but of a tangible human being who converses, who eats and drinks, who has table fellowship with his followers. But the ascension (Luke 24.51; Acts 1.9) draws to a close Jesus' earthly life and work. From then on, all of what he has accomplished will become the subject of the Church's preaching and teaching. The Church will then become a witness to all he has said and done. But more than that, it will be a witness to his life working through each believer and through the Church and in the world.

Conclusion

Luke may have been limited with regard to his sources, but his aim, to provide an orderly report or a clear sequential history of 'the things that have been fulfilled among us' (Luke 1.1), is fulfilled both in the Gospel and in Acts, for he provides not only material for the Church's preaching and teaching ministry but also a systematic account of salvation history. His idea of an orderly report is one in which each event in the scheme of salvation has its proper place and is in its rightful position. This is not the same idea as H. Conzelmann's concept of salvation history. Luke makes his starting point the plan conceived from time immemorial in the heart of God; then spoken as the 'Word of God' by the prophets of the Old Testament; then coming to fulfilment in Jesus' life and work; then continuing towards completion in the life of the Church.

Because this is a scheme of salvation, it also takes the form of a pattern or programme of mission, beginning in Israel and made available through Jesus and through the faithful in Israel (his followers); reaching out to the 'lost sheep of the house of Israel' taking in the whole of the ancient kingdoms of Israel and Judah; then finally reaching to the Gentiles, the nations; first to those already devoted to Israel's God and then in the last analysis to those lost in the darkness of idolatry and the worship of false gods. This schema is Luke's great conception of God's mission, and in the Gospel and Acts he is able to present it through a series of events, teachings, cameos and examples, so that by the end of his two-volume work, he is able to leave the world-wide mission of the Church open-ended and to invite the reader to participate in it.

Thus, as Paul is welcoming all who are searching for God at the end of Acts – both Jew and Gentile – and is telling them all about the kingdom of God, 'with all boldness and freedom' (28.31), in similar fashion the disciples of later generations are also being summoned to bear witness and in their turn, to speak with all the boldness and freedom of the Holy Spirit about that same kingdom of God. This means, in sum, that whatever other purpose it may have, the *overriding purpose of Luke–Acts* is to describe the mission of God, to outline that mission in the ministry of Jesus Christ and in the Church of the apostles and finally to call others to participate in that same mission of God, which is still in the process of being completed before the great eschatological time of harvest and ingathering, and the time of the heavenly banquet in the presence of God.

5

John's Gospel – as the Father sent me, so I send you

From time immemorial – or so it seems – John's Gospel has been regarded as 'the spiritual gospel' in comparison to the Synoptic Gospels. It has been treated as a unique work existing in a splendid isolation, even before the days of higher criticism. In contrast to the Synoptic Gospels, John has been thought to be more reflective, philosophical and theologically profound. For those on retreat, or with time to study, John has often been approached as a meditation on the timeless truths of the Christian faith.

Yet strangely enough, at a very early stage, John's Gospel proved to be fertile ground for Gnostic 'heresies'. In the early second century, Heracleon, of the Valentinian school, wrote a 'spiritual interpretation' of this Gospel which placed it outside mainstream Christian thought and aroused the suspicions of many leading churchmen, who resisted its inclusion in the canon of Scripture.[72] In orthodox Christian circles, still in the second century AD, Clement of Alexandria attempted to rehabilitate the Gospel for use in the Church, but he still followed the general opinion that it was a 'spiritual gospel' best approached by a long preparation in the study of philosophy.[73] Following in Clement's footsteps, one of his successors at Alexandria, Origen, the first great exegete of the Bible, promoted allegorical and spiritual interpretation of texts as the highest forms of criticism. John was considered to be particularly suited to such an approach. Origen's methods remained popular right through to the end of the Middle Ages and up until the Reformation.

The effect of this approach to the Gospel has been to focus scholarly attention on the *ideas and themes* of the Gospel and to examine John as a book of theology and abstract ideas; in other words, as a kind of precursor to the doctrinal formulations of the second to the fourth centuries. Inevitably, the Gospel does lend itself to such an approach, with its use of terms like 'the word', 'the truth', 'light and darkness', etc., and with its many monologues on Jesus' self-understanding. It can easily be regarded as a book mainly concerned with the search for meaning in life and with the first principles of faith. As David Rensberger puts it:

> The haunting profundity of [John's] opening words and the elusive character of its language . . . combine to make this Gospel itself seem very much like the Spirit, which 'blows where it will . . . but you do not know where it comes from or whither it is going (3.8)'.[74]

The earlier understanding of John has also had its effect on the modern critical approaches to the Gospel. In the mid-twentieth century, debate raged around the question of whether or not John had any historical foundation, or whether it was built on the philosophical reflections of the author – be it the shadowy 'beloved disciple', 'the elder' or someone else entirely, or even a 'school' of disciples. The long, rambling and repetitive discourses seemed far removed from Jesus' 'authentic' style of teaching, as represented in the Synoptic Gospels, where Jesus expresses himself in parables, terse sayings, riddles and pithy summaries. In his famous commentary of 1953, Rudolf Bultmann saw the Gospel as a late New Testament writing finally edited between AD 80 and 120; heavily influenced by second-century christological ideas, by Hellenistic philosophies and by Gnostic writings, and showing similarities in thought forms with the second-century Mandaean and Hermetic texts and with the mystery religions of the Roman Empire. Bultmann thought that the value of the Gospel lay not in its portrayal of the historical Jesus but in its presentation of the Christ who could be encountered in the existential present moment.

The British scholar, C. H. Dodd, in his *Historical Tradition in the Fourth Gospel*[75] also made use of form critical methods and like Bultmann saw parallels between the Gospel of John and the Hermetic literature of the Hellenistic world, but he did not accept the conclusion that this vitiated the fundamental historicity of John's narrative. He considered that the materials in John's Gospel belonged to a tradition of their own, and were not dependent on the Synoptic Gospels. Although these units of tradition had been embellished and expanded by an editorial hand, nevertheless, because the traditions were early, they constituted convincing evidence of a kernel of historical fact at the origin of the Gospel.

C. K. Barrett, in his widely respected commentary,[76] considered the influences from the Hellenistic world to be important, but at the same time suggested that there was indeed a historical basis to the Gospel. But Barrett contended that this basis was provided by John's knowledge of Mark.

In the 1970s and the 1980s the examination of the social, political and historical background to the Gospel became more popular and widespread. John's Gospel then came to be seen as a document which started its life with apostolic memories and eyewitness accounts; but which was later revised, overlaid, added to and re-written several times at different stages of the Johannine community's life. The historical background has therefore been analysed on two levels: a background in the real life and work of Jesus and his disciples and a background in the *Sitz im Leben* of the Johannine churches. The Gospel thus reflects historical events over a long period of time – a time of turbulent change and various crises, beginning in the 30s of the first century, with Jesus' historical ministry, and ending around the 90s, with the final publication of the Gospel. The finished Gospel in this way emerged from the heat of conflict and controversy, strident polemic and angry debate.

One of the most developed theses along these lines has come from the pen of Raymond Brown, who described the stages in the composition of the Gospel as paralleling stages in the history of the community.[77] At the first stage, a man who had known Jesus during his ministry – the 'beloved disciple' – gathered around himself, in or near Palestine, a group of Jewish believers, including followers of John the Baptist, who had accepted Jesus as Messiah.

At a second stage, Greek-speaking Jews – somewhat like Stephen and the Hellenists of Acts 8 – had a successful mission in Samaria. This group – with their converts – came into the community with a high pre-existence Christology, based originally on the idea that Jesus, like Moses, had 'seen God face to face', had been with God and 'come down' from on high to reveal this knowledge to others.

At a third stage, there was conflict developing between the synagogue and the Christian community. This was partly a struggle between orthodox Jews and believers in Jesus for the hearts and minds of the Johannine community. Some stayed with the synagogue; others were eventually expelled and were forced to make a clean break with it. The community then had to establish its own identity. Brown surmised that at some stage there may have been a move or 'exile' to the Diaspora (most likely to Ephesus) and that this new environment brought to bear new philosophical influences. The Johannine Gospel revised around this time reflects an interest in the universal search for God and in Jesus as the universal saviour of all humankind. The 'world' as a whole then became the arena in which Jesus' teaching and work was played out. At this point, the community also began making converts among the Gentiles.

The defensive concentration on a Christology aimed at 'the Jews' and also at more conservative Jewish Christians in the last phase of the community's life led to a split or a schism. This fourth stage is mainly reflected in the letters of John. Those who remained true to what was taught 'from the beginning' held onto a real, human, historical Jesus as well as maintaining belief in a divine, unique saviour. Others, who seceded from the community, believed that Jesus was divine and not fully human. He was not restricted or contaminated by 'taking on flesh'. Neither his incarnation nor his death had any salvific import. This view led by easy steps down a slippery slope to Gnosticism or to the docetic heresy.

Jesus came to be seen as one who imparted knowledge for those 'spiritual' enough to receive it. This knowledge revealed such 'truths' as the pre-existence not only of Jesus but also of all believers, for true believers were possessors of the Paraclete or Spirit. Those who retained the more 'orthodox' belief in Jesus as fully human and fully divine, in the one whose life and work and, in particular, whose atoning death, had brought about the possibility of the salvation of the world – those now in a small minority – gradually forged closer links with other apostolic churches and at length reluctantly accepted the authority of the presbyter-bishops and the church structures and discipline of orthodox Christianity. This situation is illustrated in narrative form by John's relationship with Peter in Chapter 21 of the Gospel.

At this final stage, the Gospel was the great gift of John's community to the Universal Church, but at first it was not welcomed or readily accepted, because, as already intimated, it found favour with Gnostic and heretical groups. Acting as a counter-balance to the Gospel, the letters of John portrayed Jesus as the incarnate, fully human Saviour who died for the sins of the world, and most probably served to allay the fears of the church fathers and facilitate the Gospel's eventual acceptance into the greater Church.

This imaginative reconstruction of the history of the Johannine community has been variously adopted, adapted, reassessed, and even rejected – but by and large its merits have been recognized. The test has been twofold. First, does it fit into what we know about the first-century historical background? And secondly, on close examination, does the Gospel itself evince a lively interest in those matters Raymond Brown refers to at the various stages of composition? On both counts, the general verdict has been a guarded 'yes'. J. Louis Martyn independently developed a somewhat similar thesis,[78] although his dating of the later stages of the Gospel's composition is given a longer time lapse than Brown's and he says very little about Gentile conversion or Gentile influence in the community.

Oscar Cullmann has also discussed the history of the community,[79] but he regarded the Gospel writing as the work of a school or circle of disciples originally gathered around the central figure of 'the beloved disciple'. Cullmann saw the early community as a motley collection of heterodox Jews, followers of John the Baptist, and also some Samaritans. Other writers, for example, Georg Richter, M.-E. Boismard and John Ashton, have all held modified views of Brown's community and Gospel history, but the general theory of a Gospel composed over a long period of time, reflecting the differing interests and preoccupations of different periods, has largely remained intact.

Nevertheless, new interests and new approaches to John have emerged in more recent times. Two trends seem to be apparent in the early years of the twenty-first century. First, there is an interest in John as a finished literary composition. Writers like R. Alan Culpepper,[80] Charles Talbert[81] and Mark Stibbe[82] have focused attention on John as a *purposeful narrative*: they highlight literary devices and techniques in the text as an integrated work of art; they analyse characterization, ordering of time, development of plot, use of irony, symbolism, etc. This approach has brought many new insights and has respected the integrity of the finished Gospel rather than imagining that it can only be understood properly if it is dissected into many discrete pieces.

Other critics, like John Ashton,[83] Gary Burge[84] and Maurice Casey,[85] have taken further the analysis of John as a historical document, and have looked at various special perspectives in the Gospel, for example: John's understanding of 'the Jews'; or the Gospel's interest in 'Wisdom'; or the historical basis of a 'Signs Source'. The new confidence in John as a document with a historical basis has led Richard Bauckham[86] to argue that John actually corrects and supplements the Gospel of Mark. In other words, he asserts that the author of John actually knew Mark's Gospel and filled in the gaps in Mark's account of Jesus' ministry. Accordingly, Bauckham argues that John regarded Mark as a somewhat misleading account in that Mark portrayed Jesus as having a brief ministry in Galilee, then going on a single journey to Jerusalem towards the end of his life. In contrast, John has Jesus exercising a ministry over three or four years, with regular trips to Jerusalem at the festival times. John's Gospel was therefore written for an audience acquainted with Mark, and had the express purpose of supplementing Mark's information and complementing his 'incomplete' Gospel.

The purpose of the Gospel

As we take the time to survey the various approaches to the Gospel of John over the years – even over the centuries – we come to see that the purpose of the Gospel has been envisaged differently at different times. It has been regarded as a philosophical treatise on the search for God; as a theological treatise on the nature of the relationship between God the Father, God the Son and God the Holy Spirit; and has even provided an outline for the later doctrine of Christ fully human and fully divine. At another time it has come to be seen as a polemical work, seeking to persuade readers of the claims of Christ and to oppose various forms of heresy. In more recent times, it has been analysed from the historical point of view, and pointed questions have been asked about the historicity of its presentation of Jesus' life and death. Both negative and positive conclusions have been drawn on this front.

From a different perspective, scholars have tried to read between the lines, to understand the context and background to the Gospel, and to draw conclusions about the nature of the Johannine community and to trace the changes and vicissitudes in its fortunes.

Each new period of Christian history has had its own preoccupations and vested interests – and the interpretation of the Fourth Gospel over the years reflects this very closely. Yet all of these approaches have greatly enhanced our understanding of the Gospel of John; but to this day the *exact* purpose or *raison d'être* of the Gospel seems to remain obscure. Was it written for the benefit of its own community – to strengthen faith during the fires of persecution? Was it written for the Church at large – to correct some misunderstandings and mistakes apparent in the other Gospels? Was it written to expand and clarify our knowledge of Jesus' ministry – his words and works? Was it written from the point of view of a sect shoring up its defences against a hostile world?[87] Or, again, was it written to establish among Christian believers a clear identity and a firm faith after hostility and rejection by the Jewish synagogue authorities? Then there is also the possibility that the Gospel was written to encourage outreach and mission and to turn the Church in a new direction.

The Gospel itself appears to state its purpose in unequivocal terms, in 20.31: 'But these are written so that you may come to believe that Jesus is the Messiah, the Son of God, and that through believing you may have life in his name.' This would indicate that the primary purpose of the Gospel is christological. Its intention is to clarify who Jesus was and to promote faith in him. And indeed, on a cursory reading of the Gospel, it is evident that John is preoccupied with Jesus as the Christ. The long discourses all seem to revolve around the person and nature of Jesus and his relationship with God (see e.g. 5.19–44). The miracle stories of John are 'signs', pointing beyond themselves to questions about whether Jesus' miracles prove that he is from God or has the authority of God about him (see 2.23; 6.2; 7.31).[88]

This christocentric focus in John is borne out by the absolute claims of Jesus in a series of 'I am' statements. These expression are unique to John and only ever appear on the lips of Jesus himself. Sometimes the 'I am' statements lack any predicate; for example, 'before Abraham was, I am' (8.58 see also 8.24, 28; 13.19). The apotheosis of this expression occurs in 8.24 where Jesus tells the Jewish authorities, 'You will die in your sins if you do not believe that I am [*ego eimi*] he.' This use corresponds to the self-revelation of God (Yahweh) to Moses in Exodus 3.14, but also to the divine name 'I am' uses in Isaiah (43.25 and 45.18; 51.12; 52.6 – LXX translation). At other times Jesus uses 'I am' with a predicate: e.g. 'I am the bread of life' (6.35); 'I am the good shepherd' (10.11, 14; and cf. 10.7, 9); 'I am the light of the world' (8.12); and, ultimately, 'I am the resurrection and the life' (11.25) and 'I am the way, the truth and the life' (14.6). In all of these statements, John unequivocally places Jesus on a level with God and in the closest possible relationship with God.

Some of the metaphors employed are those used of God in the Old Testament. Bread of life refers back to God's provision of manna in the wilderness (Exodus 16) and 'The Good Shepherd' relates to passages like the one in Ezekiel 34, where God declares that he himself will be Israel's shepherd in the absence of worthy human leadership (Ezekiel 34.11–31). Although the Gospel of John always makes a distinction between Jesus and God the Father, nevertheless the two are in the closest possible concord and unity.

Jesus as 'God's agent', or as 'Son of God', is sent by the Father (3.17, 34; 5.36; 6.57; 7.29; 10.36; 11.42; 17.18), knows the Father intimately (10.15; 7.29; 17.25), does the Father's will (14.31), carries out the work of the Father (5.36–7 etc.), speaks the Father's words (12.49–50), and is the one who has seen the Father (6.46; 8.38). He is loved by the Father, and, in sum, is one with the Father (10.30 cf. 5.18). Jesus states baldly, 'The Father is in me and I am in the Father' (10.38 cf. 14.20; 17.21, 24), and, 'He who has seen me has seen the Father' (14.9).

So, clearly the major purpose of the Gospel writer is to promote faith in Jesus as the 'Son of God' and as the one through whom believers come to God. The christological purpose is paramount, but, by extension, this means that it is fundamentally *theocentric* too, in that Jesus is the revealer of God's nature and will, and the agent of God's creative purposes and of his mission.[89] Yet it has been all too easy to lose sight of this central preoccupation, when other fascinating aspects of this Gospel cry out to be examined.

In recent times, Richard Burridge has done scholars a service in demonstrating[90] that the ancient literary forms of biography *(bioi)* invariably have a concentrated focus on the central figure of the story. The more minor characters are defined by how they relate to or respond to the hero or protagonist. In a similar way, the Gospels present Jesus at the heart of all that is said and done in the Gospels – even when he is not physically present.

The mission of Jesus in John

The christological purpose may be central in the Gospel of John, but there is another important aspect to this, distinguishable in principle from the general purpose of bringing people to a knowledge of who Jesus really is. The Gospel has a second and connected purpose of showing how Jesus achieves the aim of God in bringing faith and salvation to the world. In other words, it highlights *the mission of Jesus* as the one who is sent by the Father to carry out the Father's mission (John 3.16). This second and vitally important purpose of the Gospel has hardly ever been identified as distinct from the primary purpose.

Jesus' revelation of God and of the nature of God's purposes is also, by extension, a disclosure of God's mission – the *missio dei* – God's reaching out to the world in love with the offer of salvation. Jesus not only brings knowledge of the Father, but simultaneously performs the works of God in the world which lead to salvation: 'The works that the Father has given me to complete, the very works that I am doing, testify on my behalf that the Father has sent me' (5.36). This is a mission statement in the true sense. Jesus also speaks to humanity as a whole when he says, 'The Father who sent me has himself given me a command-ment about what to say and what to speak' (12.49). Jesus' miracles and healing, his teaching and preaching, are therefore all part of God's mission to the world. The overall purpose of all such 'works' is to bring glory to God and to impart God's salvation to the world.

Through the concept of bringing glory to God, John is able skilfully to link the ministry of Jesus' lifetime to his death and resurrection. For example, in the story of the healing of the man born blind, Jesus precedes his actions with the explanation that this is done 'so that God's works might be revealed in him' (9.3). In the story of the raising of Lazarus, Jesus states that this death took place in order to bring glory to God (11.4).

Of course, it is difficult for people in the twenty-first century to understand this kind of reasoning; that a man can be born blind in order that God's glory might be revealed; or that a man can be allowed to die simply in order that God's glory might be displayed in raising him to life again. Nevertheless, the import of Jesus' statements is undeniable: all that he says and does, and all that happens to him, is part of the overall purpose of his mission, namely, to bring glory to God, that the world might see and know. This also comes out very plainly when Jesus speaks of his death as the appointed hour, the ordained time, for the Son of Man to be glorified (12.23). This is the time when the grain of wheat dropped into the ground dies, but then produces a great harvest (12.24). In this way, the Son of Man is lifted up and draws all people to himself (3.14–15). Thus, the glory Jesus brings to God's name also reflects upon him and reveals the glory of the Son as the saviour of the world (see 1.14; 2.11; 11.4, 40).

The Prologue describes the mission of the Word made flesh

The mission of Jesus as the Word of God is in effect the main theme of the famous introduction to John's Gospel, the Prologue. As in the rest of the Gospel, the general theme is clearly established, namely, the intimate relationship between the Father and the Son: 'The word was with God; and the word was God' (1.1). But the passage taken as a whole describes not only the person of the Christ but also more particularly the *mission* of the Son of God. M.-A. Boismard[91] depicted this mission in the form of a parabola – following the pattern of a descent from heaven to earth, the accomplishing of the Son's mission on earth and then an ascent back to the Father in order to bestow the gift of the Spirit and to commission the work of the disciples in continuing and completing the mission. There is a form of parallelism between verses 1–14a and verses 14b–18 which becomes evident when the action is laid out in the form of a parabola.

The mission of the 'Word made flesh' is seen in various ways in the Prologue. On the downward path to this world, the Word is the agent of natural creation, with the power to perform mighty works (*erga*) and signs (*semeia*) (1.3). He brings gifts from God, in particular the 'natural' gifts of light and life. His

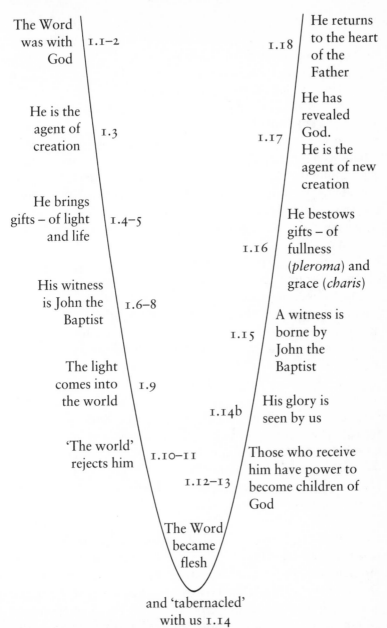

The Word was with God 1.1–2

He returns to the heart of the Father 1.18

He is the agent of creation 1.3

He has revealed God. He is the agent of new creation 1.17

He brings gifts – of light and life 1.4–5

He bestows gifts – of fullness (*pleroma*) and grace (*charis*) 1.16

His witness is John the Baptist 1.6–8

A witness is borne by John the Baptist 1.15

The light comes into the world 1.9

His glory is seen by us 1.14b

'The world' rejects him 1.10–11

Those who receive him have power to become children of God 1.12–13

The Word became flesh

and 'tabernacled' with us 1.14

Figure 5.1

glory is seen and is testified to, in particular by John the Baptist, the primary witness. As he comes into the darkness of the world, he encounters rejection by the many (1.10–11). Yet he achieves his purposes when he takes on flesh and dwells or, literally, 'puts up his tent' among the children of men.

On the upward side, the parallel phrase to the rejection by the world (v. 11) concerns the faith and acceptance of 'all who received him' (v. 12). Then the natural light of verse 9 corresponds to the supernatural light of verse 14b – 'we have seen his glory'. John the Baptist's witness is not only to the enlightenment brought by the Word, but now to his true nature. He ranks above any mere prophet or messenger of God: 'He who comes after me ranks ahead of me', says John (*hoti protos mou en* v. 15). This is a testimony to the divine status of the Word of God, who now becomes the bestower of the supernatural gifts of God – fullness of life (*pleroma*) and grace upon grace (*charin anti charitos* v. 16). He is henceforth the agent not only of natural creation, but of the supernatural creation from above, spoken about later during the encounter with Nicodemus (see 1.17 and 3.3). The difference between the old and new dispensations is made explicit in verse 17 when John states that the Law was given through Moses but grace and truth came (literally 'became' or 'were created') through Jesus Christ. The Word now receives the name of an ordinary mortal, and becomes the only-begotten son (v. 18). The emissary of God is therefore also the instigator of a new covenant between humanity and God. At length, finally, the son returns to the bosom of the Father. He has revealed the Father and made him known, and so his mission is complete. He is now in a position to send out others in his name.

This mission of 'the Word' or 'the Son' is initially conceived in the very heart and mind of God. It is therefore God's mission and God is the sender. The Son acts as the Father's agent and carries through his purposes. The beginnings of this mission are closely linked to the physical, material world. The Word is the agent of creation; the bringer of light and life. He then comes himself into the material, created world and this 'incarnation' forms the culminating point of this first movement of creation. The Word takes flesh and fully enters into the physical and the material universe.

On the 'upward' thrust of the mission, the emphasis is on the spiritual and the supernatural. God's glory is revealed; 'the Son' brings the life of God and the grace of God. The Son now becomes the agent of new creation or re-creation. He reveals God's grace and truth and makes known the Father.

The themes of the Prologue are then taken up, illustrated and elaborated in the Gospel as a whole. The theme of *pre-existence* recurs when Jesus declares 'Before Abraham was, I am' (8.58); his *relationship with the Father* is explored at length in such passages as 4.19–30 and is made explicit in phrases such as 'The Father and I are one' (10.30) or, referring to the disciples, 'that they may be one, as we are one' (17.11, 21). The Word as *agent of creation* and of *re-creation* is illustrated well by the Lazarus story of Chapter 11, at the end of which Jesus proclaims, 'I am the resurrection and the life' (11.25). The theme of *light in darkness* is explored in several ways: in Jesus' presence at the Feast of Tabernacles (Chapters 7—9); in the story of the healing of the man born blind (9.1–12); and in the discussion around the statement, 'Whoever follows me will never walk in darkness, but will have the light of life' (8.12). The *testimony of John* leads into various investigations of the theme of bearing witness. Andrew is seen as a witness to the Messiah (1.41); the woman of Samaria becomes a witness after speaking with Jesus at the well (4.29). The whole idea of bearing witness is also related to the work of the 'paraclete' or 'advocate' in Chapter 15 (especially in verses 26–7).

The reality of *rejection* and of the *hostility of 'the world'* forms another ongoing theme in the Gospel. The rejection of Jesus by the Jewish leaders is expanded into a reflection on the sinful nature of 'the world' (*ho kosmos*) and its dark and devious ways (see e.g. 15.18–23). The flipside of this is the idea of God's glory residing among his people on the earth – dwelling in a tabernacle and moving around with them wherever they go – constantly on the move and in a weak and temporary house of flesh. In the case of the Son, the glory thus shines through the 'clothing' of a physical body and is most especially and clearly seen at the 'hour of glory' upon the cross.

The contrast between *the old and new covenants* is illustrated by the changing of water into wine at Cana (2.1–12) and also in the cleansing of the Temple (2.13–21). These events are placed in sequence, and are both situated at the beginning of Jesus' ministry in John. Right from the outset he is bringing newness of life and is establishing a new relationship between God and humankind.

The *authority of Christ* (1.12) is seen in his intimate knowledge of the Father's will, and in his capacity to carry out the work of the Father God (see esp. 5.19–20). It is also seen in his power to bestow new life from above, as illustrated by the interview with Nicodemus (3.3–8). It is definitively seen in his ability to reveal the Father (1.8). Jesus' teaching is understood in this way (see esp. 6.45–6 and 7.16–17): he is portrayed as *the figure of Wisdom*, emerging from the bosom of the Father to bring understanding of the Father's will to ignorant and misguided people living in darkness. In this sense, his role can be compared to that of the female figure of Proverbs 8.

Through examination of these themes and others, a close connection can be established between the Prologue and the Gospel as a whole. Even though the Prologue has a rather different vocabulary and use of language from the rest of the Gospel (e.g. the unique use of words like *logos, charis* and *pleroma*), it has nevertheless been incorporated into the body of the text in a most thoroughgoing way. It sets the tone for the whole, highlights the major themes and provides a model for the missionary purpose of the Gospel.

In this opening chapter of John's Gospel, comprising the Prologue and the inauguration of Jesus' ministry, six christological titles make their appearance: 'word' (1.1, 14), 'son' (1.14, 18), 'Christ' (1.17, 41), 'lamb of God' (1.27, 36), 'King of Israel' (1.49) and 'son of man' (1.51). In addition, no less than seven archetypal figures enter the frame: Moses, Elijah, John the Baptist, Andrew and Peter, Philip and Nathanael.

The Prologue and the opening scenes thus summarize the Gospel and present a quintessential account of the main thrust of the work and its fundamental themes and ideas. The Prologue is in this sense the Gospel in microcosm, providing an overview of the mission of the Word made flesh. The christological interest is expressed both in abstract terms and in the form of titles, but then leads on to brief scenes which encapsulate in real-life situations what that mission means – in terms of calling, healing, challenging, liberating. The desire to clarify the status of 'the Word' or 'the Son' does not arise purely from a philosophical interest in how a human being can relate to divinity in some speculative definition; it arises from a desire to demonstrate how 'the world' or at least how 'those who believe and receive' can enter into a relationship with the Son and through him with God the Father. In this way Christology is linked to mission. The context in which the Prologue is written is one in which there were a number of different reactions and responses to Jesus. The Gospel writer wants it to be clear that the mission of 'the Son' – right from the outset – was to make it abundantly clear that right belief leads to new life and experience of the true God. Thus, the question of the person of Christ is not a matter of academic definition, but is part and parcel of the work of God in sending his only Son into the world in order to offer salvation to humankind.

The stages of Jesus' mission

The Prologue makes a subtle – or perhaps not so subtle – distinction between the Jews and the Gentiles by describing the former as 'his own' with regard to 'the Word', and the latter as 'the world': 'He came to what was his own (*hoi idioi*), and his own people did not accept him' (1.11). At the same time, 'the world came into being through him; yet the world did not know him' (v. 10). It is interesting that John uses two different verbs in these sentences. 'His own' did not *receive* or *welcome* him (*auton ou parelabon*) – this being tantamount to an old friend refusing hospitality. The world, however, did not *know* or *recognise* him (*ho kosmos auton ouk egno*). The world, being a place of darkness and ignorance, did not have enough experience of God to recognize his agent. Yet John continues the Prologue by pointing out that to whoever received him (*hosoi de elabon auton*) he gave the right or power (*edoken eksousian*) to become God's children (v. 12). Faith or belief in God's Son is the sole condition for this new status. So the Gospel writer makes an *initial* distinction between Jews and Gentiles – both being seen as potential enemies of God or rejecters of God's Son – yet those willing to receive and accept, to believe and have faith – regardless of race or any man-made distinctions – are enabled to become God's children (v. 13).

This pattern laid out so early is one which is seen over and over again in the body of the Gospel: a pattern of rejection by some Jews – especially the religious leaders from Jerusalem (e.g. 5.15–16, 18; 6.41, 52, 60; 7.1, 12, 20, 30; 8.37, 40, 44, 52, 59; 9.16, 24, 41; 11.50, 53, 57), alongside a pattern of ignorance and lack of recognition among non-Jews. For example, the Samaritan woman at Jacob's well is told, 'You [Samaritans] worship what you do not know; we [Jews] worship what we know, for salvation is from the Jews' (4.22). Then Jesus prophesies that in the future 'true worshippers will worship the Father in spirit and in truth . . . God is spirit, and those who worship him must worship him in spirit and truth' (4.23–4). Here, as in the Synoptic Gospels, the coming of the Holy Spirit marks the time which 'is coming, and is now here' – set for the future but already present in Jesus' ministry – a time when Jews and Gentiles will come together in a new way to worship God.

A similar situation is again envisaged in Chapter 12 when some Greeks (*hellenes tines* 12.20), who had gone to Jerusalem for the Passover festival, approached Philip and said, 'Sir, we wish to see Jesus' (12.21). There is an openness and curiosity evident in this enquiry, but a certain ignorance is also implied. Jesus' answer appears to be completely irrelevant and unconnected to this incident – one of the many *aporia* of John's Gospel – for he starts to tell a parable about a grain of wheat which must fall into the ground and die in order to produce many grains (12.24). But despite appearances, this answer is in line with what Jesus told the Samaritan woman. It is not until Jesus' own earthly mission has been completed that the time will be right for the mission to the Gentiles to begin. It is *after Jesus' death* – beyond the moment of self-revelation to the whole watching world – and also after the giving of the Holy Spirit (20.19–23), that 'the Greeks' will discover what they are tentatively beginning to search for. Once again, in John, as in the Synoptic Gospels, we discover an assumption that there is a timescale and a pre-ordained plan of salvation history, which begins with the Jewish mission and eventually encompasses the mission to the Gentiles.

The Jewish mission in John

As we move beyond the Prologue, we immediately discover that the words in the Prologue about John the Baptist are not idealized abstractions about the nature of John's testimony; rather they are an effort to establish from the very outset that John is not the Messiah, but is only a witness – 'the voice of one crying out in the wilderness' (1.23). When John himself is asked about his role, he humbles himself in relation to Jesus, saying, 'I am not the Messiah' (1.20); then he adds that he is not Elijah returned (*Elijah redivivus* 1.21a); nor is he the eschatological prophet of the Last Days (1.21b). He is a mere herald, a voice announcing Messiah's coming. His function, in other words, is to point away from himself to the one who is to come, the one who baptizes not just with water, but with water and the Spirit. His testimony comes to a head in verses 29–30 when John is made explicitly to acknowledge Jesus as 'the Lamb of God who takes away the sin of the world' (1.29). Again, John repeats that Jesus is the one who has priority over him, who is in fact greater than he is (1.30).

Now, what is the purpose of the self-effacement of John the Baptist all through this section of the Gospel? It is certainly not motivated by theological concerns alone; there are more polemical undertones, which more than likely reflect the real historical context and the life of the Johannine community. The view of John the Baptist expressed here must surely reflect the fact that many of John's followers have been weighing the different claims to allegiance of John and Jesus. Some perhaps regard John as the Messiah; others as a great prophet. But the Gospel writer wishes to convince the whole community around John the Baptist of the superior claims of Jesus. Even if John is a great prophet, he is not the Messiah. Jesus is. And, more than that, John himself has borne witness to this very fact.

This scene with John the Baptist reveals something very important; that the Christian mission has already had some measure of success among those Jews who see the need for repentance and renewal, and especially among those who have accepted John's call to be baptized, those who had sought forgiveness for their sins and wished to make a fresh start in life. The Gospel writer and the followers of Jesus surrounding him are desperately now trying to convince the rest of the Baptist community that there is a need to go further, a need to accept Jesus as Messiah and Son of God, a need to be baptized in water *and in the Holy Spirit*. The story of John's two disciples in 1.35–42 now becomes more than a story of Jesus choosing his first followers: it becomes in the Gospel writer's hands an archetypal story of how John the Baptist encouraged his own followers to turn to the Messiah and to become followers of Jesus. That is why John openly declares Jesus to be 'the Lamb of God' (1.36) and without demur allows two of his leading disciples to go after Jesus. This change of allegiance leads directly to the recruitment of Simon Peter through Andrew.

Still in the orbit of the Jewish mission, we next come across Philip and Nathanael. Jesus calls Philip (1.43), but it is Philip himself who finds Nathanael and bears witness to Jesus as Messiah (1.45). Philip, like Andrew, is the type of an evangelist. It might perhaps be equally true to say that he is the type of a Christian witness – one to whom Jesus is sent, and who is then sent out in his turn. Nathanael, however, is a disciple who does not appear in the Synoptic Gospels. Here, in John, he represents the genuine seeker in Israel. As Jesus himself says, 'Here is truly an Israelite in whom there is no deceit' (1.47). Nathanael has become sceptical about the old religion – at least in the way it is taught and practised in Jesus' time. His disillusionment shows up in another way in the story, 'Can anything good come out of Nazareth?' (1.46). Does this also reflect the attitude of the authorities (mostly from the south of the country) who see the north as an area full of troublemakers, fomenters of rebellion and prophets of the end times? Be that as it may, Nathanael is quickly convinced by Jesus' word of knowledge (1.49) – his scepticism has not turned into cynicism and he shows himself more than willing to believe.

So in the very first chapter of John's Gospel we encounter two groups from among the Jewish people: the followers of John the Baptist; then the ordinary, rather disillusioned Israelites who will now have something – or someone – to believe in.

The next group we encounter are the corrupt Jewish Temple authorities and those who have turned the Temple into a market place and a place of commerce. Jesus confronts these authorities, overturning the moneychangers' tables and thereby storing up trouble for himself by engendering an animosity which will eventually result in his own persecution, arrest and demise. The Jewish leaders now already have grounds on which to oppose him and attack him. This is – from the perspective of the Gospel community – no doubt the group seen as opposing the acceptance of the Gospel preaching, hostile to the mission of the Church. They are followers of Moses, and not of Jesus; they look to the man-made Temple for their worship, instead of worshipping within the temple of Jesus' Body (i.e. among the new People of God); and they dispute and rail over Jesus' teachings and over his authority.

In Chapter 3 we find that, despite appearances, not all the Jewish authorities are single-minded in their opposition to Jesus. The figure of Nicodemus represents yet another sub-group within the Jewish community. He is a Pharisee, and a leader of the Jews. He comes to Jesus by night, yet he is not in total darkness (in the eyes of the Gospel writer). He already believes that Jesus has come from God and that his teachings and miracles are signs that God is with him (3.2). Jesus' reply once again seems to be quite off-key and irrelevant to the question: 'No one can see the kingdom of God without being born from above' (*ean me tis gennethe anothen* 3.3). But on closer examination the meaning of the answer becomes clear. Jesus is saying to Nicodemus that the old Jewish way of believing is now inadequate. The revelation and power of the Holy Spirit is now necessary in order that one may enter the kingdom and become a true follower of God. This idea is made quite explicit in verse 6: 'What is born of the flesh is flesh, and what is born of the Spirit is spirit.' Nicodemus seems quite ignorant about the Spirit's role; Jesus then has to explain to him that he is speaking of what he knows, in other words, from experience of the Spirit. The implication is that Nicodemus is following God from afar – through observance of the Law and the reading of the Scriptures – but he does not 'know', that is, have experience of God at first hand.

Nicodemus is not given the opportunity to respond to Jesus' words, but it is obvious from what he says that he falls into a category of Jews who have a foot in both camps. He holds a position of respect and authority as a religious teacher in his own community, but at the same time, he secretly admires and follows Jesus. From the vantage point of the evangelist, writing at a later date, Nicodemus is one who wants to hedge his bets. He has remained within the safety of the synagogue, but is sympathetic to the Christian message – perhaps even a covert Christian.

This was presumably a time when relations were becoming strained and Christians were coming increasingly under attack and had even been expelled from the synagogue (16.2–3). It was then necessary to make a decision for or against. In the evangelist's eyes, Nicodemus is not so much an honest enquirer; rather, he is the indecisive type, who will not make a clean break with the old traditions, who will not give up his privileges, nor give up everything for Jesus' sake. He falls into the category of those Jews the Christian Church has successfully reached, but who do not go far enough in their commitment. Their Christology is not sufficiently high – or, to put it another way, they do not have a high enough regard for Jesus, to make a break with the past and embrace him as Messiah. This surely reflects a situation as much fitting the time of the Johannine church(es) as Jesus' own time. In short, this whole context reveals something of what is happening in the Christian mission of the latter part of the first century.

There is a footnote to the Nicodemus story, however. We encounter him once more near the end of the Gospel, after the crucifixion. Joseph of Arimathea is permitted to take away the body of Jesus, and Nicodemus assists him with the preparation of the body for burial, embalming it with spices. Nicodemus clearly partially redeems himself (19.38–40). The way is open for him to join the Johannine community. Yet John, even at this juncture, is quick to point out that Joseph of Arimathea – like Nicodemus – is only a 'secret follower' of Jesus 'because of his fear of the Jews' (19.38).

The Samaritan mission

After the first encounter with Nicodemus, the evangelist moves beyond the Jewish community, along with its various groupings and their differing responses to Jesus. At a time when Jesus' followers were baptizing more disciples than John (4.1), Jesus decided to extend his mission into Samaritan territory. He deliberately went through Samaritan land on his way back from Judea to Galilee, a direct route but one usually avoided by the Jews. He came to a town called Sychar and there met a Samaritan woman by the village well, known as Jacob's well. This setting for the story in John 4 is most unconventional: a Jewish rabbi alone with a woman, a Samaritan woman and a woman of ill repute, who must collect water alone, at a time when nobody else is around.

Without going into the detail of this fascinating narrative, suffice it to say that Jesus does not set Jewish worship over against Samaritan worship; nor does he enter into traditional arguments over Samaritan heresies. What he does is to insist that salvation comes through the Jews (4.22), but then speaks of the future, of a time when all people of faith, whatever their background or allegiance, will come to know the One they worship through the power of the Holy Spirit. This coming age is not only impending but is already present, according to Jesus (4.23). The woman grasps immediately that Jesus is talking about the messianic age. But Jesus will not let her rest on traditional clichés, and releases a thunderbolt: 'I am he' – that is, the Messiah to come – 'the one who is speaking to you' (4.26).

The woman demonstrates her faith and then goes off to tell others. She becomes a witness to her own community, so that 'Many of the Samaritans from that city believed in him because of the woman's testimony' (4.39). When the townsfolk came out to see Jesus, they begged him to stay with them (4.39–40) and Jesus agreed to stay two further days. Because of this, 'many more believed because of his word' (4.41). The Samaritans show a spiritual hunger and an openness which many Jews in John's Gospel are lacking. The implication may be that John sees the Samaritan 'heresy' as a defective religion in some ways, but that Jesus is able to provide new hope and spiritual sustenance for them.

The story has often been interpreted in recent times in terms of Jesus' dealings with women, or perhaps with Israel's traditional enemies, or perhaps even with an untouchable, outcast race; but surely the main theme of this story is really about the spread of the Gospel; it is a story about mission. It may well be the case that in the Gospel, John has linked this story closely with the later mission to the Samaritans carried out by the Early Church. This story is to be compared with Acts 8.4–25 where Luke describes the beginnings of the Samaritan mission.

The interest of the townspeople in general and their openness to Jesus does not seem to have any follow-up in his ministry – in this Gospel or elsewhere. It is at a later date that we find Samaritans joining themselves to the Christian community. However, there seems little doubt, given the consensus of evidence in the Gospels and in Acts, that there was a relatively successful mission to the Samaritans in the earliest days of Christianity. Not only that, but the pattern of mission in John follows precisely the same sequence as in Acts: first, there is a reaching out to the Jews, with varying responses and results; then to Jews on the margins of society; then to the Samaritans (part of greater Israel); then to the Jews and Gentiles together. Thus, the Samaritan woman at the well is once again an archetypal figure, or an exemplar, who is representative not only of *women* in Israel, but also of the Samaritan community and her community's reaction to the coming of Jesus.

Reaching out to the Gentile world

After the Samaritan adventure, Jesus then moved on to Galilee, but interestingly John at this point chooses to insert the declaration, 'a prophet has no honour in the prophet's own country' (4.44), which Jesus had apparently said previously. In the Synoptic Gospels (Mark 6.4 and parallels) the saying is directed against unbelief in Jesus' own home town of Nazareth, but here John prefers to apply it to the unbelief in Judea, whereas Galilee is praised in the following verse: 'When he came to Galilee, the Galileans welcomed him, since they had seen all that he had done in Jerusalem . . . ' (4.45). This saying is a floating unit of tradition, attached here as the introductory note to a healing in Cana – the healing of the son of a government official (*tis basilikos* – a ruler or governor). This official was in King Herod's service. He was either a Gentile himself, or closely connected to the Gentile rulers of Israel who came from around the Roman Empire. The official came from Capernaum to see Jesus and asked him to accompany him back to Capernaum. Jesus did not agree to go with him, but promised him help: 'Go, your son will live' (4.50). The official trusted Jesus' word and received the news on his way home that his son was recovering (4.51). The time of improvement corresponded with the time when Jesus made the promise.

This whole episode is highlighted by John as the second sign that Jesus performed (4.54). It is a healing miracle which stands alone and which concludes a whole section of the Gospel. After this account – in other words, from Chapter 5 onwards – Jesus is engaged in visits to Jerusalem and in debates with the Jewish authorities. It seems extremely likely, therefore, that John wished to attribute some significance to this event, standing as it does as the culmination of a long sequence of events. The significance is surely that the story represents Jesus' first tentative reaching out to the Gentile world.

Astonishingly, such an interpretation is dismissed out of hand by as eminent a commentator as D. A. Carson, who bluntly asserts, 'There is no evidence that this official was a Gentile.'[92] Yet this narrative in some ways parallels Jesus' healing of the Syrophoenician woman's daughter (in Mark 7.24–30). There are perhaps even more points in common with the healing of the centurion's servant/slave in Matthew 8.5–13 and Luke 7.1–10 (from the 'Q' source). In both accounts there is the place – Capernaum; the approach of the Gentile (rather than Jesus seeking the person out); the seeming rebuff by Jesus; the request made with great humility; the healing at a distance; the rejoicing of the household and their demonstration of faith; the coincidence of the time Jesus prayed for the healing and the healing itself. The only clear difference is that in the Synoptic Gospels the healing is stated specifically to be of a *Gentile* official's servant; whereas, in John, the ethnic status is not specified.

But this aspect might not have been at all obscure to John's first readers. The word 'official' (*basilikos*) may well have been an obvious reference to a Gentile, just as the word 'navvie' used to bring to the mind of English people an *Irish* railway worker. The fact that the official had heard of Jesus without having had any personal contact with him (4.47) is a further indication. The Synoptic Gospels link the story of the centurion's servant to faith found outside of Israel, but John has the comment right at the start of the story that Jesus was like a prophet not accepted *in his own country* (4.44). He highlights in a different idiom the fact that Jesus had to go beyond his normal sphere of work to look for true faith.

Regardless of whether the Synoptic stories are variants of the same tradition as John's story,[93] the story in John has enough signs within it to show that this involves Jesus reaching out towards the Gentile world; and if the man himself is not certainly a Gentile, he is nevertheless certainly within the orbit of the Gentile world, being closely associated with Gentiles.

Raymond Brown is astute enough to comment on this story:[94] 'Even though John's story has nothing specific to do with the salvation of the Gentiles, we shall see that this theme may be represented by subtle allusions.' But Brown draws back from giving any theological significance to the story from a missiological point of view, and expresses 'doubts that John intended a progression in faith from the Jews of chapters 2–3 through the Samaritans (half-Jews) to the Gentiles at Cana'.[95] At the same time he keeps all his options open by adding later that 'there is no *a priori* objection to the symbolic capsulization of the history of the Christian mission' in this section of John. The problem is that Brown finds the allusions upon which such an interpretation is based 'subtle and uncertain'. He prefers to isolate the unit and to see its purpose as drawing out the themes of 'light' and 'faith', but he is nevertheless right on target in seeing this story as 'the conclusion to part two of the gospel'.[96] It could well be that this comprises a section of the Gospel, or even a kind of early form of Gospel in itself, which Brown himself entitles *The Book of Signs* in his commentary.

The allusions Brown mentions are not so 'subtle' or 'uncertain' if Chapters 2 to 4 are taken as a series of illustrations of the mission of Jesus, and if they are regarded as a progressive and integrated narrative within the Gospel as a whole. Because of the use of the weekly, or even daily, liturgical readings, it is easy to become used to studying short passages in isolation from one another. The same technique has been employed in commentaries, in which short passages are analysed in discrete or fragmented form. That means that readers of the Gospels rarely gain the opportunity to see the Gospel as a whole, as a complete literary construction, or as a work conceived as a whole. The exception to this is the Passion Narrative, which is treated as an integrated piece of writing during Holy Week. Such an approach has resulted in the scholarly understanding of the Passion Narrative as a single literary unit existing before the final composition of the Gospel.

An overview of a whole Gospel from the point of view of redaction criticism has yielded many interesting insights and new understandings of the author/editor's theological intentions.[97] To his credit a commentator like C. H. Talbert[98] attempts to remedy the piecemeal approach and instead examines John in larger sections, analysing the Gospel through a series of themes. But unfortunately another problem then arises, namely, that Talbert follows a traditional approach, considering the *theological* themes of the Gospel and ignoring, by and large, its missiological emphases. An example of this is the way he links together the stories of the Samaritan Woman and that of the Official's Son (4.43–54) and concludes that these stories are revelations of Jesus as 'The saviour of the world'.[99] Another problem is that in this case Talbert regards the Samaritan Woman's story as the beginning of a new section, and not as the continuation of a previous section. Thus, Jesus' earlier mission to different Jewish groups is simply subsumed under another title: 'The object of the Baptist's praise'.[100]

Having said all this, however, Talbert does in fact make some helpful comments about Jesus' mission in Chapter 4, arguing for example that 'Jesus supersedes traditional Jewish worship in whatever form.'[101] He also states rightly that the background to Chapter 4 'is the overall Johannine understanding of mission', and adds, perceptively, that John makes a distinction between Jesus' mission and that of the disciples. The disciples 'bear witness to Jesus and attempt to lead others to Jesus, but it is Jesus who is ultimately the evangelizer (1.40–2, 43–9; 4.29–30, 39–42; 17.20)'.[102] Talbert then sheds light on the story of the Official's Son, when he says that even Jesus' return to Galilee would hint at an approach to Gentile territory, for the name 'Galilee' (*galil ha goyim*) means literally 'the circle of the Gentiles'.[103]

In the story of the Official's Son, we have a pattern of events reminiscent of the welcome afforded to a visiting dignitary in the Roman world: the ruler goes out to greet Jesus, invites him into his town, humbly petitions him and all the while defers to his authority and status. This official is representative in John of those who have not seen and yet believe (cf. 20.29). Jesus has not yet embarked upon a Gentile mission as such: perhaps that fact accounts for John's reticence in the account. He – unlike the Synoptic Gospel writers – does not have Jesus praise the great faith of the Gentiles. But all the same this does represent a first step towards the Gentile world. The official does not obviously become a follower of Jesus, but his faith is obviously increased. This pattern is repeated at a later stage, with the tentative enquiry of the Greeks. They approach Philip as an intermediary with the request, 'Sir, we wish to see Jesus' (12.21), but Jesus is not ready to engage with them. Even so, he makes it clear that such an hour will come later, when he has been through death and resurrection (12.24).

Thus, the pattern for the first four chapters of John is as follows: first there is an overall description of Jesus' mission in the Prologue (1.1–18); then there are illustrations of that mission in narrative form. There is a movement through Jesus' contact with various group representatives: followers of John the Baptist (1.19–42); the 'guileless' ordinary Israelite people (1.43–51 and 2.1–12); the Temple authorities (2.1–25); the covert believers among the Jewish religious leaders (Nicodemus – 3.21); the remnant of John the Baptist's followers (3.22–36); the encounter with the Samaritans (4.1–42); and, finally, a reaching out to the Gentile sphere of influence (4.43–54). This pattern follows a clear progression and comes to a logical conclusion. Thus, there is no doubt that this pattern is intentional on the part of the evangelist.

Apart from the Prologue, the literary techniques employed in John to convey theological truths are very much like those employed in the Synoptic Gospels. Examples and real-life stories serve as exemplars to highlight an aspect of Jesus' teaching or mission. Individuals or characters often serve as archetypes to represent whole groups of people and to typify their responses to the challenge of Jesus.

John also seems to have an assumed or unconscious understanding of mission which is remarkably similar to that of the Synoptic evangelists; namely, that there are stages in the unfolding of salvation history, and that every stage has its own time and place in the scheme of things. The Gospel of John has so often been viewed in splendid isolation, and similarities of approach between this Gospel and the other three have tended to be treated with suspicion. Some useful insights have been lost as a result. An analysis of the theme of mission in John brings to light the fact that although many of John's traditions may come from different sources as compared to the other Gospels, nevertheless *John's treatment* of his sources displays some similarities with the other evangelists' treatment of their sources. A fixed focus on the *differences* between John and the other Gospels obscures the fact that all four evangelists do evince similarities in the handling of source materials, especially in so far as they are seen as *vehicles to convey theological ideas and themes.*

The mission of the Spirit

Just as the Father sent the Son to execute his mission, so the Son sends the Holy Spirit. This theme recurs at various points in the Gospel narrative, but is particularly carefully explored in Chapters 14 through to 17 – in a long section of discourse which forms a contrast with the narrative form of 1.18—4.54. The descent of the Spirit is mentioned in John 1.33 in the context of Jesus' baptism. The Baptist is told, 'He on whom you see the Spirit descend and remain is the one who baptizes with the Holy Spirit.' Right from the outset, the Holy Spirit is linked with Jesus and with promises for the future. In the Synoptic Gospels, the focus is on the Father commissioning the Son, but in John the contrast is made more explicit between the one who baptizes in the water of the Old Covenant (John) and the one who baptizes in the Holy Spirit (Jesus). In addition, the commissioning of the Messiah in the Prologue of John takes place from all eternity, when the Word was first prepared for mission to the whole world; but now the emphasis is on Jesus as the Son of God (1.34) fulfilling that mission to all people in the power of the Spirit. This is further elucidated in the Nicodemus interview, when Jesus insists that now is the time when anyone seeking God can be and must be born spiritually of the Spirit (3.5, 8).

Thus, Jesus inaugurates the Age of the Spirit. He is able to speak words from God because they are inspired or conveyed by the Holy Spirit (3.34); and the authority or power carried in the words and works are owing to the communication of God's power by the Holy Spirit (3.35).

Although John makes it abundantly clear that Jesus is the bearer of the Holy Spirit, or, more precisely, the one who bestows the Spirit, the *main* emphasis in the Gospel is on the Spirit as the one sent by Jesus for the empowerment of *the disciples' mission*. For example, if Nicodemus truly wants to become a follower, he must be 'born again' or 'born from above' (the Greek *anothen* can carry either meaning). When we come to Jesus' long discourse in Chapters 14–16, we find that he is speaking about the Spirit's role in the *Church's* mission. The Spirit is going to do for the Christian community what it did through Jesus during his lifetime on earth. The Spirit will be with them (14.16), will teach them (14.26) and will guide them into all the truth (16.13).

In the context of the Gospel as a whole *the truth* relates closely to Jesus' mission and specifically refers to God's plan for salvation.[104] This is 'truth' as understood in apocalyptic terms; that is, as the unveiling of God's purposes, the unfolding of a divine plan, as seen in the events of history. Jesus, as God's agent, features centrally in this plan: 'I am the way, the truth, and the life' (14.6). The word 'truth' is used 48 times in John, as compared to 4 times each in Mark and Luke and only 2 in Matthew. An examination of the uses throughout John reveals that the Holy Spirit is above all a Spirit of *revelation*, imparting a deeper understanding of Jesus' teaching and the reason for his coming, as well as a deeper knowledge of the risen Jesus as a personal friend.

The Spirit's ultimate responsibility is therefore to replace Jesus' presence or, perhaps better, to make Jesus' risen presence a living and vivid reality. The whole of Chapter 15 of John is devoted to the idea of Jesus' presence, not as a person of flesh and blood, but as 'the real vine' giving power to the branches (the disciples), who are then empowered to bear much fruit. The disciples are enabled to abide in the risen Christ through the instrumentation of the Holy Spirit (15.4, 5, 7, 10). The *paracletos* or 'encourager' or 'counsellor', assists the disciples by assuring them that the Son is in the Father, and that they, the disciples, are in Christ (14.20).

They are strengthened to obey his commands (14.21; 15.10) and his teaching (14.23). They are also helped to love one another and to remain in unity. Unity is a powerful theme in this Gospel, just as it is also in the letters of John. It is by remaining in Christ's love that the disciples can live in harmony and in agreement (5.12, 17). The Spirit's task is to intensify the presence and power of the risen Lord in the community, so that they 'remember' and so go on to do the works Jesus did, and 'even greater works' (14.12).

The 'even greater works' firstly mean works in continuation with Jesus' own works – signs of God's greatness, healings in God's name – but John clearly wishes to convey something else in addition. This saying occurs in the context of Jesus going to the Father, and of his being one with the Father. Hence, another aspect of doing greater works must be that the followers of Jesus will spread the knowledge of God the Father further abroad than Jesus was able to. They can multiply the impact of this revelation. Further, doing greater works relates to Jesus' own exaltation and glorification. Through this, the disciples come to know that they have one who intercedes on their behalf at the right hand of the Father. Jesus confirms this by saying, 'I will do whatever you ask in my name' (14.13). So the 'greater works' of the disciples must relate both to the revelation of God as Father and of Jesus as risen, exalted Lord, now with the Father in authority. The disciples' works are 'greater' quite simply because they are done in the name of Jesus.

The latter half of Chapter 15 then adopts a new tone, and the Spirit takes on a new role. Whereas before, the Spirit has been very much a facilitator of Jesus' continuing presence, now the Spirit becomes the disciples' witness and advocate when they come face to face with a hostile world, or have to confront enemies intent on persecuting them. The community Jesus is addressing at this point seems to have the aspect of a sect huddling together in a threatening environment, in a world which is full of hatred for the believers: 'If the world (*kosmos*) hates you, be aware that it hated me before it hated you' (15.18).

We need to bear in mind, however, that this is the same world which is in John the target of God's mission and the object of God's love – in short, the arena of God's salvation:

> For God so loved the world that he gave his only Son, so that everyone who believes in him may not perish but may have eternal life. Indeed God did not send the Son into the world to condemn the world, but in order that the world might be saved through him. (3.16–17)

Yet, as the Prologue makes clear very early on, the world is also a place of darkness, in both senses of 'ignorance' and of 'evil intent'. It is 'the world' which rejected the Son and brought about his death. Thus, the attitude to 'the world' in John is deeply ambivalent. 'The world' is a mission field for the disciples, but it is also a minefield for the Christian community. The world can be a place where faith is awakened, and also the place where faith is threatened or distorted, the place where life is created, and where life can be prematurely extinguished.

So in John the Spirit has a very specific function: as the advocate who bears witness to the Truth and who defends those disciples who stand by the Truth. That Truth is the truth in and about Jesus: 'the Spirit of truth . . .', says Jesus in John, 'will testify on my behalf' (15.26). Even when the Christians are expelled from the synagogues and are persecuted, the Spirit will be their protector. Like a brilliant lawyer in a courtroom, he will prove the disciples' case and secure their acquittal: 'He will prove the world wrong about sin and righteousness and judgement' (16.8). In these Chapters 15 and 16 – more than any other sections of John – the atmosphere and imagery of the law court are ubiquitous. It is as though the disciples are on trial and are at risk of the death sentence. They are literally following in the footsteps of their master. It is then the task of the Holy Spirit to mount a defence and to secure their innocence and subsequent release. Because of this situation, it is the primary task of the Spirit to be a witness or indeed more than a witness, an expert counsel for the defence.

Was this passage (Chapters 15 and 16) written at a time of great danger and anxiety for the Johannine church, when its enemies were mounting reprisals and breathing threats of murder? If so, according to John, such enmity seems largely to be stemming from the synagogue (16.1–4). In Chapter 17 Jesus resumes this theme and this time prays that the disciples may be kept safe and protected (17.11b–12, 15).

Yet the risk of persecution and the joy of bringing the world to faith in Christ go hand in hand. The disciples are bound to encounter opprobrium, because their mission is to the very world which has rejected God in Christ (17.18). Yet they will know joy as well as heartache and danger (17.13). The Christian community is not 'of the world' but lives in it and is called to work in it and accomplish Jesus' continuing mission to it (17.14–18).

In the final analysis, 'the world' in John is a metaphor for humanity itself. The Christian community itself is not outside 'the world': as a corporate entity and as individuals Christians will find something of the world within themselves – if they fail to abide in Christ, if they do not love one another, if they do not have the spirit of service, if they do not avail themselves of the Holy Spirit. Similarly, among both Jews and Gentiles there will be those who receive and those who reject Christ – as the Gospel stories demonstrate. The important thing is that Christians do not give up or abandon their faith because of the influences or threats present in the world. The task of the Holy Spirit is primarily to ensure that this does not happen.

The Spirit is active in promoting faith and unity, and is also a catalyst for mission in and to the world. So the mission of the disciples is effectively triggered, energized, guided and directed by the Holy Spirit (see 15.25–7). So long as *the disciples themselves* initially receive the Spirit and live by the Spirit, they will also have the courage and the power to reach out in mission to others. This fact is illustrated by the acted parable of Jesus towards the end of the Gospel. He breathes the Spirit into them, first to show in an unequivocal way that the same Spirit who worked in and through him will now be working in and through them, then secondly to indicate that the full authority to carry out God's mission will now be the prerogative of the disciples. Jesus makes this explicit:

'As the Father has sent me, so I send you.' When he had said this, he breathed on them and said to them, 'Receive the Holy Spirit. If you forgive the sins of any, they are forgiven them; if you retain the sins of any, they are retained.' (20.21b–3)

As the Father sent the Son, so the Son sends the disciples. John's Gospel outlines a procession of missionary endeavour.

The mission of the disciples

The disciples' mission is essentially the same as the mission of the Son and of the Spirit – to bring glory to God and to bring to the world forgiveness of sins and spiritual life. Raymond Brown explains this continuity of mission in the following way:

> The special Johannine contribution to the theology of mission is that the Father's sending of the Son serves both as the model . . . and the ground . . . for the Son's sending of the disciples. Their mission is to continue the Son's mission; and this requires that the Son must be present to them during this mission, just as the Father had to be present to the Son during His mission.[105]

According to the evangelist then, all Christian mission must be conceived through the commissioning of the Son by the Father – it is God's idea in the first place: then it is derived from and modelled on the mission of the Son. The closest possible connection is drawn here: the disciples are to abide in the Son, to imbibe his teaching, to imitate his ways and then to impart all these things – along with his living presence – to others. That is the essence of mission. Accordingly, the disciples, like Jesus, teach the world about sin, righteousness and judgement. They bring the same challenge and demand the same response as Jesus himself did – and for one simple reason: they carry the presence and power of Jesus himself – the risen Lord – wherever they go, and they bear witness to that fact.

However, there is one crucial difference to note between the mission of the Son and that of the disciples. It is the Son alone who can make possible the intimate knowledge of God as Father. He it is who reveals the Father's will and nature, for the obvious reason that he has always known and still knows the Father in a relationship of unbroken communion. He knows the Father directly and intimately. The disciples need to have this knowledge imparted to them: they are taught and reminded about all the things of which Jesus himself had immediate and intuitive knowledge. It is only the Son who can make possible the forgiveness of sins – through his atoning death. So although the disciples are witnesses to the glory of God, and are filled with the life of God, and although they preach the forgiveness of sins and even offer absolution on Jesus' authority, nevertheless their experience and knowledge is *mediated* from the Son through the Holy Spirit.

In this way, the missions of the Son and of the disciples are in continuity, for both are part of God's overall mission; but the disciples' mission is not identical with the Son's mission. The nature of the Son and the remit of his mission are, in certain respects, unique. The Son's mission is also *delegated* to the disciples who act on the authority of the one who sent them and not on their own authority.

The fact that the disciples need to receive an understanding of the truth and the power of the Spirit in order to be equipped for mission is conveyed *in narrative form* in the body of the Gospel. In fact, in the first half of the Gospel, the disciples' participation in mission is very limited. At the feeding of the five thousand they are instructed to go and buy food (4.8); then to help with the distribution of the food and the clearing up of the leftovers (6.5–13). Beyond that, they are learners or novices. The Greek for 'learner' or 'disciple' (*mathetes*) occurs no less than 70 times in John's Gospel. Beyond being learners, the disciples are helpers or assistants, engaged on in-service training! They participate in the work Jesus does (4.2, 8, 27, 31, 33, 38, etc.). Only gradually do they come to occupy a place of responsibility (6.3, 8, 12, 16, 22, 24, 60–71). On the way to Jerusalem they begin to play a more important part in the proceedings (9.2; 11.7–16, 54; 12.16,

21–2). At that time they receive detailed instructions about their future mission. Then from Chapter 13 through to Chapter 17 they are regarded as potential leaders in the mission of the Father, Son and Holy Spirit.

The change of role, from being learners and novices, to becoming mission leaders, is marked by a change of relationship with Jesus – from subservience to more intimate friendship. In the first verse of Chapter 13 the evangelist speaks of the disciples in relation to Jesus as 'his own, whom he loved' (*agapesas tous idious* cf. 17.6, 10). They are then addressed as 'children' in 13.33 (*teknia* cf. 21.4–5); then later as 'friends' (*philoi*), for whom Jesus would lay down his life. The promotion from 'servants' to 'friends' is made explicit by Jesus in 15.15: 'From now on I do not call you servants . . . but I have called you friends.' The reason given is that Jesus has now imparted everything to them that the Father has made known to him. In other words, they are fully equipped for their mission.

Then, at a final stage, Jesus refers to the disciples as 'brothers' (*adelphoi* – 20.17) and says to Mary Magdalene, 'I am ascending to my Father and your Father, to my God and your God' (20.17). Mary and the others are now admitted to the inner sanctum, where their knowledge of and love for God is deemed similar to Jesus' own. This happens just before the commissioning of the disciples in 20.19–23), when Jesus puts the last piece of the jigsaw of mission into place – the baptism in the Holy Spirit – when Jesus breathes something of his own self into the disciples and gave them authority to forgive sins (20.22–3).

So in this very subtle way, the evangelist follows the progress of the disciples from servants and students to assistants and helpers, to companions and friends of Jesus, to brothers and then leaders of the Church's mission. As Andreas Kostenberger writes: 'In the second half of the Gospel [of John], the emphasis is on Jesus' vision of a unified, loving, faithful, suffering and witnessing community of believers through which Jesus' mission would continue to be carried out.'[106]

The vision of this unified community engaged in mission to the world is expressed in various ways, but most vividly in the images of a flock of sheep (10.16; 17.6–26; and 21.15–17), and of the branches of a vine (15.1–11). Both of these images enable John to distinguish Jesus clearly from the disciples or the church. He is the good shepherd: they are the flock; he is the vine: the disciples are the branches.

The image of a flock is of course a traditional and longstanding biblical image for Israel, God's people (e.g. Psalm 23; Isaiah 40.11; Jeremiah 23.1; Ezekiel 34.11). In John 17 Jesus prays for the flock – for its unity in love, its purity of life and its protection from the world (17.17–21). Interestingly, here the future Church is envisaged – the Church of the time of the Gospel's writing, perhaps. It is described as 'those who will believe in me through their word' (17.20). Moreover, there are sheep in more than one sheep pen, for Jesus mentions the sheep 'not of this fold' (in 10.16). This appears to link up with the words addressed to Peter in 21.15–17, when he is instructed several times over to care for (or feed) the sheep. It is in the words about the flock that we gain a glimpse of the situation in the Church in the time of the final redactor of the Gospel. There is surely an indication here that the Johannine churches were aware of – if not yet in fellowship with – the mainstream Petrine network of churches. Some scholars call this network 'the great Church'.

Not all historical reconstruction is pure speculation. Rather, it can be an attempt to dovetail the Gospel account with what is happening in the real world of historical events. In this case, the probabilities are clear: the Johannine church has been too long out on a limb, and has suffered from both internal and external attack, has become vulnerable and weakened and is ready to throw in its lot with the churches looking to Peter as founding apostle. This will guarantee the future of the Johannine communities and will also enrich 'the great Church' at a single stroke.

With regard to the image of the vine, the emphasis here is on the fact that the Church must take on itself the mantle of the true Israel – being both faithful to God's original will and intent, as well as fruitful in terms of mission. Three aspects of discipleship are stressed in this regard: the need to be dependent upon Jesus who is the very sap and lifeblood of the Church; the need to be in unity with one another as branches of the one vine; and, finally, the need to go and bear good fruit (15.16). This last aspect gives a missionary perspective to discipleship. The followers of Jesus are appointed to live and work in such a way as to bring a harvest. This involves, among other things, being witnesses in the power of the Spirit (15.27) – a clear reference to the future mission of the Church.

In the final analysis, the disciples are not called to *represent* Jesus: they are called to *re-present* him; that is; they are to bring to the world the impact of his risen life. To this end, according to John, the Lord himself will be with them and will be the life coursing through the veins of the Church (the vine), and will also act as the leader of the Church (as the Good Shepherd). The disciples, for their part, must operate from a base of solidarity, unity and corporate witness. They must not allow themselves to become exposed and isolated, for the world is perceived as a place of danger and the lone disciple is very exposed and vulnerable. In carrying out their mission, the disciples are to dwell in or remain in the Father, who as vinedresser or gardener frames and shapes the mission, pruning and nurturing to produce the best yield. They are also to dwell in or abide in the Son, who guides the mission and accompanies it at every turn. And they are equally to dwell in or live by the Holy Spirit, who inspires and empowers the mission.

John's vision of mission is thus Trinitarian and corporate. Even if the doctrine of the Trinity is not expressed explicitly in John, and if the word 'Church' (*ekklesia*) is not used, all the same, from the perspective of mission, the logic of a Trinitarian procession (or pattern of sending) and of a Church commissioned for service are both necessary to the outworking of the life of discipleship. A pattern of sending and indwelling can be shown in diagrammatic form. The disciples are encompassed by Father, Son and Spirit in circles of protection and enfolding love.

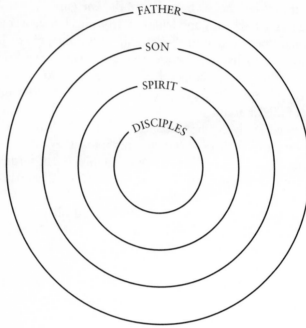

Figure 5.2

Conclusion

Both the concept and the practice of mission are integral to the philosophy of the Gospel of John. The concept is explored in a strikingly original way in the Prologue (1.1–18); while examples of the practice are featured episodically in the first four chapters of the Gospel in particular (1.19—4.54). Those chapters following on (5.1—12.50) are more concerned with Jesus' relationship with the religious authorities in Jerusalem, as he attends the festivals and Temple services: the Passover (6.1–71), the Feast of Tabernacles (7.1—8.59) and the Feast of Dedication (10.22–42). Jesus is portrayed as the one who replaces the Temple and who is consequently Lord of the Festivals. His claims are explored through the discourses and the miracles of Chapters 5–10. Then the signs and christological claims reach their zenith with the healing of Lazarus (11), at which time the Jesus of the Gospel claims to be 'the resurrection and the life' (11.25). This is a culmination point and sums up Jesus' ministry of teaching and healing. John makes use of various methods of persuasion in order to convince his readers or hearers of the truth of Jesus' claims. After this, from Chapter 12, and especially from Chapter 13, John's Gospel is concerned with the eschatological events surrounding Jesus' atoning death, his resurrection and the sending of the Spirit.

During the discourses about eschatology, the mission of the disciples and of the Church also comes into view. That too is seen as a sign of the Last Days; especially the ingathering of the Gentiles. As already indicated, John links mission with an eschatological time frame. The preparation of the disciples for mission takes place in the discourses of Chapters 14–17, and the commissioning of the disciples then takes place in the aftermath of the resurrection (20.19–23). At that time the conditions are right for mission to the world at large to take place, and for Jesus to be declared 'saviour of the world'. The gospel of the forgiveness of sins and faith in Christ can then be universally proclaimed.

In all these ways, not only is the theme of mission integral to the theology of the Gospel but also the implications of Jesus' mission are explored through his relationship with his disciples. They are prepared, taught and drawn into the inner life of the *rabbi* who is also the Son and the Word. Through such training they come to understand and take to heart the realities of mission in a threatening and hostile world. The commissioning of the disciples thereafter involves the imparting of the Holy Spirit, who brings both enlightenment and empowerment to the disciples. They are commissioned at the same time as they receive the Holy Spirit, using the terms Jesus has employed throughout: 'As the Father has sent me, so I send you' (20.21).

This all makes it clear that mission is a procession or a sequence: a movement from Father to Son, from Son to Spirit, from Spirit to Church, in an unbroken chain. The mission is ultimately the mission of God the Father, who has sent the Son, who has sent the Spirit, who has sent the disciples. As such, this gives the Church's mission both its impetus and its authority.

The purpose of the Gospel, summed up in the concluding words of the original version of John (at 20.30–1), is seen to be both christological – 'that you may come to believe that Jesus is the Messiah' (v. 31a) – and also missiological – 'that through believing you may have life in his name' (v. 31b).

It is not certain to whom these words are addressed, partly because there is a textual variant around the words 'that you may believe' – either *hina pisteuete* (present subjunctive) or *hina pisteusete* (aorist subjunctive). The early manuscript evidence is evenly divided on this matter. The former possibility would mean 'that you go on believing' or 'so that you continue to believe' – implying that those already in the Church community are being addressed. The latter possibility would mean 'that you may come to believe' or 'that you might come to faith' – implying that those outside the Christian community are envisaged. John much favours the aorist forms in most other cases,[107] and he uses this form 88 times in the Gospel as a whole. On these grounds alone, it is perhaps better to assume that the mission of the Church to the world is in the mind of the evangelist. And once again, in the context of the whole Gospel, and viewed from a mission perspective, this point of view is confirmed. In conclusion, the missionary purpose of John's Gospel can be expressed in this way: 'that you may come to believe that Jesus is the Christ, the Son of God, and by your faith have life through him'.

The twin thrust of John's Gospel is therefore first to show that Jesus was sent from God and was the revealer of the truth or truths about God. He is the Son of God who has first-hand and intimate knowledge of God as his Father. Secondly, it is to demonstrate how Jesus reached out to the world God loved in order to present himself as its saviour. Even the death of Christ is depicted as the Son of Man being lifted up in order to draw all people to himself, and as the time when God's glory is displayed most openly. The disciples in John take up the work or mission of Jesus, and are trained and commissioned to convince or persuade the world that Jesus is indeed the Christ. They are to bring faith to all people and, through that, new life to the world.

6

The life and mission of
the Early Church

Lessons from the Gospels

Up to this point, we have been looking at mission through bi-focal lenses: one lens has focused on the mission of Jesus, and the understanding of that mission in the Gospels: the other has focused on the mission of the Early Church, which was in full flow at the time the Gospels were edited and given their final form. A major assumption has been that the churches out of which the different Gospels emerged had some kind of influence on the way in which mission was presented and understood in the relevant Gospel. According to this supposition, because of their different geographical and cultural locations, the Matthean community, for example, would have had a different perspective on mission from the Johannine community.

Nevertheless, it should be borne in mind that although the Gospels were all written from within a particular context, from varying social, cultural and religious terms of reference, nevertheless they were in all likelihood also written with all the Christian churches in mind, or at least with an awareness that the Christian Church was one nation or people spread all over the known world. Just as Israel had understood herself as one single chosen race scattered among all the nations of the world, so with the Church of Christ. In the earliest documents of the New Testament, Paul's letters, it is clear that there is a concept of the Church as being both the local congregation of believers and yet also the whole people of God – or Body of Christ – spread far and wide by God's mission.

At first, in the early days, a largely oral – or partly written but piecemeal – version of the good news of Jesus Christ had sufficed for the local Christian communities; but, as Richard Bauckham suggests:

> It was distance that required writing, whereas orality sufficed for presence . . . The obvious function of writing was its capacity to communicate widely with readers unable to be present at its author's oral teaching.[108]

Bauckham's argument does, however, seem to go too far in then concluding that the Gospels were not written for a particular community or group of communities. Even if we concede that they were not written *primarily* for a particular church group, all the same, the context or *Sitz im Leben* of a local community is bound to influence the theology and viewpoint of each particular author: and we have seen this to be self-evidently the case. In the earlier chapters a great deal has been written about mission from the point of view of one particular Gospel as opposed to another. Each Gospel has been shown to be subtly different in its interpretation of Jesus' mission and what it meant to reach out to different peoples with the gospel message. In fact, it is possible to consider each Gospel's understanding of mission without a great deal of repetition or overlap.

When Richard Bauckham contrasts the writing of the Gospels with the composition of Paul's letters, he writes this:

> The more gospel scholarship envisages the Gospels in terms approximating to a Pauline letter, addressing the specific situation of one community, the more odd it seems that the evangelist is supposed to be writing *for the community in which he lives* [italics in original]. An evangelist writing his Gospel is like Paul writing 1 Corinthians while permanently resident in Corinth. Paul did not do this, so why should Matthew or the other evangelists have done so?[109]

But Bauckham's argument surely backfires on him at this point and proves the opposite of what he intended. Paul may not have been resident when he wrote to Corinth, but he had lived there and is precisely concerned with that particular community: the maturity (or otherwise) of its faith, its grasp of Christian lifestyle, its specific problems and difficulties, its groups and factions, its witness and mission. It is abundantly evident that Paul was writing almost all his letters to a particular community living in a particular social situation. If Paul had wished to preserve some of the teachings and actions of Jesus and ensure that eyewitness accounts were available to posterity – which is of course the case for the Gospel writers – then we can say with confidence that he would have preserved them at least partly for the instruction and edification of his own community – in other words, in order to address their particular concerns.

The fact that Paul's letters were fairly soon disseminated, copied and read across a wide spectrum of Christian churches is simply evidence of the fact that right from the start the Church conceived itself as both local and universal, both in a real and particular place and context, while at the same time being part of a great worldwide movement or mission.

Our knowledge of the social, religious, cultural, historical and political settings of the first-century churches – even down to fairly specific local variations in geographical settings – has grown exponentially since the 1970s, through the work of scholars like Martin Goodman, Wayne Meeks, Gerd Theissen, John Stambaugh and David Balch. In addition, methods of literary criticism have become far more subtle and sophisticated with the advent of various forms of narrative, rhetorical and reader-response approaches applied to the Gospels. It is there-fore not mere speculation to see the fourth Gospel for instance as a narrative of the Johannine community's expulsion from its local synagogue. The quotations in the text of John are very specific and pointed, reflecting real historical events. On the lips of Jesus we have, 'They will put you out of the synagogues. Indeed, an hour is coming when those who kill you will think that by doing so they are offering worship to God' (16.2; see also

John 12.42). It is also known from later Jewish writings that the *birkat ha-minim* clause condemning 'the Nazarenes and the heretics' was introduced into synagogue liturgy in the late first century.

To take another example, it is obvious from its preoccupation with matters of legal interpretation that Matthew's Gospel was written for a community which had been used to adopting or adapting forms of Jewish religious practice to its own daily life. And at the same time, the emphasis on Jesus' personal interpretations of Torah and on the terms for Gentile membership of the Church make it equally clear that here was a community wrestling with new ways of worship and practice in a multiracial environment. These conclusions are not speculative: they arise out of a serious and intelligent reading of the text. Similarly, the different theological emphases one finds in the different Gospels also reflect not the personal preferences of the authors but the different contexts in which they were written.

So it is true to say that the Gospels were written for all Christians and with an awareness of the universal Church. But this does not imply in any way that the Gospels were not also written with the interests and needs of their own local community or communities in mind. As with any genre of writing, they are contextualized before they are universalized. Thus, the Gospels were written to address concerns within the local churches, but had wider aims: namely, to convince readers in general of the truth of the gospel of Christ's coming, and Christians in particular of the paramount significance of the Church's role in the history of salvation.

It is possible to take this line of argument a step further. We can now perceive how each of the four Gospels has an understanding of mission peculiar to itself. Let us look at the example of Matthew first. He regards the duty of the Christian missioners or evangelists as follows: they are first and foremost apprentices or learners. This means that study and reflection on Christ's work and teaching should lead them to imitate the pattern of Christ's life and obedience to Christ's instruction and 'law' (Matthew

28.20). But paradoxically evangelists are also teachers: they can guide and instruct, prepare for baptism and confirm the seeker in the truths of the Christian faith, bringing treasures old and new from their storehouse of wisdom. The risen Christ prompts and directs them in this process, for he accompanies and inspires them: 'I am with you always, to the end of the age' (28.20). This is more than an image of the rabbi and his apprentice, for there is a new focus on the presence and person of the risen Lord, on the community's worship and on the Church's mission to the whole world.

If we take Mark as a second example; his Gospel conveys a sense of the urgency of the Christian mission. It is in the light of the coming *eschaton* – the end of time, when the Messiah will return – that the Church's mission is carried out. But even more, it is because the kingdom of God has already broken into the life of the world, through signs and wonders, and is already spreading like a forest fire, that the Church must gird up its loins and join in the work. Just as Jesus responded to the clamour of the people with the words, 'Let us go on to the neighbouring towns, so that I may proclaim the message there also' (Mark 1.38), so the Church must embrace its mission, must be constantly on the move, must adapt to new situations, be ready for new challenges, must be in step with the restless movements of the Lord himself. Consequently, the evangelist is to travel light, go without luggage, live without possessions, leave family and friends, depend upon the hospitality of well-wishers: 'He [Jesus] ordered them to take nothing for their journey except a staff; no bread, no bag, no money in their belts . . . "Wherever you enter a house, stay there until you leave the place"' (Mark 6.8). This is a gospel without baggage, without many rules and regulations; in fact, some luggage has even been left behind already: the laws of ritual purity have been laid aside (Chapter 7), the work continues even on the Sabbath day (3.1–6) – the old wine cannot be contained in the new wineskins; 'otherwise the wine will burst the skins, and the wine is lost, and so are the skins; but one puts new wine into fresh wineskins' (2.22). Even the demons are unable to resist the inexorable advance of God's kingdom (see 1.23–6, 34, 39; 3.11;

5.6–13). Because the coming of the kingdom is so closely linked to the person and mission of Jesus Christ himself, it may be assumed that the primary task of the disciples is to proclaim the gospel in terms of Christ's coming and the Lordship of Christ in this life. Peter, in a central passage in the Gospel, is inspired to say in a moment of revelation, 'You are the Messiah' (8.29).

It is Mark who places the spotlight clearly on Jesus as the one who ushers in the kingdom of God and who begins to spread the good news (gospel) of the kingdom, bringing their reality to the world in an ever-widening arena. The disciples then continue Jesus' ministry of preaching linked to healing and exorcism:

> These signs will accompany those who believe: by using my name they will cast out demons; they will speak in new tongues, they will pick up snakes in their hands, and if they drink any deadly thing, it will not hurt them; they will lay their hands on the sick, and they will recover. (16.18)

If this does not come from the pen of Mark himself, it is the community's understanding of his theology nevertheless. And the point here is perhaps not to interpret the precise phrases too literally, but to see that the spread of God's kingdom through the preaching of the gospel will be followed by 'signs' – as the gospel message is vindicated and confirmed and as the new age of the Messiah is inaugurated.

If we briefly turn to Luke, then there is a slowing of the pace: the advent of the kingdom is not so imminent or so swift; the Church now has time to become established and to spread the Word far and wide, until every nation and people has heard and responded to the Gospel. The age of the Church stretches into the future, for the far corners of the earth must be reached before the return of Christ. The mission of the disciples is therefore now the mission of the Church, and this has a universal reach and application. As this gospel extends far beyond the bounds of Israel and the greater Israel of the Diaspora, so it also reaches beyond the usual limits of religious belief and practice into the most remote and

darkened corners of human life. It must reach beyond the righteous, the orthodox believers, the respectable and the admirable.
It must reach even beyond the chronically sick, the disabled,
the demonized, the marginalized, beyond the prostitute and the
tax collector. It must be able to liberate even the self-satisfied
'Pharisee', the 'heretical' Samaritan, the 'stranger in the midst'
and the 'outcast'. The universal reach of the gospel in Luke not
only means the gospel for all nations, but also the gospel for all
people, and for all kinds of people: for all people from the supposed highest and most important to the lowest, the poorest and
the least regarded.

There is in addition another universality about Luke. His
Gospel does not bear only a spiritual message; it is for the whole
person and for every aspect of life. Jesus' manifesto in Luke
encompasses release for prisoners, recovery of sight for the blind,
liberation of the oppressed and the cancellation of debts. So the
gospel extends to those owing money as much as to those who
have sins weighing heavily upon their conscience (Luke 4.18–19).

In Luke the connection between the work of God, the mission
of Jesus and the work and mission of the Church is the empowering of the Holy Spirit. As Senior and Stuhlmueller put it: 'For
Luke, the concept of the Spirit sealed the kinship between God's
universal will to save, the liberating ministry of Jesus, and the
worldwide mission of the church.'[110] But it is vitally important to
realize that the mission of the Church in Luke goes well beyond
the confines of Church life. The mission of Christ in the Gospel is
acted out in the world at large and among people conventionally
considered non-religious or even 'irreligious'. We are forced to
draw the conclusion that the Church – in imitation of the Spirit
of Christ – is not only called to go where she is needed, but where
she is needed the most. The Church's mission is not 'a campaign
to make converts', nor is it the imposition of a set of beliefs upon
individuals. Rather, the wind blows where it will and is active in
the most unpromising and surprising of places. As Jürgen
Moltmann insists, the Church 'has no need to look sideways or
in suspicion or jealousy at the saving efficacies of the Spirit outside the church: instead it can recognise them thankfully as signs

that the Spirit is greater than the church'.[111] This insight is especially true of Luke's understanding of the Church's mission.

In John's Gospel, there is again a rather different perspective on mission from the other Gospels. Mission is regarded essentially as a response to God's call and to the love of God for the world. Thus, as David Bosch puts it, 'To participate in mission is to participate in the movement of God's love towards people, since God is a fountain of sending love.'[112] Mission is therefore not something the church decides to engage upon or that evangelists feel gifted to carry out; rather, mission is the constraint of love for all people which is already in the heart of God, which is revealed and enacted by Christ and which is – or should be – the motive force for those who believe in him.

John has the clearest understanding of mission as originating in the heart of God, and then proceeding through the Son and the Spirit to the people of God. It is God who inspires and equips the mission of the Church, and that mission must inevitably be a response to God's love for the world, and a response to God's life in the world and in the lives of all people. Mission is therefore not something Christians take upon themselves – however nobly they may conceive their duty or obligation. Rather, it is something God draws his people into, preparing their hearts with that same love and compassion that he has for the world and for humanity in particular. This is a reassuring doctrine, for it militates against the Church being unduly anxious or duty-bound with regard to mission. The success or failure of the Church is ultimately God's concern and is in God's hands. To be faithful in small things, and to co-operate in small ways with God's grand design – that is the true responsibility of the Christian and of the Church at large.

John's vision is that mission is the opportunity to be a witness – to demonstrate through one's own life and example that God is at work in the human heart and in the world. Being a witness is a humble role. The image is not of one person telling another how to think or how to behave (certainly not at the initial stage, if at all); it is more a bearing witness to that grace and mercy which has surprised and delighted the believer. It is also bearing witness to the life of Christ active in the world. 'The world' has an ambivalent sense in this Gospel. It is the place of darkness and ignorance and unbelief; yet at the same time, it is the place where the Holy Spirit is active and powerfully at work. Thus, as Rowan Williams puts it in his book *On Christian Theology*, Christians should not assume to know 'a totality of truth about God or about the human world, or even a monopoly of the means of bringing divine absolution or grace to men and women'.[113] Their task is simply to be faithful witnesses to the mission of God at work.

For the author of John's Gospel, there is no place for pride in the Christian life. Jesus condemned the disciples for wanting the best places in the kingdom and attacked the arrogance of some Pharisees who set themselves up as judges of God's truth. Rowan Williams's further words about what it means to be a Christian today are particularly true to the Johannine understanding of the Christian life:

> To be 'in Christ', to belong to Jesus, involves a far-reaching reconstruction of one's humanity: a liberation from servile, distorted, destructive patterns in the past, a liberation from the anxious dread of God's judgement, a new identity in a community of reciprocal love and complementary service, whose potential horizons are universal.[114]

This 'humility of love' displayed in the Johannine Gospel does not always appear to extend beyond John's own community and into the world. Perhaps his churches were on the defensive, with their backs to the wall, huddling together for safety and security in a hostile environment. Yet the wider *implications* of John's theology of mission are that the attitude within the church should extend to the work and witness of believers beyond the church. The notions of 'witness', of 'service' and of 'friendship' surely leads to an idea of mission conducted in a particular spirit or with a particular ethos.

John's first-century world of Christianity in the midst of other faiths bears some similarity to the twenty-first century situation of the Church. Kenneth Leech's words in this regard are as appropriate for the early Johannine Christians as they are for Christians today:

> Christian testimony within a context of plurality of faiths should be marked by reality, not fantasy; by humility, not aggressiveness and arrogance; fidelity, not embarrassment; and openness, not inflexibility . . . We need to learn from the early Christians, but also learn the lessons of Christendom.[115]

Those 'early Christians' referred to could fit the Johannine community or communities, whose view of the world was hard-headed and realistic, yet whose lifestyle was marked by service in the manner of foot-washing, whose relations were based upon equality and on love for one another, whose beliefs were not predicated upon lists of doctrinal truths but upon faith in Christ alone and abiding in him. Their idea of 'witness' and 'testimony' was a form of openness and dialogue, rather than a didactic approach to faith and a treatment of others as objects who needed to change.

We now move on to a more general consideration of the life of the Church at the time the Gospels were written – say, between AD 70 and 90. Our approach will concentrate on life within the Church itself – and so it will focus particularly on the sacraments of baptism and the Eucharist (or Holy Communion). However, from these starting points other aspects of the Christian life will emerge.

The Eucharist and table fellowship

One of the best-known features of Jesus' work – and one to which all the Gospels bear testimony – was his policy of open table fellowship with anyone who wished to be allied to or associated with his movement. Most writers would agree that eating and drinking with 'sinners' was one of the most characteristic and striking marks of Jesus' ministry. The unusual and even scandalous nature of this activity is noted in the Gospels. Early on in Mark, we read that 'many tax collectors and sinners were also sitting with Jesus and his disciples – for there were many who followed him' (2.15), and then Mark also notes the reaction of the scribes:

> When the scribes of the Pharisees saw that he was eating with sinners and tax-collectors, they said to his disciples, 'Why does he eat with tax-collectors and sinners?' When Jesus heard this, he said to them, 'Those who are well have no need of a physician, but those who are sick; I have come to call not the righteous but sinners.' (2.16–17)

Mark goes on to add that Jesus and his disciples were condemned not only for sharing table fellowship with the 'unclean' but also for feasting and celebrating instead of fasting. Jesus' response to this is that while the disciples have the bridegroom with them they should celebrate; when he is no longer with them they will indeed fast (2.18–20). These passages have their parallel in Matthew and Luke. Matthew (9.9–15) adds a second justification in addition to the saying about the sick needing a physician. He has Jesus say, 'Go and learn what this means, "I desire mercy, not sacrifice." For I have come to call not the righteous but sinners' (9.13). By quoting this from Hosea 6.6, Jesus places himself squarely in the prophetic tradition which often saw a need to criticize the ruling establishment in order to make clear God's will. In Luke's account, the evangelist makes this moral dimension of Jesus' mission explicit: 'I have come to call not the righteous, but sinners to repentance' (*eis metanoian*) (5.32).

In all three Gospels this event is attached to the parable about the new wine in old wineskins; with the implication that Jesus is doing something so radically different that it will not fit into the old mentality or mindset or the Jewish religious establishment (see Mark 2.21–2; Matthew 9.16–17; Luke 5.35–9). Luke describes this meal in Levi's house as a 'great feast' (*epoiesen doksen megalen*), which gives the impression that he attaches a special significance to the occasion: it is an anticipation of the great banqueting feast in the kingdom of God. N. T. Wright[116] picks up this theme. He argues that Jesus acting as a private individual sharing table fellowship with unsavoury people might not have been so remarkable (although this, in my opinion, is debatable), but then he adds:

> But when it is allied with the claim, made in praxis and story, that Jesus was inaugurating the long-awaited kingdom, it becomes deeply symbolic. That is why, as we saw, it aroused controversy. Jesus was, as it were, celebrating the messianic banquet, and doing so with all the wrong people.

Jürgen Moltmann also picks up on this eschatological dimension of Jesus' table fellowship with 'all the wrong people':

> The fellowship at table of the men and women who follow Jesus and enter into his messianic mission must be open for the meal which accepts and justifies 'tax collectors and sinners', and must be seen in the perspective of the universal banquet of the nations in the coming kingdom.[117]

Moltmann takes the significance a step further with this comment. The table fellowship of the gospel is no longer simply a scandal to the religious establishment, nor is it even only a foretaste of the banquet in the kingdom. It is now a coming-together of different groups and people in reconciliation and peace. Thus, Moltmann sees table fellowship as an anticipation of the Church's life, as well as of life in the kingdom; for in the Church Jew and Gentile, slave and freeborn, women and men – all are united in fellowship and in Christ. So Moltmann highlights in this way the link – not often noticed – between table fellowship in the Gospels and the churches' practice of Holy Communion or the eucharistic meal:

> Because the fellowship of the table unites believers with the triune God through Christ, it also causes men to unite with one another in messianic fellowship. The common bread and the

common cup point to the oneness of the people who partake in the one Christ, and in him all participants at all times and in all places ... The open invitation of the crucified one to his supper is what fundamentally overcomes all tendencies towards alienation, separation and segregation. For through his giving himself up to death for the fellowship of men with God and with one another, the godless and inhuman divisions and enmities between races, nations, civilisations and classes are overcome. Churches, which permit this deadly division in themselves, are making the cross of Christ a mockery.[118]

In John's Gospel it is the story of the feeding of the five thousand (6.1–15) which appears to make the link between table fellowship and the eucharistic meal, as many scholars have intimated. First, John specifically connects this meal to the Passover: 'Now the Passover, the festival of the Jews, was near' (6.4). The two early mentions of 'a large crowd' (*ochlos polus* vv. 2,5) seem to indicate an unrestricted fellowship open to all-comers. The feeding centres upon Jesus, who, in words reminiscent of the communion liturgy 'took the loaves, and when he had given thanks, he distributed them to those who were seated; so also the fish, as much as they wanted' (6.11). The action at the end is also reminiscent of the liturgy: 'he told his disciples, "Gather up the fragments left over, so that nothing may be lost"' (6.12). The whole event is seen by the people as 'a sign' (v. 14) and they acclaim Jesus among themselves as 'the prophet who is to come into the world' (v. 14), thus attributing eschatological significance to the event.

The fellowship meal in Jewish life and thought – even without all the connotations of John's Gospel – is an expression of acceptance, affirmation and friendship. It would be impossible to sit at table and share food with an enemy or with someone considered 'unclean' in some way. This is significant in itself, for Jesus' willingness to share the same table as tax collectors and sinners meant that the Early Church could later justify its own acceptance of Samaritans and Gentiles without separation or segregation and without pre-conditions.

However, there is no doubt, as we have seen, that the Gospel writers also saw table fellowship in Jesus' ministry as a powerful and profound sign of the kingdom of God. It not only anticipated the great banquet which would be the reward for all who had found God's favour, but it showed – controversially – that this banquet would throw up many surprises. If Jesus as Messiah was willing to accept and to bless at table people whose lives were deemed unrighteous and tainted, then presumably all could potentially be made righteous by making friends with Jesus, or, to put it another way, by putting their trust in him.

The acceptance of all people at the fellowship of the meal portrayed in a form of acted parable what acceptance and forgiveness could look like in society at large. Saying words was not enough, preaching alone could not ensure acceptance; but the actions of Jesus put the seal on forgiveness and reconciliation, through the assent to sharing the mealtime. This messianic sign Jesus gave by eating with all those willing to accept *him* illuminated the true meaning of love, reconciliation and freedom, and, more than that, made it a reality through praxis.

The fact that the evangelists recognized the eschatological dimensions of Jesus' fellowship with tax collectors and sinners meant that the eucharistic meal of the Church also had the same overtones of reconciliation through the presence of Christ, shared fellowship, acceptance of one and all as equals, and the anticipation of the banquet in the kingdom of heaven. Through the common sharing of bread and wine all who followed Christ were able to find acceptance in him and among his people, and also to be drawn into the mission of Jesus to 'seek out that which was lost'.

The Last Supper is portrayed as a Passover Meal in the Synoptic Gospels, but at the same time what is written about it (in Mark 14.12–21; Matthew 26.17–25; and Luke 22.7–14, 21–3) also reflects the liturgical practice of the Early Church, at the time the Gospels were composed.

What then are the elements in common between the Jewish Passover, the Last Supper and the Christian Eucharist? The Passover was essentially linked to the time Israel spent in captivity in Egypt, but the name itself implies an anticipation of the liberation from captivity as well. To assist this recollection, no less than four cups of wine are drunk during the mealtime. The first is accompanied by benedictions, the second by the question, 'Why is this night different from other nights?' The answer relates to the food: this night unleavened bread only will be consumed; the lamb is roasted; and bitter herbs will accompany the main dish. The Bible reading beginning, 'A wandering Aramaean was my father . . .' is read, and the significance of the Passover and the elements of the food is explained. These explanations and readings begin in 'disgrace' but end with the 'glory' of liberation and redemption. The singing or chanting of the *Hallel* Psalms then introduces the third cup and is completed by the time of the drinking of the fourth cup, with which the meal – or *seder* – concludes.

One interesting detail in the meal is that a piece of bread is broken from the main loaf at the beginning and is then hidden and later revealed, as a sign of the coming of the Messiah. Thus, in the Passover, there is not only a strong aspect of remembrance but also an aspect of eschatological anticipation – a looking forward to the age of the Messiah, when God's rule or kingdom would be established.

In the Gospel accounts, there is mention of dipping the bread in the dish (Mark 14.20), and of the thanksgiving prayer at the breaking of the bread (14.22), the thanksgiving prayer which accompanies the drinking of the communal cup (14.23) and the singing of a hymn at the end of the meal (14.26). The eating of bread is given especial prominence, and the liturgy of the four cups has been reduced to the one. This of course closely parallels the practice of the Early Church at its eucharistic celebration. The 'hymn' in Mark's account may reflect Christian singing as opposed to the chanting of the *Hallel* Psalms.

The elements which seem to depart from traditional Passover practice are the pronouncements of Jesus: 'This (is) my body' over the bread and 'This (is) my blood' over the wine (Mark 14.22, 24). In Mark, Jesus also vows not to drink wine again until he drinks the new wine of the kingdom of God (v. 25).

Matthew adds that this covenant is 'for the forgiveness of sins' (26.28); but by and large he retains Mark's tradition faithfully. Luke transfers words about drinking wine anew in God's kingdom to the beginning of the meal, however, and he adds the words at the breaking of the bread, 'Do this in remembrance of me' (22.19). Elsewhere, Paul's account (1 Corinthians 11.17–25) adds to our knowledge of Early Church practice in his, the earliest, account of the Last Supper. Paul is aware that he is guarding an honoured tradition (11.23) and insists on the memorial aspect of the meal twice, after the breaking of the bread and the taking of the cup (11.24, 25). He lays further emphasis on 'proclaiming Jesus' death' in verse 26, but in the context of his return or Parousia. The covenant is here 'God's new covenant' (11.25), linked to the cup, which signifies the blood of Jesus. After the bare description, Paul explores the pastoral implications of taking the bread and wine.

Clearly, according to the early traditions, the Christian observance of the Lord's Supper transferred the remembering connected to the Passover to the remembering of Jesus' life and death. The bread and wine both pointed to the Passion. It was also regarded as a covenant observance, and the blood (wine) sealed the covenant, which came to be seen as a *new* covenant, replacing the old. The element of anticipation or looking forward, related to the Messiah's coming in the Passover, now became an anticipation of two things: the coming again of Jesus Christ in glory and the banqueting feast in the kingdom of God.

The fundamentally *new* element or emphasis in Christian worship is not so much a wholesale replacement of Passover by Eucharist – far from it. Rather, it lies in the understanding of Jesus as Messiah. First, he is associated with the suffering servant figure of Second Isaiah, whose blood is poured out 'for many' (*hyper pollon*) (Mark 14.24, Matthew 26.28). This is really a semitism meaning that his sacrifice would be efficacious 'for all' or perhaps 'for all who avail themselves of it'. He is the one who will be faithful and establish God's covenant, thereby making possible reconciliation to God for others. Secondly, the Parousia, or second coming of the Messiah, is associated with Jesus' presiding over the final establishment of God's kingdom, which leads into the great celebration of the banqueting feast. Thirdly, the Eucharist, by contrast with the Passover, becomes a present communion with the risen Lord, and the worship of Jesus is at its most intense in the Early Church as the sacramental bread and wine are consumed. Both the remembering and the present experiencing of Jesus became 'participation in Christ' or the re-presentation and re-enactment of his sacrifice and his self-giving. In the communion, believers in some sense received Christ as he offered himself anew.

The missionary aspects of this now become clear. First, Jesus as Messiah is regarded at an early date as a universal saviour. No one can be beyond redemption, whether Jew or Gentile. Secondly, the gathering around the Lord's Table reinforces a sense of unity and fellowship among disciples, who are in a covenant relationship with God as the Body of Christ. This imposes a sense of discipline and solidarity upon the people of God and their mission to the world. Thirdly, this mission quickly came to be understood as God's mission – a sending out from the place of blessing and commissioning. It is a mission which in the eyes of believers is bound to succeed – for it ends with the coming of Christ and the banqueting feast which celebrates Christ's victory. In the *Didache* (early second century?), the description of the Eucharist includes references to the gathering of God's scattered flock from the ends of the earth, in the same way as the one loaf had been prepared from many grains of wheat (*Didache* 9.4).

The Early Church also forged a link between Jesus' ordinary table fellowship with any who would join with him and the special celebration of the Passover supper. Paul makes it clear in 1 Corinthians 11 that a general or ordinary meal (the *agape* meal) was closely linked with the special taking of the bread and wine of communion (see 1 Corinthians 11.20-2, 33-4). So the Last Supper would have been seen as the culmination of that series of meals Jesus had with his disciples – and with many other people too. In the first century, the table may therefore have been 'open', as it was in Jesus' own ministry. But the ethical dimension

– eating worthily, arriving after prayerful preparation, fasting before partaking, etc. – first expounded by Paul (1 Corinthians 11.27–34) – eventually dictated that only those who had first proved themselves worthy to take part could come to the Eucharist proper. The Eucharist itself took on more and more the aspect of ethical efficacy, as the rite of word and spirit. It was believed to purge the recipient of sins committed after baptism, and would complete the cleansing which the believer had already begun through repentance, prayer and fasting.

Purification and baptism

Baptism was the process by which converts first became affiliated to the covenant people of God – the Church. The training and nurturing process, culminating in the rites of initiation, made its impact with regard to the Church's understanding of God, Christian morality and mission. These processes gradually became more lengthy and complicated over a period of time and the baptism rite itself became linked to Easter.

In the Early Church, baptism, seen as entry into a new life, was held in even higher regard than the Eucharist. The beginnings of a systematic catechetical training are seen in the *Didache*, but, by the end of the second century, the postulant (new convert) had to go through a long examination at the hands of the trainer or catechist. Often a letter of recommendation or a testimonial had to accompany the postulant's application for baptism. The moral life of the candidate came under close scrutiny – a married man or woman must be faithful, a single man or woman chaste. No unlawful trade or profession should be pursued. These included actors in the theatre, teachers in pagan schools, charioteers and gladiators, military governors, magistrates, as well as harlots, sodomites and magicians.[119] Then followed a period of instruction, which could last up to two years, with a twofold emphasis, on doctrine and ethics.

Before Easter came round the catechists selected those deemed sufficiently advanced for baptism. A second moral examination ensued, to witness to their moral suitability. Throughout the 40 days leading up to Easter (later, Lent), there were daily exorcisms, regular days of fasting and penitential exercises. On the Wednesday of Holy Week, a final examination took place before the bishop, on Thursday there was a purificatory bath, on Friday a fast, on Saturday solemn exorcisms and then before Easter Sunday an all-night vigil, prior to the appearance at the baptistery on Sunday morning at dawn. The bishop blessed the water and the oils, and the baptism candidates were undressed and clothed again in white. The service itself involved exorcism – either with oil or the laying on of hands. At the font the candidate made a short confession of faith in response to questions, covering the main articles of the Creed. The baptism itself would then be a threefold act (corresponding to the work of the Trinity) – by full immersion, by the pouring of water over the head, or by placing the candidate under a jet of water. The newly baptized would be anointed with oil, have hands laid on with prayer, the sign of the cross made and a holy kiss given. Often feet were also washed in a special ceremony. Then after confirmation – often closely linked to baptism – new members could take part in the whole liturgy as communicants. A special feature for them alone was the offering of bread and wine and, in addition, two cups – one of water and one of milk and honey. These were administered after the thanksgiving to symbolize inward washing and the entry into the Promised Land.

This complicated and long-drawn-out process reflects the importance attached both to the training of new converts and to the act of baptism itself. The basic rite of baptism was in fact built on the foundation of the Jewish baptism of proselytes, although the interpretation of Christian baptism came from several sources, including the mainstream Jewish understanding. As with the baptism of proselytes, Christian baptism denoted incorporation into the people of God; but unlike the Jewish practice it was at an early stage extended to whole families, including children of Christian parents, and thus the practice of infant baptism became widespread.

It also presupposed repentance and pointed to the coming of the Messiah to consummate God's purposes for Israel. In this way, it stood closer to the emphases given to it by the Essenes of Qumran and by John the Baptist and his followers. As with John's baptism specifically, it was a once-for-all event and, significantly, was accessible to all, whether Jew or Gentile. It also symbolized entry into the community of the Messiah.

The most important and specifically Christian aspect of baptism was the recognition that the Messiah had already come in Jesus Christ. This focus on the person of Jesus also went further, because baptism was early on seen as conformity with the life and death of Christ (as in Romans 6.3). In this way, baptism was regarded as a dying to the past and a rebirth into a new way of life. This corresponded to the cross and resurrection as understood and expressed in various ways: for instance, as a transfer from the realm of darkness into a kingdom of light; as the embracing of a new community and an alternative society; as the purification of life and acquisition of a new power over thraldom to sin; and, perhaps most important of all, as the imitation of Christ and conformity to his life. Much of this symbolism can be found in Paul's writing – especially in Romans 6 and, in more metaphorical language, in Colossians 3.1–17.

Baptism was clearly a highly exclusive commitment both to Christ and to the Church. The commitment to Christ involved, among other things, being a witness and living a life worthy of Christ. The commitment to the Church involved becoming part of a society within society at large, part of a disciplined order strongly committed to one another in mutual solidarity and with its own rules of conduct. Both of these commitments had a clear missionary dimension.

The roots of baptism in the Gospels themselves must inevitably focus on Jesus' own baptism. This, like the Last Supper, is described in the Synoptic Gospels, but only alluded to in John. The first point on which all three Synoptics agree is that Jesus aligned himself with the baptism of John. This is outlined by the evangelists as a once-for-all baptism of repentance and for the forgiveness of sins (Mark 1.4). Jesus evidently agreed with the need for a turning from sin and the living of a new life, but he added in Mark the positive message of the imminent coming of God's kingdom and the need for faith (Mark 1.15). Matthew introduces a debate between John and Jesus, to the effect that Jesus does not require baptism; but Jesus insists that this is God's will for him (Matthew 3.14–15). In Luke, Jesus is baptized 'after all the people', perhaps implying that his preparation was long and serious. There is no interaction with John, but John's preaching and life is reported at some length by Luke (3.2–20). In all three accounts an essential ingredient is the coming of the Holy Spirit upon Jesus like a dove (Mark 1.10; Matthew 3.16; Luke 3.22). In addition, in all three accounts this is accompanied by the voice of God announcing that this is God's own son, in whom he is well pleased (Mark 1.11; Matthew 3.17; Luke 3.22). In Mark and Matthew there is also an apocalyptic sign – the heavens opened (Mark 1.10; Matthew 3.16). The empowerment of the Holy Spirit for Jesus' mission is given due emphasis by the story immediately following – the temptations in the wilderness. Jesus requires superhuman strength to confront and resist Satan.

The Gospels do not record Jesus baptizing anyone, so the next significant mention of baptism comes right at the end of Matthew's Gospel in the commissioning story (28.16–20), when the disciples are instructed to go to all peoples everywhere, make disciples and 'baptize in the name of the Father, the Son and the Holy Spirit' (28.19). This is characteristically linked in Matthew with the need for training: 'teaching them to obey everything that I have commanded you' (28.20). Presumably, these injunctions reflect the practices already established in Matthew's church: there, baptism is in a Trinitarian form, and is preceded by some kind of catechism. Other parts of the Gospel are so arranged that the existence of a systematic scheme of training seems quite feasible.

In the Acts of the Apostles, Luke describes Christian baptism in various places, but on examination it becomes clear that there is a pattern or inner logic to these descriptions. There is also a close – and somewhat intriguing – connection between baptism and the Holy Spirit. The sequence begins with Peter's speech on the day of Pentecost. At that time the Jews from every part of the

Diaspora are gathered, and the sermon Peter preaches is aimed especially at a Jewish audience. The speech ends with Peter crying, 'Save yourselves from this corrupt generation' and Luke concludes, 'So those who welcomed his message were baptized, and that day about three thousand persons were added' (2.40–1).

After this spectacular event, Luke does not mention baptism again until the Christian mission takes a new turn; with Philip's adventures in Samaria. First, in Acts 8, Philip confronts Simon the magician (Simon Magus) and a crowd of Samaritans. Interestingly, Philip's message is a proclamation of 'the good news about the kingdom of God and the name of Jesus Christ' and, after his word, Luke adds, 'They were baptized, both men and women. Even Simon himself believed' (8.12). In a fascinating way, the gospel of Jesus and the Early Church's mission are linked together by the words, 'kingdom of God' and 'the name of Jesus Christ'. Next, Peter and John come down to Samaria. This time, Luke regards it as important that the work receives the seal of the Holy Spirit as well as the sanction of the church leaders:

> The two went down and prayed for them that they might receive the Holy Spirit (for as yet the Spirit had not yet come upon any of them; they had only been baptized in the name of the Lord Jesus). Then Peter and John laid their hands on them, and they received the Holy Spirit. (8.15–17)

The Samaritan mission is a kind of half-way house between mission to the Jews and mission to the Gentiles. This transition continues when Philip returns and is placed in the path of the Ethiopian eunuch. He presumably represents the god-fearing Gentile, who is already attached to the synagogue – he is certainly shown already reading the Jewish Scriptures. When Philip explains Isaiah's prophecies to him as predictions about Jesus' coming as Messiah, the Ethiopian calls out, 'Look, here is water! What is to prevent me from being baptized?' (8.36–7).

The next great leap is to the Gentile mission proper. This begins with the conversion of Paul, who, after his encounter with the risen Lord 'got up and was baptized' (9.18). Shortly afterwards, Peter is led by the Spirit to the house of Cornelius, the Roman centurion. Peter speaks about the coming of Jesus and then Luke interjects, 'While Peter was still speaking, the Holy Spirit fell upon all who heard the word' (10.44). Peter's response is to say. '"Can anyone withhold the water for baptizing these people who have received the Holy Spirit just as we have?" So he ordered them to be baptized in the name of Jesus Christ' (10.46–8). In this instance, it is the reception of the Holy Spirit which gives God's seal of approval to the conversion and inclusion of the Gentiles.

In order to reinforce the importance of this new departure, Peter justifies his actions to 'the circumcised believers' in Jerusalem (11.2). He explains about the Holy Spirit falling upon the Gentiles and then, significantly, adds, 'And I remember the word of the Lord, how he had said "John baptized with water, but you will be baptized with the Holy Spirit"'(11.16). Peter obviously appeals not only to the witness of the Spirit but also to the authority of Jesus' words to vindicate his own actions. He finishes his speech with, 'Then God has given even to the Gentiles the repentance that leads to life' (11.18). Peter is to repeat his explanation and his justification of Gentile membership of the Church at the Council of Jerusalem, and there again he argues that the seal of the Spirit ensures God's approval of the new mission (15.8).

Once Luke has taken his readers through these steps where baptism is related to the mission of the Church – to the Jews, the Samaritans, God-fearing Gentiles and to hitherto unbelieving Gentiles – then there is not a great deal of further interest in baptism. However, there are just a few other mentions which actually bring out new points of significance for Early Church practice.

First, when Paul and Silas are in prison, the jailer is converted, and Luke concludes the narrative with these words: '[T]hen he and his entire family were baptized without delay'(16.33). And just in case any might regard the mention of the entire family as incidental to the plot, Luke reinforces the same point at 18.8, where Crispus, the synagogue official, is converted: 'Crispus . . .

became a believer in the Lord, together with all his household; and many of the Corinthians who heard Paul became believers and were baptized.' The importance laid by Luke on baptism of whole households must surely pave the way for the Church's justification of the practice of infant baptism. The Holy Spirit, whose role is not central in these instances, is not mentioned at all.

Finally, Luke brings out the meaning for the Church of an isolated incident in Ephesus when followers of John the Baptist are challenged by Paul: 'Did you receive the Holy Spirit when you became believers?' he asks (19.2). They respond that they did not even know there was such a thing as the Holy Spirit. They were baptized into John's baptism of repentance only. Paul then goes on to explain that John pointed to 'the one who was to come after him, that is . . . in Jesus' and they were accordingly baptized 'in the name of the Lord Jesus' after which 'the Holy Spirit came upon them and they spoke in tongues and prophesied' (19.4–6). From the point of view of the Early Church, those who had been baptized by John and who had become Christians nevertheless had to take a further step of a second baptism in the name of Jesus. At this stage, the Trinitarian form of baptism does not seem to have been firmly established. However, the Holy Spirit is again an agent in baptism.

It is now apparent that all the stories concerning baptism in the Acts of the Apostles are not only narratives highlighting the spread of Christian mission. They each have the further specific purpose of elucidating and justifying Early Church practice. They demonstrate how the Church was able to move from mission to the Jews to the incorporation of 'fringe' communities, and then the Gentiles. At the same time, Luke is eager to link the Holy Spirit's work to baptism and to the Christian life.

In the Early Church baptism is connected both to mission and to church discipline. There is a strong conviction that the Church, as the people of God, should bear witness to Jesus Christ through its unity and holiness of life. The Holy Spirit is regarded as the powerful instrument by which this reconciliation and new life can come about. The development of a rather stringent and legal-istic disciplinary code of practice from the end of the first century, and the moral testing of baptism preparation may well have been seen as helping the churches to conserve their evangelistic thrust.

The stress on 'observance of the law' in some strands of early Christian thinking induced many writers later on to seek to demonstrate Christian distinctiveness and ethical purity of life in visible and tangible ways and, of course, over against the perceived corruption of the world.

In Matthew we have a fairly early example of these links between baptism, the Christian life and witness or mission to the world. Matthew holds two aims in tension: the preservation of the Church's holiness and the restoration of offenders through the pastoral discipline of the Church.

The Sermon on the Mount (Chapters 5—7) speaks of the need for the practice of piety, and puts it in the context of Jewish ethical understanding. In concrete terms Matthew stresses the need for almsgiving (6.2–4), prayer (6.5–15) and fasting (6.16–18). He also strengthens the observance of Torah by taking it into the motives and inclinations of the heart (5.17–20; 15.3–9; and 19.17). In that way, Christians can exceed the observances of the Pharisees and their search for purity and adherence to God's way. For Matthew, observance in the way of Christ means having rightly guided motives and a true love for God. So Jesus is able to say in Matthew's Gospel at the culmination point of the sermon, 'Be perfect, therefore, as your heavenly Father is perfect' (5.48 cf. 15.17–20; 23.23).

The witness of the Church is frequently stressed in Matthew – especially in passages relating to pastoral discipline. In 5.23–6, the believers must be reconciled together in unity before taking their gift to the altar. And if someone has a grievance against another, then to avoid revenge or angry remonstrance, witnesses are called upon to adjudicate in the matter and to pass judgement (18.15–17). Christians must not be stumbling blocks or bad moral examples to others (18.6–7). If they do have a grave fault or weakness, then it would be better to cut off or to take out the offending limb or organ than to continue in sin (18.8–9). The eye must be full of light, not darkness in a world which judged inner health by the state of the eye as window to the soul (6.22). The worst-case scenario for a believer is to be like the Pharisee – pretending to be upright yet full of corrupt motives within – in other words, like a whitened sepulchre (23.25–8). The Christian must have his or her house swept clean – and make sure it is kept clean in case other 'demons' take advantage of the new location (12.43–5).

Even the Last Judgement is seen by Matthew in terms of the practice of good works. The sheep who meet with the Lord's approval are paradoxically surprised and bewildered by the final judgement: 'When was it we saw you hungry and gave you food, or thirsty and gave you something to drink?' (25.37) This might serve to show that a focus on obedience to God and the worship of Christ leads naturally to service of others as the result of grace operating in the believer's life. Whatever the case may be, Matthew insists on the living of a serious and devout moral life, a life which begins with the teaching and testing prior to baptism, and which then follows on naturally from baptism itself.

Matthew's understanding is quite intelligible: as believers are baptized into Christ, they put away the old life and past sins in order to live for (and work towards) a life of righteousness (*dikaiosune*). The Christian life – both as an individual and as a member of the Church – is marked by a Jewish understanding of good practice – almsgiving, prayer, fasting – and by conformity to Christ's own life and teaching. Matthew does not have a developed theology of baptism, but his understanding of Christ's death and resurrection is surely about living in the power of new life, the power of grace and the presence of the risen Lord.

This understanding is then geared to two longer-term aims: unity, love and faithfulness within the Church fellowship; and the witness of the Church in the world, that is, the Church's mission. Pastoral discipline was therefore intended to be the means by which new life was brought to the inner and outer life of the believer and also brought to the world at large, through the witness of the Church, whose witness could be regarded as a sign of the kingdom (see Matthew 10.7–8) and which could best be conceived in terms of justice, mercy and faith offered to all people (23.23).

In John's Gospel these matters receive a rather different kind of treatment: there is a deliberate internalizing of the external forms of Church life. This means that John makes considerable use of symbolism and imagery. For example, the one who comes to belief moves from darkness to light. This process is seen as having its origin in the witness of John the Baptist: 'He came as a witness to testify to the light' (1.7). The Word (*logos*) is pinpointed as the true light, but the association with John gives this image of light a connection with baptism. Also, a few verses further on, we read, 'To all who received him, who believed in his name, he gave power to become children of God, who were born, not of blood, or of the will of the flesh or of the will of man, but of God' (1.12). Here there is not only an indirect allusion to baptism, but also an indirect reference to the work of the Holy Spirit. John and his community clearly regard baptism as the way to be 'born again' or 'from above' (3.7). A close link between baptism and the empowering of the Holy Spirit is forged here, and the link is made even more explicit later on in the conversation between Jesus and Nicodemus. The way of the old religion will not suffice of itself; it needs to find the key to the kingdom of God – and that key is the Holy Spirit: 'Very truly, I tell you, no one can enter the kingdom of God without being born of water and Spirit. What is born of flesh is flesh, and what is born of the Spirit is spirit' (3.5–6). Then Jesus goes on to speak of the contrast between darkness and light once again – in this way drawing attention to the moral and spiritual consequences and implications of baptism:

> For all who do evil hate the light and do not come to the light, so that their deeds may not be exposed. But those who do what is true come to the light, so that it may be clearly seen that their deeds have been done in God. (3.20–1)

Here the link between the light, baptism and Christian discipline or good works is made crystal clear.

Baptism gives us two tremendous insights into the life of the Early Church: it shows us how the first Christians linked baptism to faith in God as Father, Jesus as Son and the Holy Spirit as agent of new life – giving impetus to the nascent doctrine of the Trinity. This is extremely important, for it is in these areas that we see a parting of the ways with Jewish belief and practice. It is true to say that many aspects of Christian worship – more than generally recognized – are taken over either wholesale or in adapted form from Judaism: for instance, the practice of public prayer, and especially thanksgivings, adoration and confession (notably on the Day of Atonement); the reading of Scripture passages, the interpretation of Scripture – both in textual commentary and in preaching generally; the singing of Psalms and sacred songs; the observance of feast days and fast days. However, the worship of God as Father has concomitant elements of intimacy and assurance almost unknown in Second-Temple Jewish worship. The worship of Jesus Christ as Lord is altogether a new departure, and a huge step for a strict monotheistic Jew to take. We shall shortly look in more detail at this. The worship of the Holy Spirit and the attribution to the Spirit of power over sin at baptism and power to live a new life – a power regarded as accessible and available at all times throughout the Christian life – as well as the work of the Spirit visible in the Church and in the world, these ideas of the Spirit also represent a whole new departure. It is a far cry from the Old Testament understanding of the Spirit as a rare inspiration of the prophetic voice – and a creative power largely external to the individual human life. Now, in the Christian life, the Holy Spirit is seen as the personal guide, the motivator, the strengthener, the counsellor and the inspiration behind mission.

The risen Christ – worship and mission

The most surprising and unusual fact about early Christian worship was what Larry Hurtado[120] calls 'Christ devotion': that is, the introduction into a fiercely monotheistic religion of the worship of Jesus Christ as Lord and God. Whether this spelt a move away from monotheism deserves further investigation; but at this point it is simply to be noted that this change of emphasis was like a revolution in the thinking of those Jews who became Christian believers; and working out the implications of such a change required many years, if not centuries, of discussion and debate.

Hurtado argues that this factor is all the more remarkable in that the very chief characteristic of Jewish religion in the first century was 'its defiantly monotheistic stance'.[121] He goes on to contend that Jewish monotheism nevertheless played a powerful role in shaping 'Christ-devotion'. The clearest scriptural expression of pure monotheistic belief and practice is found in the second part of Isaiah (43—8), in the section most probably deriving from the time of the Babylonian exile – that is, the sixth century BC. When we consider that Isaiah featured in the Gospel writers' interpretation of the mission of Jesus and that of the Church, then it is also highly likely that the close study of Isaiah contributed to the early Christian understanding of the exclusive worship of the one true God. In the first century there was a consistent Jewish resistance to worshipping any but the God of Israel over against the deities of other peoples and traditions, over against divine beings or agents of any sort, and certainly over against the worship of the emperor as a god.

The accommodation of Jesus Christ as an object of devotion in the worship and life of the early Christians was therefore a most significant counter-cultural step that simply cannot be accounted for on the basis of any tendency in Jewish religion. It is an intriguing phenomenon, often overlooked or taken for granted today. Jewish belief did allow for an exalted status for the likes of Elijah and Moses, for angels and messengers, and for the figure of wisdom, a personified emanation from God. However, a sharp line was drawn between any such figure and the one God, alone worthy of worship.

The New Testament reflects the monotheistic tradition of Judaism – and upholds it. Paul refers to pagan religious ceremonies as *eidolothyton* (1 Corinthians 8.1, 4) – 'offerings to idols' – showing his scorn for such 'gods'. Paul places over against what he calls 'the so-called gods in heaven and on earth' the 'one God, the Father, from whom are all things and for whom we exist' (1 Corinthians 8.5–6), but significantly he adds, 'and one Lord, Jesus Christ'. In Chapter 10 of the same letter Paul insists that Christians completely shun 'the worship of idols' – *eidololatria* – and this is in the context of the eucharistic meal, where participation excludes joining in with any cultic rites associated with other deities, here called 'demons' (10.20–1).

From this it is clear that for Paul – and for all the early Christians – devotion to Jesus Christ was somehow regarded as compatible with a strictly monotheistic faith and practice. The worship of Christ cannot be understood simply as apotheosis – the exalting of Christ to the status of a god, or making Christ an additional god in the pantheon of divinity. Jesus is not revered as 'another deity': something more subtle is at work here. The constraining influence of monotheism must have itself determined the contours that the worship of Christ took in the Church's life.

The divine significance of Jesus Christ is primarily expressed early on in terms of his relationship to God the Father. Any worship of Christ is justified by reference to his exaltation 'to the right hand of God' – in other words, to the action of God in conferring divine status upon him. In the Gospels, the resurrection is always understood as Jesus Christ being raised by God. He did not simply come back to life through some power of his own, nor did he raise himself out of the sleep of death. In addition, John's Gospel consistently regards Christ as 'one with God' – the channel through which God's life is poured, the revealer of all that God is and does. But at the same time, John sees Jesus as somehow subordinated to the Father in terms of being sent, and in terms of deriving all he is and has from the Father as author and prime mover.

Thus, an early development in the Church was the notion of praying to God in or through the name of Jesus Christ. As Larry Hurtado says: 'Christ functions as God's principal agent, Christ's revelatory and redemptive actions constantly portrayed as done on God's authority, as expressions of God's will, and as serving God's purposes and glory.'[122] Yet the worship and adoration of Christ as equal with God are unparalleled and marks a major development in the Jewish understanding of monotheism.

The Early Church must have come to this understanding – which, as suggested, was very much against the grain for Jewish believers – because of their religious experience; and, more specifically, because of their experience of Christ as risen Lord. These experiences must have been so striking that for the believers they had the force of a new revelation. They were powerful enough to re-orientate or re-configure the worship life of the Church and cause it to come to a new definition of the godhead and central beliefs as compared to Judaism.

If we examine the resurrection accounts in the Gospels, it becomes evident that these stories are not only written as descriptions of what was believed to have happened after Jesus' death and burial: they are also written to describe the experiences of the first Christians and to show how they now related to Jesus as risen Lord. This could then give Christians of later generations insights into how they themselves should relate to Jesus, who, though now ascended and invisible to their earthly sight, is still in a real sense the risen Lord living the resurrection life. In other words, for the Gospel writer there is a clear and direct continuity between the experiences of the first witnesses to the resurrection and the members of the Church at a later date.

In John's Gospel in particular, this concern is very transparent. First there is the open tomb and the element of surprise at its discovery. Mary Magdalene finds the stone rolled away, and goes to tell a sceptical Peter, 'They have taken away the Lord' (20.2). Peter and 'the other disciple' go to investigate for themselves and find the linen clothes and head cloth neatly wrapped up and laid aside. Surprise now gives way to faith – the faith of those who are beginning to relate to Jesus in a new way. In the next episode, Mary stands weeping. The fact that the tomb is empty only means to her that 'They have taken away my Lord' and Mary does not know where he is (20.13). When Jesus appears to her, she does not at first recognize him, presuming him to be the gardener (20.15). Then Jesus calls her by name, and she responds *rabboni*, 'master'. She tries to grasp hold of him. But at this stage Jesus rebukes her: 'Do not hold on to me, because I have not yet ascended to the Father' (20.17). From the Gospel writer's point of view, a new stage in the relationship has been reached: Mary has to relate to Jesus as risen Lord and not as an ordinary human being – in other words relate to him in a new way. In addition she has a new task; she is to go to the other disciples and explain that Jesus is ascending. Jesus makes it clear to her how this will affect her and the others: he is ascending 'to my Father and your Father, to my God and your God' (20.17). The new relationship with Jesus is going to mean a new relationship with God. The Father has up to this point been Jesus' Father; but now all the disciples may relate to God as Jesus himself relates – 'my Father and your Father'. Mary's task is to be a witness to the resurrection; but she also has another equally important task, namely, to tell the others that a new relationship with God has been made possible for them.

In the next episode John outlines the meeting of Jesus with the disciples (20.19–20). Jesus reassures them with his blessing of *shalom*, peace. Then they are commissioned for a task of mission. Jesus says, 'As the Father sent me, so I send you' (20.21) – and he breathes the Holy Spirit into them, to empower them for the task and to give them the authority to forgive sins in his name (20.23). Thomas was not present at this meeting and refuses to believe unless he sees and feels the nail-marks in the hands and the wounds in Jesus' side (20.24–5). His wish is granted, and then, in one of the most significant moments in all the accounts he is told not to doubt but to believe, and then responds with 'My Lord and my God' (20.28). From now on Jesus has become the focus for the worship and devotion of the disciples. And Jesus then adds that Thomas has come to this point through seeing and touching, but 'Blessed are those who have not seen and yet have come to believe' (20.29). Patently, all future generations of Christians are in this situation of blessing: they have faith and are therefore able to enjoy a personal relationship with the risen Lord, despite not having literally been witnesses to the resurrection.

Although Chapter 20 of John's Gospel seems to come to a climax and a fitting conclusion, there is then appended the extra chapter – 21, with its second set of stories of resurrection appearances. In the first incident, the disciples are shown going on a fishing expedition. This in itself is very odd in the light of what took place in Chapter 20, but the provenance of Chapter 21 is not our main concern. The disciples go out on the lake and catch nothing, then at daybreak Jesus appears on the lakeside and tells them to cast out the net on the other side. This time the net is filled to breaking point with fish. Peter jumps out of the boat to wade ashore and greet Jesus. The others drag the net in and find it contains 153 fish. Then they all have breakfast with Jesus.

This story has many strange elements, but what seems most obvious is that it is a story relating both to the past and the future. It looks backwards to the time when the disciples were simple fishermen without any greater purpose in life. They should not have gone back to the old life: it is fruitless and they achieve nothing. But, looking forward, with Jesus in their lives they are able to embark upon a new adventure. In the power of the risen Lord they will catch many fish – in other words, they will have a successful mission as witnesses to Jesus as Lord. And the fact that this relates directly to the Gentiles is clear in the number of fish: 153 represents the number of Gentile nations in the world at large. So it is a story about new life, being a witness, and going on mission.

The final story is ostensibly about the restoration and reinstatement of Peter as Jesus' trusted servant. But, more than that, it is about Peter as pastor of the sheep. Three times he is asked if he loves Jesus, and he is told in different ways, 'Feed my sheep' (21.15–17). So the story looks to the time when Peter will have great responsibilities in the infant Church, and particularly with regard to those who have been following 'the beloved disciple'.

Finally, the relationship between Peter and 'the beloved

disciple' is explored. This passage appears to have been written in response to one or more pastoral problems: for example, why has the beloved disciple died before the Lord's return? Or again, what is Peter's position and status in the churches John founded? But there is a further point about the Early Church. The way in which Peter is able to find forgiveness from Jesus as risen Lord and the way in which he is commissioned and gifted as church leader and pastor is indicative of the way Jesus will work in and through the Church of the first century, and especially the Church of the time when the Gospel was written.

So in John we see not only accounts of Jesus' rising from the dead and the circumstances relating to his appearances but also a progressive understanding of the new ways in which disciples of Jesus are to relate to him as risen Lord: in other words, how they will worship him in their devotional lives. This all culminates in a few snapshot impressions of the Early Church, its mission to the Gentiles and its leadership and ministry.

If we continue to work backwards through the Gospels, moving on to Luke, we find that he follows Mark in his brief opening account (24.1–12), mentioning the women as the original witnesses to the resurrection (24.1–10), the discovery of the empty tomb (24.2–3), the appearance of men or angels in dazzling clothes (24.4), the passing on of the news to the disciples (24.9, 11) and Peter's discovery of the empty tomb and the grave clothes (24.12). In Luke, the women are simply not believed by the other disciples: 'these words seemed to them an idle tale' (24.11).

The reactions mentioned in this account move from perplexity (v. 4) to terror (v. 5) to amazement (v. 12). The new relationship is unexpected, in fact a total surprise, and the responses are very human ones. Then, in the long account of the disciples on the Emmaus Road (24.13–35), the two disciples whom Jesus accompanies on their journey begin in non-recognition and sadness (24.16–17). They have a discussion with Jesus about 'the things that have taken place' (24.18) and mention that they 'had hoped that he was the one to redeem Israel' (24.21). Then they go on to speak of the testimony of the women about the empty tomb and the vision of angels (24.22–4). Jesus rebukes their unbelief and declares that all this happened in accordance with the Scriptures, which he then interprets himself. As they come near to their destination, the travellers urge Jesus to stay with them and, as they share the evening meal together, the scales fall from their eyes, they recognize him, and suddenly he vanishes from their sight.

This story has very clear allusions to the worship and life of the Early Church. First, the vital need for faith in the risen Lord is made plain. Without that, even the women's tales of resurrection mean nothing. Secondly, the Scriptures need to be interpreted in order to show how the resurrection was always in God's plan. The Early Church quickly engaged with this task. Thirdly, as the believers come together in fellowship, and especially around the Lord's table, they will discover that he is there in the midst, and their hearts will burn within them (24.32). The sadness now gives way to rejoicing and excitement, as the two on the road return to tell the eleven and their companions. The watchword is now 'The Lord has risen indeed' (24.34) – a phrase which soon became part of the Easter liturgy.

In the last section of Luke's Gospel (24.36–50), we have two stories compressed or conflated into one. The first demonstrates that Jesus in his risen body is not like a ghost, but is solid and real: 'Touch me and see; for a ghost does not have flesh and bones as you see that I have' (24.39). He then proved it by eating broiled fish with them.

This brief episode highlights Luke's concern to portray the resurrection as a real happening, a real rising again. It is demonstrably a physical resurrection, not a separation of the soul from the body, nor a reconstitution or resuscitation of a physical body alone. In the context of the Hellenistic world, both of these ideas could have taken hold in some circles.[123] Believers who worship Jesus should, in Luke's eyes, realize that Jesus is the first fruit of a new age, the time when God will resurrect to eternal life all those who believe. We see at a later stage that this is important to the Early Church in its formation of doctrine and belief.

Finally, Luke includes a commissioning story beginning, as in John, with words about fulfilment: the Scriptures show that the Messiah had to suffer and die, and then to rise on the third day (24.46). Then the mission of the Church enters into the frame: 'repentance and forgiveness of sins is to be proclaimed in [the Messiah's name] to all nations, beginning from Jerusalem . . . ' (24.47). The disciples are to be witnesses.

So Luke has important similarities to John's Gospel: reactions to Jesus' rising again move from alarm and unbelief through to faith and joy; Jesus is not always recognized at first, but a new relationship is eventually forged; the disciples have to be convinced that Jesus really is risen, body and soul, and to feel his wounds; the resurrection is shown to be a fulfilment of the ancient Scriptures – in other words, has been God's plan all along; and, finally, the disciples are sent out on a new task of mission to the whole world. In all these ways, the resurrection relates closely to the worship of the Early Church and to its witness and mission among the nations.

Matthew's Gospel bears some of these same features too. There is the discovery of the empty tomb by the women; there is a movement from terror through fear to joy (28.4, 5, 8); there is the instruction to go and tell others the news (28.10); there is the commissioning of the disciples for their mission to the nations. And at the end, there is a new relationship – 'Remember, I am with you always, to the end of the age' (28.20). However, the emphasis in John on the ambivalence of Jesus' appearance is not mentioned – non-recognition is not a motif in Matthew. The emphasis on doubt giving way to faith is not apparent either. What Matthew does add to the other accounts is the story about mounting an armed guard on Jesus' tomb and making it secure (27.64–6). Presumably, the Early Church had to counter stories about the body being smuggled away and hidden, so that Jesus' resurrection could be announced. Matthew also speaks more of earthquakes and angels and, strangely, of an apocalyptic style resurrection of people in Jerusalem emerging from open graves (27.52–4). The point here may be to assure the members of the

Early Church that Jesus' own rising was the guarantee of the resurrection of all believers at a future date. Paul faced difficulties over belief in a future resurrection in 1 Corinthians 15.12–23 and in 1 Thessalonians 4.13–18.

Once again we see that the resurrection accounts have a historical referent in the life of the Church. They are intended to show that Jesus really did rise from the dead and came out of the tomb. But the importance for the Early Church is that he is alive for ever and can be known in worship and prayer. The very mission of the Church is the last command of the risen Jesus before his ascension (at least, according to Matthew) and the Church is acting out this calling to mission in the age of the resurrection – in the company of the risen Jesus.

The Gospel of Mark ends most abruptly, as we have seen, and it is difficult to give a full and coherent account of Mark's aims in writing up the resurrection narratives. For reasons already given it seems probable that the ending at 16.8 was not the final verse of Mark's Gospel. The early predictions of Jesus' suffering and death point forward to his resurrection as having great significance (8.31; 9.31; 10.31–4). The disciples are told in 16.7 to go to Galilee where they will meet again with Jesus. This meeting is of course never subsequently described, for the Gospel ends with the next verse. Some of the themes of Mark seem incomplete without a longer account of Jesus' actions after the resurrection. The fear at the end seems logically to be the prelude to faith, with excitement and joy following on, as in the other Gospels, and in Mark itself elsewhere (see 4.40 and 6.50).

The closest parallel to the women running in fear from the empty tomb in 16.8 is the story in 5.25–34 where the woman with the haemorrhage touches Jesus' cloak and then falls down before him in fear and trembling (5.33) and then confesses the truth. Jesus' reply to her is one of reassurance: 'He said to her, "Daughter, your faith has made you well; go in peace, and be healed of your disease."' (5.34). It does not seem farfetched to suppose that Mark is here highlighting the very message that the fearful women at the tomb will finally receive from the risen Jesus. Yet at 16.8 they are left in fear and trembling.

Mark does have the common themes of the empty tomb with the great stone rolled away (16.4) and of the women being the first witnesses of the resurrection. There is also the 'young man' dressed in white (16.5), who tells them that '[Jesus] has been raised; he is not here' (16.6). These themes are important for reinforcing the faith of the Early Church. The later disciples do not worship a Jesus who is dead and buried, whose body is located and venerated in a tomb somewhere. They worship a risen Lord who 'is not here' (16.6). The disciples are told to meet with Jesus in order to hear their mission instructions; to be told about their future work (16.7). The numinous awe at realizing that Jesus is risen is the starting point of a more reassured and joyful faith.

All our detailed investigations into the Gospel resurrection accounts serve to demonstrate that Jesus' resurrection is absolutely central to the beliefs, worship, life and mission of the Early Church. Only in the light of Easter does the full meaning of the Gospel themes become clear. Each Gospel writer tells the story of Jesus' resurrection in his own way, even when one source is used by a second author. Yet, despite a lack of close verbal similarities, there is a consistency of themes in the stories; a basic outline which is constant: the themes are conveyed and communicated in subtly different ways and even through different stories, stories which are fitting to each Gospel and which are in no way interchangeable. The resurrection is throughout seen not only as a climax to the gospel story but also as an introduction to the next or new phase of the work of Jesus Christ. He is now Lord of the believer, object of worship, bestower of the Spirit and guide of the work and mission of the Church.

7

The Gospels and mission today

After chapters of close analysis of the Gospel texts, the time has now come to stand back a little and to reflect on the content of the Gospels from a more detached point of view. The task in hand is no less arduous than the earlier analysis, however, for the business of evaluation and assessment requires a search for connections between the life of the Early Church and the Church of today. It is a question of discerning those principles which are applicable at the time of the writing of the Gospels and applying them – perhaps in slightly different ways – to the very different world of the third millennium. The hermeneutical task of linking these two worlds together across what G. Lessing described as a great, ugly ditch is not a task to be underestimated. Constructing a bridge to cross the divide is a perilous piece of work.

It seems logical to adopt a similar policy to that in the earlier chapters – namely, to look at each Gospel separately, and to ask what its distinctive contributions might be. This sounds suspiciously like the old science of redaction criticism, but in fact it has a broader remit than the isolating of the particular theological viewpoints of particular authors and examining the detailed differences between the Gospels as finished works. In our case, it is a matter of examining the evidence of the written text in order to tease out the individual understandings of each Gospel with regard to the mission of the Church.

To begin with John's Gospel may appear to be a rather cavalier or illogical approach, but it is John who provides us with the most developed theological understanding of mission and the clearest outline of the abstract principles relating to mission.

John's Gospel – God's mission

The first principle of the Gospel of John is the overarching one of *missio dei*, God's mission. From the outset, the life and work of Jesus is set in the context of a sending mission in the heart of God from the beginning of creation.

This notion of mission as having its origins and beginnings in God's nature and will has in recent times become a popular place to embark upon an investigation into the true nature of mission. It was first used at the Willingen Conference of the International Missionary Council of 1952. The question it seeks to answer is almost as vast as that posed by Douglas Adams in his Hitchhiker's Guide – 'life, the universe and everything' – for it ponders the purpose and will of God and his relationship to the world. The Gospel of John has a ready answer to this speculative thinking; God's mission derives from his love and concern for the world:

> For God so loved the world that he gave his only Son, so that everyone who believes in him may not perish but have eternal life. Indeed, God did not send the Son into the world to condemn the world, but in order that the world might be saved through him. (3.16–17)

These sentences are not about individual salvation, as they are so often deemed to be, but about God's purposes for the world as a whole. This is a vitally important point. God does not seek to save people by extracting them from a corrupt material universe (the gnostic view); nor does he seek to save only those willing to obey him (the sectarian view); his concern is with the whole world and with all people.

John's assertion also assumes that God is a personal God who has a personal interest in the world of humankind. This is not a philosophical God who escapes all definition and cannot fit the categories of human language at all: nor is this an impersonal 'first mover' or even 'the ground of our being'. Mission cannot be carried out by this type of God – for mission is an activity which presupposes a personal and a compassionate God. John makes it clear in these few lines from Chapter 3 that it is appropriate to use human analogies when speaking of God – and himself uses images of a divine Jesus such as 'the vine', 'the gate', 'the good shepherd' etc. By extension we can also apply human categories to God and speak of his justice, his mercy, his anger (wrath) or his love.

At the same time, if all language about God is *no more* than a human construct, an attempt to unify and harmonize our disjointed and arbitrary experiences, then, as Andrew Kirk suggests, 'it would be better to speak of *missio hominis*'.[124] Such mission is no more than an invention of the human mind and a need of the human psyche. But the Gospel makes it clear that such language is analogy – no more and no less. The God of John's Gospel is personal, but is supra-personal as well.

John's deceptively simple phrases tell us something else: that God is actively involved in his creation and, in the words of Emilio Castro, purposes 'to gather the whole of creation under the lordship of Jesus Christ, in whom, by the power of the Holy Spirit, all are brought into communion with God'.[125] Thus God is active in seeking to bring his mission to completion or fulfilment in history.

If God's mission is broad enough to encompass the whole of creation, then it must be conceded that this mission is far broader than the common conception of the mission of the Christian Church. If the Church is the spearhead of God's mission, it obviously takes a lot more than the work of the Church alone to bring justice and peace to the world as a whole, and 'to safeguard the integrity of creation and sustain and renew the earth' – to quote the words of the fifth 'Mark of Mission' as promulgated by the Lambeth Conference of the Anglican Church in 1988.[126] Christians have to consider carefully how to co-operate in certain ventures – without compromising their own identity – with government organizations, other faith communities, secular agencies and charitable concerns.

For the Christian Church, to speak of *missio dei* is to speak of God as Trinity, or of *missio trinitatis*. The mission of God has of necessity to flow from the true nature of God. Thus, if creation is an act of love, then love must have been in the heart of the godhead from before time began and before anything was created.

Such love can only be conceived as having an object, or, in other words, in terms of personal relationship or reciprocal caring. And this talk of reciprocal relations also gives rise to other concepts, such as community, harmony, unity in diversity, compassion, forgiveness, equality and, above all, love itself. All of these qualities can only be understood in terms of one personal being relating to another, or to others. In addition, it means that God's love is not a self-absorbed self-love. It is rather a constant reaching out for the other: 'It is a passion which wishes the very highest and best for the other, and is willing to sacrifice all that this might be achieved.'[127]

Love is not an abstract quality; it must express itself in action. Ultimately, the action of Jesus in dying on the cross to reconcile those who before were enemies of God is the action par excellence which expresses the nature of God's love. Thus, in David Bosch's succinct summing up: 'There is mission because God loves people.'[128] And the logical consequence of this is that 'to participate in mission is to participate in the movement of God's love towards people, since God is a fountain of sending love'.[129]

Mission would therefore express the nature of God and also should be carried out in close relationship with God. But God himself has the overall or ultimate responsibility for mission – and for its success. Very often, church members are hesitant about 'having a mission' and are reluctant to be involved in mission. Perhaps it conjures up images of high-pressure evangelism or of slick worldly methods of persuasion, or even of hidden motives to offer spiritual gifts in exchange for worldly gifts of money. Perhaps it presents an insuperable obstacle to the shy and private Christian who finds it embarrassing to 'share faith' or expose their innermost feelings. Perhaps others again feel themselves to be inadequate or too feeble to face the task. Whatever the case may be, it is easier to subscribe to the Church's mission if one feels that God is taking the responsibility and assuming the main body of the task – that is, working in the secret places of the human heart. It is also easier if one is happy to acknowledge and take to heart the fact that mission is the very heartbeat of God and the fulfilment of his purposes for the world.

Mission is, from a human perspective, carried out in weakness. The Christian, or even a whole church, can never feel fully adequate to the task. The leaders' vision for a church can easily outrun the reach of most of the members. They will find it difficult to envisage change and growth, and inevitably will imagine that they need expert or specialist skills. Yet mission – God's mission – does not depend upon the genius or expertise of church members entirely: it is always carried out in a spirit of human weakness. For Christians what is important is to have faith in God's strength and in God's compassion for ordinary people.

The average church member may be reassured to know that mission is instigated by the simple act of praying, and of listening to God, and following God's guidance. In such fundamental activities all Christians can participate. In addition, it is reassuring to know that God's Spirit is at work in the world prior to our engagement in any relationship or any work of mission. The presence of God in the world means that anyone embarking upon God's mission already has an ally and accomplice in the work. It becomes 'mission alongside' rather than mission alone. And in fact, John's Gospel makes it clear that mission is *always in relationship*. Just as God the Father and the Son are portrayed as being in constant communication, so the Holy Spirit is represented as a helper or counsellor, an advocate, who is one like Jesus (John 14.16–17), who ministers to those involved in God's mission and who protects and guides them while they work in the world at large.

All this must mean that mission should be at the heart of the Church's life; so much so that it is not an optional extra on the agenda. It is rather that which defines the essence of the Church. The Church's self-understanding and sense of identity is closely bound up with its conception of its own mission and work in the world, its call to live out the gospel and be a witness for Jesus Christ at all times and in all places. Emil Brunner said that the Church exists by mission as a fire exists by burning. And the Second Vatican Council had it that 'mission is not the work of the church: it is the church at work'.[130] *Missio dei* shows that mission is not merely an activity of the Church, but is the Church's very reason for being. The Church would not exist but for mission. And God's mission is greater that the mission of the Church – for it involves the total redemption and transformation of the world. But the Church is seen as the body called and privileged to participate in God's plans and to share in God's desire for the world. In the well-known words of Archbishop William Temple, the Church is the only organization which exists for the sake of its *non*-members.

Incarnation

The second key concept in John's Gospel is that of incarnation. This is the Gospel of the word made flesh, and at the heart of the commanding passage introducing the Gospel – the Prologue – John lays open the mind of God: 'And the Word became flesh and lived [*eskenosen* – literally, set up a tent] among us, and we have seen his glory, the glory as of a father's only son, full of grace and truth' (1.14).

In the Gospel, Jesus is portrayed as descending to the very depths in reaching out to the most disaffected and ostracized, the sick and the disadvantaged. At the same time he encounters hostility from the very people he should have been able to count on for support – the religious leaders. John's early words come true in the story – 'He came to what was his own, and his own people did not accept him'(1.12). The other side of this is that, for those prepared to accept him, Jesus adopted, in this Gospel, a one-to-one ministry, dealing mainly with individuals and addressing individual needs and requests. In this way he showed the human, incarnate nature of pastoral ministry.

In an incarnational model of mission, those who join with Jesus are those who reach out to the marginalized. They do not simply offer a 'spiritual' salvation – forgiveness of sin or experience of God – but associate themselves with those most in need of a friend – with the Christ who asks a loose woman for water, and speaks at length to her; who is on the side of the woman taken in adultery, and stays to talk to her. The incarnate Christ is the one who sweats and agonizes with the little ones of the earth, who bleeds for those who are victims of corruption and the brutal misuse of power. Those who follow such a Christ in the world are in solidarity with those he most obviously came to help – not the righteous, but the lost.

The difficulty for those following the way of incarnation has been to maintain a clear Christian identity and spirituality. It is easy for one in solidarity with others to become like them, and to be subsumed under their identity or, worse, to be consumed by their problems. It is also easy for the Christian deep in the world's life to become frustrated with the Church, seeing it as part of the oppressive and powerful establishment. Solidarity with the poor and the oppressed must be in concert with Jesus' own thinking and acting – that is, from a strong base of unity with God, unashamed purity of life, integrity of faith and with a spirituality unafraid to spend time apart in prayer and fasting and reading the Scriptures. If a Christian follows Jesus in giving up the glory and ambition of this world and pouring him or herself out in a form of *kenosis* or self-emptying, this must be in order to be filled not with anger or frustration, but with God's love and the power of the Holy Spirit. Otherwise, such mission will end up being conducted in the spirit of a political campaign.

Incarnation must surely mean bringing God's life to the life of the world. This was the essence of Jesus' incarnation. He was able to reveal the Father to others – to show God's nature and to explain God's will in human terms. More than that, he was able to reflect God's character in and through his own life. So, conducting mission after this model of incarnation means some-how being Jesus Christ for others – carrying something of God's Spirit into any situation or place. This lays a heavy burden upon the Christian-on-mission, for it means living up to a high calling. In life and behaviour, it means being beyond reproach, with utter integrity and, unfashionable as it may sound, living in purity of life in terms of motives as well as actions. This high ethical lifestyle – when without pride or self-righteousness, and when with humility and kindness – is still one of the most powerful forms of witness to the world. The fact that representatives of the

Church still, even now, often hold a position of great respect in society and among many who do not attend a church is testimony to the fact that many have earned such esteem by the nature of their moral lives.

However, the mission of incarnation is not just a rather unappealing brand of moral stature or untarnished character; it is also the human face of God's love. Incarnated mission must always have a human face: it must be personal, warm, attractive and caring – just as Jesus himself presented an appealing personality to all kinds of people and was welcomed by all of good will. He told the disciples in John's Gospel: 'No one has greater love than this, to lay down one's life for one's friends' (15.13). This is the end or goal of incarnation – being prepared to love others so that one is even prepared to die for them. In that is encapsulated the self-sacrificing love of God.

In the thirteenth century, the orders of mendicant friars – the Franciscans and Dominicans – represented a new and radical departure from the monastic tradition of the past. They adopted a rule of communal poverty, refused to accept endowments or to own property, and in this way were able to break from a sedentary and fixed mode of living. They abandoned the seclusion and enclosure of the often isolated monastery to engage in an active and itinerant pastoral ministry to the crowded towns and cities of late medieval Europe. They mixed with ordinary people and lived as the poor among the poor. They preached in the vernacular and made use of stories and anecdotes in order to communicate clearly. They portrayed a Christ who had suffered and who felt strong emotions – in other words, a Christ that people could feel for and identify with. This radically incarnational model of ministry had then – and is continuing to have – a tremendous impact.

A more modern example is that of L'Arche (The Rainbow) community, founded by Jean Vanier in the middle of the twentieth century. Its members would work among the physically and mentally disabled – in other words, the most needy and neglected people in society – and a central aim was to empower them by giving them the skills to work productively themselves. By fashioning a loving and creative environment, L'Arche was able to give such people useful employment and fullness of life. This is again the Church with a human face.

By way of contrast, the Church still firmly stuck in the 'modern' paradigm has, too often, a rather inhuman face: presenting itself as impersonal, efficient, businesslike, rational, wordy, objective, controlling and distant. It seems to lack warmth in its worship too, being only willing to believe in the evidence of the senses, usually ruling out mystery and the supernatural. This is a Church which can normally manage its financial and property affairs very well, but when confronted by the question 'How is the work of God progressing?' or 'What is your mission?' is often reduced to an embarrassed silence.

The Church needs urgently to move from the cold efficiency of doing things 'the right way', observing the traditions faithfully, maintaining the external concerns, to a somewhat looser and more relaxed way of operating, a warmer and more personal way of dealing with people, giving more time to people's real concerns, ensuring that all are made welcome and given a feeling of belonging and reassured that they have something useful to contribute. This is a Church capable of tolerating different points of view, trying a variety of experiments in worship and organization of Church life, being prepared to take the risks involved in engaging with the world outside its doors in mission and service.

Incarnation is also adaptation to context, or, to use a favourite word of theologians, 'inculturation'. Christians need to know the area in which the Church is situated, the community or communities to which they relate, the ways people live their lives who do not often frequent the church. Such understandings should then provide 'ways in' for the Church to engage with people, to minister to their needs, to speak to them in their own language and to understand what interests or excites them. Inculturation does not mean compromising the Gospel in either its message or its content. Rather, it means concentrating on those aspects of the gospel which speak to people's hearts, expressing the gospel in ways they understand, presenting the gospel in ways which engage rather than alienate.

Often people outside the Church imagine that the Church is judging them and that those who attend church consider themselves superior to those who stay at home or who go elsewhere. These things may not be true, but the Church has somehow to overcome these prejudices, and the best – perhaps the only – way to ensure this is to be the Church with a human face, that is, to enter into real relationships with real people – in other words, everyone without exception. Those who come to know the minister or church member through real contact often gain a new image or understanding which overthrows old prejudices.

This would seem to lead us to conclude that the Church's role in pastoral visiting is of first importance. That is true, but it is also important that this work is shared around and that people understand the face of the Church to be far more than the face of the minister or vicar. In addition, pastoral groups need to engage with a much broader constituency than the church membership or even the attenders and the penumbra which attends occasionally or is slightly connected. There is a great need, but also a great opportunity, when the Church considers its pastoral role in the community at large.

Love and service

The third and final aspect of John's Gospel I would like to draw attention to is that of love and service. This, according to John, is our primary means of witness. John's is the Gospel in which the Last Supper is represented, not by Jesus establishing a new covenant in his body and blood as he distributes the bread and the wine, but by Jesus insisting on washing the feet of his disciples (13.1–17). He explains his action by drawing attention to the fact that he who is rightly called 'teacher' and 'Lord' is also the one who serves and humbles himself (v. 14). He goes on to say, 'So if I, your Lord and Teacher, have washed your feet, you also ought to wash one another's feet. For I have set you an example, that you also should do as I have done to you' (13.14–15).

The witness of the Church in times past, and often even today, is of a proud institution in league with the established rulers of this world, and in authority over the destiny of many people. After the accession of Constantine as emperor in the fourth century, the Church rapidly became fashionable, powerful and worldly. Many at the time saw it as fatally compromised, and the beginnings of the monastic movement were set in motion, with many who were serious about the search for God becoming hermits or monks. Later, in the high Middle Ages, the Church vied with the State for influence and political power, property and possessions. Could the emperor crown himself, or must he be crowned by the pope? Which was the greater power – the temporal or the spiritual? What would a ruler give to the Church – in terms of land or endowment – to receive the Church's blessing and God's favour? Could the Church allow Jerusalem to be taken over and controlled by 'infidels' or should she recruit an army to recapture the holy sites? With such worldly questions and preoccupations the Church of the Middle Ages lost its way, and, eventually, also its sway and influence over many people.

The Church on mission has to be a humble Church. It can never further its mission by resorting to coercion or violence, as in the days of the Crusades, whose baneful effects we are still suffering today. Nor can it further its mission through worldly methods of influence – patronage, prestige and political power. It cannot be great in any real sense, in the eyes of God or the world, by the manipulation of people or the arrogance of control.

The mission of the Church is like the mission of Jesus, who came not to be served but to serve, and to give his life as a ransom for many. Jesus also spoke about the world's misuse of power and methods of control in Matthew's Gospel, and he warned his disciples to shun these ways:

> You know that the rulers of the Gentiles lord it over them, and their great ones are tyrants over them. It will not be so among you; but whoever wishes to be great among you must be your servant, and whoever wishes to be first among you must be your slave. (Matthew 20.25–7)

This passage shows a practical and down-to-earth understanding of the ways of the world; and Jesus recognizes that pride and worldly acclaim are the most alluring temptations for Christians and for the Church. But the way of Jesus is the turning of worldly values on their head: in weakness is God's strength shown. This is the very difficult way of renouncing human strength and trusting in God's strength. It is in Jesus' death – as he hangs helpless nailed to a cross – that God's glory and power are displayed; and it is in the likeness of a powerless servant that God's son lives out his life on earth.

The mission of the Church – and of individual Christians – must find expression not in domination or standing in judgement, but in acts of kindness, friendship and compassion. The Christian way is the way of self-sacrifice and *agape* love – self-giving. Such a witness can change the view of the recipient from resentment and depression into gratitude to God and love for God's people. But even if this does not happen, the way of service and humility, the way of weakness when all is said and done, is still the right way for the mission of the Church.

It is only when pride and the desire for admiration are overcome that the Christian allows God's light to shine through and God's love to be seen in action. The Holy Spirit will take up the cause even when Christians feel their witness to be feeble and acted out from mixed motives. The very act of listening or of being present is sometimes enough to make the right impression, or to make the difference.

The third 'mark of mission' of the 1988 Lambeth Conference was 'to respond to human need by loving service'. This takes many forms: pastoral care, visiting, listening, offering sanctuary and assisting and helping in practical ways. But the important thing is the spirit in which mission is carried out. Even service can sometimes be 'doing to others' or 'doing for others' – doing good in order to boost (subconsciously) our own reputation or self-esteem. In serving humbly, Christians should not seek recognition or reward, but be happy to be alongside, to receive as well as to give, to learn as well as to offer advice. John's Jesus tells the disciples to love one another, and then adds a new commandment to those of Moses: 'This is my commandment, that you love one another as I have loved you' (15.9). 'Those who love me will keep my word, and my Father will love them, and we will come to them and make our home with them . . . ' (14.23).

The promise is this: that when the mission of loving service is enacted in the right spirit, God will be present and active through the believer. For this to happen the disciple must first relate to others as the Father, Son and Holy Spirit relate to each other – with mutual respect, reverence, love, equality and mutual support. This is what John understands by loving service, and such a witness in mission is automatically a witness to the Father, Son and Holy Spirit; in other words, it is a manifestation of God's love.

Although John's Gospel does not have a developed understanding of God as Trinity, it does reflect the relationships within the godhead, and shows how these relationships inform the life of the Christian community. Thus, the words of Catherine LaCugna are not out of place here:

> It is the essence or the heart of God to be in relationship to other persons; that there is no room for division or inequality or hierarchy in God; that the personal reality of God is the highest possible expression of love and freedom; that the mystery of divine life is characterized by self-giving and self-receiving; that divine life is dynamic and fecund, not static or barren . . . The Christian community is supposed to be an icon of God's triune life . . . [131]

The Church of the twenty-first century must fulfil the commands of Christ in a thoroughgoing way, without exception, partiality or preference, and with total inclusivity, if it is to maintain its own integrity and to make inroads into the scepticism prevalent in the world at large.

Mark's Gospel – the kingdom and liberation

The central focus of Mark's Gospel is the kingdom of God. This is a somewhat strange and unfamiliar phrase to modern ears. To some it conjures up undesirable connotations of authoritarian power and masculine domination. The real meaning of the phrase *basileia tou theou* – as used in the Gospel – is 'the rule of God' or 'the government of God'. It is not about being in a place or 'kingdom', but rather under the protection and care of God as king.

The coming of God's rule was anticipated in occasional passages of the Old Testament, and more fervently wished for in the apocalyptic writings between the testaments. In Mark, the coming of the kingdom is regarded as imminent and, in Jesus' ministry, its power is actually present. Jesus proclaims at the inception of his public work, 'The time is fulfilled and the rule of God has come (*engiken he basileia tou theou*): repent and believe in the good news' (my translation) (Mark 1.15).

As we have seen already, the coming of the kingdom is expressed through a series of mighty deeds (*dunameis*) in Jesus' ministry – healings, exorcisms, miracles. They are understood as liberating people from all the forces which enslave humanity. They are the enemies of life and freedom. The final enemy to be destroyed is death, through the crucifixion of Jesus. Mark does not express this in theological terms, unlike Paul – for example in 1 Corinthians 15.24–6 – but he sees death as being annulled and overcome by Jesus' rising again (8.31; 9.31; 10.34). The forces of life and liberty have the final word.

Mark's Gospel is revolutionary in the sense that Jesus is viewed as liberator from all the forces which oppress and restrict human life and fulfilment – even from religious traditions which bind and create heavy burdens. He will not tolerate the idea that some people can be regarded as 'unclean' (7.15) – for this puts them in a straitjacket. He will not allow the Sabbath to be life-denying (2.27–8; 3.4) – he wants it to reflect God's creative life-enhancing power. He is angry at those spirits which can possess and control a person (1.14; 3.5; 10.14).[132] He will not allow his family to restrict and dictate his ministry (3.33–5); and he warns very severely those who try to force a child's thinking into a mould, or to destroy a child's faith (9.42; 10.14). He is often at work releasing people from the bondage of crippling illness; and even death is not allowed to cut short a life – especially a child's life – or to restrict a person's development and growth (5.41–3).

Wealth is regarded as an encumbrance, a hindrance which holds people back and denies their freedom (10.21–2). To leave possessions and ties behind is regarded as a way of entering the kingdom (10.29–30). In forgiving sins on his own authority, Jesus is able to liberate people from past guilt and all that creates a spiritual obstacle and holds people back. He restores hope and makes it possible for people to take their lives forward. When he heals the paralysed man, he announces, 'Son, your sins are forgiven' (2.5), and declares that the Son of Man has authority on earth to forgive sins (2.10). With regard to the Pharisees, he attempts to release them from those man-made rules or rigid understandings which confine and oppress. Faith in Mark is therefore universally portrayed as *that which liberates*.

This theme of liberation is not only very strongly expressed through the narratives of Mark's Gospel; it is also a major theological theme of Paul's writings – most notably in the Letter to the Galatians. One of the key themes of the atonement – that of ransom or redemption – evokes the image of someone being bought out of slavery and being set free. Yet here is an understanding of salvation, or of life in the kingdom of God, which has not normally been at the forefront of people's minds in the modern era when they think of the impact of Christianity. More often, people have had an image of belonging to a Church which restricts life by rules and regulations, and which binds people through authoritarian structures.

Mark, however, shows another way. His description of the kingdom – as he follows Jesus teaching and healing – highlights God's power to release human potential and to bring creativity and fulfilment into human life. The parables of the kingdom are all about plants growing and blossoming out (e.g. 4.26–32), seeds overcoming obstacles to bring forth fruit – producing up to a hundred new seeds for each one sown (4.8). In another case, the lamp must not have its light extinguished – it must be enabled to shine out and fulfil its purpose (4.21–2). Jesus' watchword in Mark must surely be, 'All things can be done for the one who believes' (9.23). For the Jesus of Mark's Gospel, faith is a power which invariably liberates – from sin, from legalism, from dominating influences, from the crippling effects of past guilt, from all that prevents a person from developing and reaching their potential.

But Mark does not see liberation only as 'freedom from . . .' but also as 'freedom for . . .'. In the modern world, freedom has somehow become a byword for all that is good: from Mrs Thatcher's freedom of choice for the individual consumer to the popular existentialist idea of freedom of choice in personal lifestyle. There are evident dangers in such secular notions of 'freedom'. It is for a start a very individualistic concept, as expressed in common phrases such as, 'It is my life', 'It is my body', 'I'm free to do as I like' – all of which deny accountability to God. Individualism can easily lead to a selfish disregard for others and a lack of concern for the good of the community as a whole. Freedom of choice for consumers gives opportunities for self-development and introduces greater variety and interest into life: but at the same time it can break society up into small sub-groups and sub-cultures which relate neither to one another nor to the community as a whole.

Freedom of choice in personal lifestyle can lead to an unending search for the good life; for more personal wealth or more leisure-time – perhaps for the idyll of life by the sea in a Spanish villa. This may have its good side, for people then discover more opportunities to live life to the full. But there is again a serious downside: modern lifestyles can often be self-centred, can cause environmental damage, transport chaos and congestion and the exploitation and depletion of the earth's natural resources.

In addition, a search for personal fulfilment can end up in an empty freedom or spiritual poverty, as well as in the weakening or even destruction of community life. In his hymn *Lord, for the years*, Timothy Dudley-Smith sums up this danger:

> Lord, for our land in this our generation
> Spirits oppressed by pleasure, wealth and care:
> For young and old, for commonwealth and nation,
> Lord of our land, be pleased to hear our prayer.

The danger of 'freedom from . . . ' is also that it leads to greater wealth and privilege for the few, while leaving the many heavily in debt, sometimes impoverished and isolated. The ideal of 'freedom from' spells, in short, privilege without responsibility.

In Mark's Gospel, however, Jesus points to a freedom which means personal human growth in wisdom and faith, in love and compassion and in godliness of life. This freedom also means service and commitment to others – the sharing of life and goods, mutual helpfulness and care, and the possibility of personal sacrifice for the good of the many. This 'freedom for' is expressed in stark terms in the Gospel, in terms of giving up one's own life in order to find life in God and in community. It is the taking up of a cross which paradoxically leads to fulfilment: 'For those who want to save their life will lose it, and those who lose their life for my sake, and for the sake of the gospel, will save it . . . ' (8.35). The following of Jesus promises to give a life which is like Jesus' own life – a life lived for others, but which somehow blesses the giver.

The implication of all this is that personal choice can be mis-guided and can lead down a cul-de-sac, which is like being drawn to the lights of a distant city only to find that they lead to a concrete jungle and to the superficial glitter of advertising hoard-ings. 'For what will it profit them to gain the whole world and forfeit their life?' (8.36).

This is a stark message which militates against modern ideas about freedom and freedom of choice; but it ultimately brings a different kind of freedom, characterized by Paul as 'the freedom of the glory of the children of God' (Romans 8.21). It is seen in the Gospels as being like the great banqueting feast in God's presence where justice, peace and joy become not those things Christians strive for and agonize over but present realities and real possessions.

The message of liberation or freedom is one which strikes a chord with the Western world in the twenty-first century. The fight against terrorism is regarded as a struggle for freedom; the overthrowing of extreme oppressive regimes in Afghanistan and Iraq are seen as battles of liberation for the peoples of those

countries. Even where 'freedom' in the world's eyes means something very different from freedom in terms of the gospel of
Christ, nevertheless freedom is the banner behind which many
will gather: 'freedom' is the value many will subscribe to.

The Church needs to present the gospel as a liberating power;
as that which can free people from the shackles of past mistakes,
from personal problems in the present and from oppression
and domination by evil influences, many of which are actively
promoted in the Western media. It should also be presented
positively as 'freedom for . . .': freedom for the promotion of fair
trade and justice; for the sanctity of every human life; for human
rights; for community solidarity; for educational opportunities
for all and at all ages; for the blossoming of human potential
and gifts; for human happiness and flourishing; for freedom of
worship and the living of a good and useful life.

Andrew Wingate, in his book *Free to Be: Discovering the God
of Freedom*[133] highlights the paradox of a Church which stands
for the glorious freedom of the sons and daughters of God and
yet so often appears to stand for a burdensome, duty-bound religion. Speaking of the gospel proclamation of Christian liberty,
he writes,

> So often the impression given is the opposite [of freedom]. To
> be a follower of Jesus Christ, or at least to be a member of the
> Church we call his Body, is to enter an oppressive society con-
> cerned with preserving the past . . . The popular view is that it
> is a society dominated by restrictions and negatives, to be a
> member of which encourages inhibition and narrowness. This
> is surely the verdict of most young people, as they pass by
> churches on the other side.

The whole of Canon Wingate's book is devoted to this theme of
freedom and to the idea that 'for freedom Christ has set us free'
(Galatians 5.1). Or to put it another way, 'If you continue in my
word, you are truly my disciples; and you will know the truth,
and the truth will make you free' (John 8.31–2). Through the
liberal use of illustrations, examples and stories, this brief but

important book points the way to a form of religion or spirituality which can liberate and bring a fuller and richer life to all.

It is true that the Church at the beginning of the twenty-first century has an image of straitjacketing, binding, restricting, limiting. Yet the gospel ideal is actually living under the rule of God, which means protection against oppressive and binding forces and powers in the world. It also means an environment where one can find oneself, make many friends, know the support of a caring community, be accepted and affirmed, belong to a place of creativity and new ventures in living. Is that not a kingdom which should have a wide appeal and offer many people beset by problems and worries relief and new hope?

Mark teaches us that this can only become possible when we have faith in Jesus, for he represents the kingdom of God in himself. The kingdom is available through him and there is no kingdom without him. That is the uncompromising message of this Gospel. In relating to Jesus we find liberation and inner freedom; acceptance and affirmation; healing and wholeness. The true message of Mark is an exciting and challenging message – not just in itself, but also for the mission of the Church.

Luke – good news for all

In moving on to Luke, we discover a more detailed unpacking of the inner meaning of the term 'God's kingdom' or 'the rule of God' and see how it relates to practical issues in the real world. In the sermon Jesus preaches in the synagogue at the inception of his ministry, he quotes from Isaiah (61.1 and 58.6 in Luke 4.17–19) – and in these few words Luke makes it clear to the reader that the kingdom is about the transformation of life in every area: in the realm of politics, social justice, economics, healing and health, and spiritual well-being. It is good news for the poor, release for prisoners, recovery of sight for the blind, the time for remission of debts, and the time of God's favour and blessing for all. In a few brief words, Jesus conveys the comprehensiveness of the kingdom. The additional phrase Luke inserts from Isaiah 58.6 – 'freedom for the oppressed' – comes from a section of Isaiah's prophecy particularly relating to *social* conditions. The prophet rails against social inequalities in Judah and the exploitation of the poor by the rich. He mentions the slave-driving mentality of employers who even make employees work on days of fasting (v. 3) and who are without mercy towards their creditors. The Lucan phrase is framed in Isaiah 58.6 by the words 'Is this not the fast that I choose . . . to share your bread with the hungry, and bring the homeless poor into your house; when you see the naked, to cover them?' Luke is also the champion of God's option for the poor. Through Jesus' announcement of Jubilee, the fate of the dispossessed, the refugee and the impecunious would be reversed. The wealthy are called upon to recognize their obligation to remember those worse off and to share with those who were victims of exploitation or of tragic circumstances.

This all means that Christian mission must be comprehensive too. It must have a broad brush stroke in its approach to the world's problems. It will not change everything, it cannot care for every ailment, nor solve everyone's problems – far from it – but it will have a vested interest in being involved in every part of life and in paying attention to everything which is not right in God's sight.

The nineteenth-century missionary movement which took Christian mission from Europe – and later, America – to every part of the globe had many faults as we examine it with the wisdom of hindsight. Western civilization at that time was all too easily regarded as Christian civilization: Western imperialistic interests often went hand in glove with Western missionary endeavour. However, in one way the missionaries had the right approach: they went not only to preach the gospel and to found churches and build church structures but also to provide health-care and to build and staff clinics and hospitals. They encouraged agricultural development and new methods of farming, good working practices and freedom from corruption in business dealings. They brought with them many teachers and educationists and built schools and colleges.

In my own time spent in Cameroon (between 1986 and 1991),

it was remarkable to see how these foundations had remained in place and had given people new values, new opportunities and a pride in certain aspects of the country's development. For better or for worse, the mission hospitals, schools and colleges were still regarded as superior to government-founded or funded institutions. The values attributed to the mission foundations were also ostensibly Christian values: pastoral concern for the individual; freedom from corruption or personal preference (nepotism); and the ideal of excellence in both moral and intellectual spheres of life.

Many Western churches find that their work in the area of social welfare and social justice has now been taken over by the State. They feel they can only work 'in the gaps' or at the very bottom of society, with people who have fallen through the net either by falling foul of the authorities or by avoiding engagement with the social services. Nevertheless, the twenty-first century has arrived with Western society in crisis and ill at ease: there seem to be more and more social problems and there are growing concerns over sexually transmitted diseases, the spread of AIDS, drug and substance abuse, crime and anti-social behaviour, binge-drinking and alcoholism, breakdown of family life and lack of community spirit or support. For a large number of people life seems to be aimless and empty.

Surely the Christian message, as presented by Jesus in Luke, has a power to reach people in whatever situation they may find themselves. Surely it can speak to politicians about solutions which start with God and which can make a difference in any and every aspect of society. The message may be a spiritual one in tone, but it has an application to every area of life. In truth it is far more than a spiritual message. It is a message about God's Jubilee, when debts are cancelled and the land returned to its original owners. Jesus challenges the rich to give away a significant proportion of their wealth and to perform social actions, such as the giving of loans and the cancelling of credit owed.

The idea of 'almsgiving' is also central in Luke, as it is in Matthew (see Luke 11.41; 12.33; Acts 3.2, 3, 10; 9.36; 10.2, 4,

31; 24.17). In today's terms this might correspond to the idea of church members' tithing their income, in order that inequalities in society may be addressed. The rich man is condemned in Luke's story about Lazarus (16.19–31). He shows no compassion or mercy. Thus, the use of money, or material aid, to redress economic imbalances is advocated in Luke not as a way to remedy the injustices in society, but as a witness to right relations and as a response to God's will. Similarly, the Church cannot hope to put right social injustices in any large-scale way, but can bear witness to the importance of remembering responsibilities to others when we have plenty, bearing witness to a single and united community, which is a Christian ideal. The Good Samaritan is one who gives without counting the cost and puts himself out and makes sacrifices. The spiritual message emerges from the action, but it is material help that makes the difference to the victim of the mugging (Luke 10.30–7). As David Bosch says, 'Where self-centred values reign supreme, the rich cannot claim to be involved in mission and cannot be in continuity with the Lucan Jesus and church.'[134] Luke reminds us in Acts 2 and 4 that the first church communities were prepared to share everything they had (2.44; 4.32) and the outcome was that there was no needy person among them (4.34).

If well-off Christians in the West were more willing to share and to give generously, this would not solve society's problems, nor those of the world at large, but it would be a powerful missionary tool – creating reserves for the Church to move beyond maintenance towards projects outside its own doors and inspiring goodwill between people of different classes and races. But first of all, the Church must become a mission enterprise, one which instils vision and confidence in its ordinary members, so that they feel that they are giving their money to a worthy and worthwhile cause.

Hospitality

If the Church feels weak and sometimes helpless in the face of enormous social and political problems, Luke's Gospel also points to at least one area where the individual can make a huge difference. This is in the area of hospitality.

The concept of hospitality is a very important one in the Bible as a whole. The Old Testament laws regarding strangers and visitors are framed in accordance with the spirit of hospitality (Leviticus 19.33, 34, etc.). Even before the giving of the law of Moses there were many instances of the entertaining of strangers (e.g. Genesis 18.2, 3). The Greek word for hospitality *philoxenia* (see Hebrews 13.2; Romans 12.13) means literally 'love for the stranger' or 'kindness to strangers'.

Luke's Gospel demonstrates how hospitality is capable of great things. In Luke, Jesus' insistence on eating and drinking with sinners enables him to come close to people, to build relationships and thereby to change lives. The case of Zacchaeus (Luke 19.1–10) is well known. An unpopular tax collector, largely friendless and ostracized by normal society, he climbs a tree to see Jesus go by; and then finds himself giving hospitality to the great preacher. In the course of the meal his whole outlook and understanding of life is turned upside down and he decides to reform his life and make good his past wrongdoing. He will repay those he has exploited and give half of his possessions to the poor.

In the Acts of the Apostles the simple theme of hospitality becomes the great engine for bringing together the Jews and the Gentiles in reconciliation, unity and peace. Peter has his dream about eating even what he considered unclean up until then; and immediately afterwards he finds himself receiving hospitality in the home of Cornelius the Gentile.

The cause of table fellowship between Jew and Gentile is taken up by Paul later on in Acts, when he convinces the 'pillars' of the Jerusalem church to accept Gentiles without (serious) preconditions into fellowship with Jews. Hospitality is in this way taken to new levels; for it enables the Early Church to draw all peoples and races together in one body and to bring a new witness to the world – that through mutual sharing and hospitality, people can settle their differences and learn to love one another in a setting where equality and mutual respect have to be observed. Luke shows how table fellowship must mean new life and transformation of life, because to people in the ancient world no one can sit down at table to eat with an enemy. The one who eats and drinks with you is automatically your friend.

In our own times and in Western culture, mealtimes still have a certain symbolic power attached to them. The formal meal is often seen as a 'special' occasion for celebration or for reunion – a graduation dinner, a wedding reception, the receiving of relatives or neighbours into the house. Many families, however, hardly ever gather to eat around a table. This makes such an occasion even more special. Part of the appeal and success of the initiation courses like *Alpha* is owing to the focus on a meal at the heart of each session. It is a time when people get to know one another and begin to forge friendships; when open discussion takes place on a basis of equality; when each person's point of view, comments or jokes are treated with respect and granted a ready and sympathetic audience. The meal is something enjoyable. It cuts across class divisions to a large extent, and allows people to relax in each other's company.

Nowadays, conversion to Christianity is regarded as most likely to take place when trust is acquired through friendship or through circles of friendship. It is seen as requiring time to build understanding and openness, through a process of questioning, debating, searching and sharing. When people have the time to laugh and cry together, to discover common links and interests, and to debate shared topics of discussion – then the ground may indeed be prepared for new thinking, new decisions, new directions; in short, for Christian mission. This should never be regarded as a deliberate form of manipulation of a person or a situation. Rather, it should be the natural consequence of people's uncovering of their inner selves – the opening up and exposing of hopes and fears, dreams and ambitions, loves and hates, beliefs and cherished ideals – to one another and to God. These private and sensitive matters can only surface – in an inhibited society where deep thoughts and feelings are usually hidden – through the kind of relaxation and friendship that a shared meal engenders and facilitates. Thus, hospitality can be a key to mission today.

The spirit of mission

Christian mission is not, however, purely a matter of good planning, building friendships, even demonstrating care and love. There is always an element of mystery and surprise when the mission is God's mission. It is always carried out in the company of a partner who is unpredictable, constantly on the move, impossible to control. In Luke this partner is of course named as the Holy Spirit. God's Spirit is the prime mover in mission, who takes on the work of Jesus and ministers the will of Jesus in a new way. First of all, according to Luke, it is pre-eminently through the Spirit that the risen Lord is present in the community. In Mark and Matthew, the Spirit is not so prominent, nor so thoroughly linked to mission. For Luke, the new challenges and tasks that mission presents to the infant church need the power and guidance of the Spirit, the one who is active here below, in and through the believer, in the Church and in the world.

The disciples cannot begin their mission until they are 'clothed with power from on high' (Luke 24.49; Acts 1.8). Just as Jesus was thrust into his mission by the Holy Spirit immediately following his baptism (Luke 3.21), so the disciples are driven into their mission by the initiative and guidance of the Spirit. At every point in the progress of the Church's mission, the Holy Spirit inspires and enables each new move, manifesting his presence with unusual experiences and signs following.

The work begins with the outpouring of the Spirit at Pentecost (Acts 2). This is a 'second baptism' corresponding to Jesus' reception of the Spirit at his baptism in the Jordan. Thereafter, the Spirit is involved in every aspect of mission: where the disciples ought to go, how they should proceed and what happens during the course of a particular campaign. When asked by the authorities – the priests, Temple leaders and Sadducees – 'By what power or by what name did you do this?' Peter answers, as Luke puts it, when he was 'filled with the Holy Spirit' (Acts 4.8). Stephen's 'signs and wonders' (Acts 6.8) are also attributed to the Spirit: 'They could not withstand the wisdom and the

Spirit with which he spoke' (Acts 6.10). Philip encounters the Ethiopian eunuch through the agency of the Spirit: 'The Spirit said to Philip, "Go over to this chariot and join it"'(Acts 8.29). Paul is filled with the Spirit after his conversion, when Ananias laid hands on him (9.17). The acceptance of the Gentiles into the Church is confirmed when the Spirit is poured out upon Cornelius and his family (10.44–8); and later, the ratification of this acceptance at the Council of Jerusalem is described as taking place under the impulse of the Spirit (15.8, 28). Paul and Barnabas were set apart and sent off on their special mission to Antioch by the Spirit (13.2–4). Paul is later stopped from going further east through the vision of a man from Macedonia calling for help – so Paul turns his attention to Europe (16.6–9). This pattern continues all through the Acts of the Apostles.

The Spirit is seen as a Spirit of power (*dunamis*), enacting miracles to progress and confirm the work of mission (e.g. Luke 4.14; Acts 10.38). This is seen in the boldness and openness of the disciples' witness (*parresia* – e.g. Acts 4.13, 29, 31, etc.), as well as in the conversion of Jews, Samaritans and Gentiles (e.g. 2.41; 8.12; 10.44). It is the Spirit who links together the coming of Jesus into the world (Luke 1.35), the confirmation of Jesus as God's Son (3.22) and the powerful initiation of Jesus' ministry (4.1). The whole of Jesus' work is under the aegis of the Spirit (4.14, 18) and then the disciples take on the mantle of Jesus to continue his mission in the power of the Spirit (Acts 1.4–5; 2.1–4). Thus, in general terms, the Spirit is the Spirit of God's mission. As David Bosch puts it: 'The gift of the Spirit is the gift of becoming involved in mission, for mission is the direct consequence of the outpouring of the Spirit.'[135] And this mission is portrayed not as an external command, but as an inner inspiration or compulsion; a conviction which impels or even propels the disciples into mission; at the same time, encouraging and strengthening them wherever they encounter obstacles, hostility or opposition.

Clearly, the Holy Spirit's inspiration is the most vital and essential ingredient for mission today, just as it was for mission in the first century. A Church which is lacking confidence needs the emboldening touch and convicting power of the Holy Spirit. A Church which is uncertain about how to proceed with mission needs the guidance and direction provided by the Holy Spirit. A Church which senses itself to be weak and powerless needs the strengthening and energizing work of the Holy Spirit.

One particular aspect of Luke's presentation of the Spirit's work should afford today's Church some succour and support. The Spirit is at work not only during the work of mission as such, but before and after the human engagement and activity we call 'mission'. Therefore, the Spirit should be presumed to have been effectively engaged and employed even before the Church arrives on the scene. By prevenient grace the Spirit prepares the ground for those going on mission.

It is in this context that we can understand the appearance of Saul at the stoning of Stephen (Acts 7.54—8.1). Even at that point in Luke's narrative the Holy Spirit is making ready the conditions in which Saul will be converted and become Paul. The story of the Ethiopian eunuch is another situation in which the Spirit has been at work. When the eunuch encounters Philip, he is already reading Isaiah's Servant Song (Isaiah 53.7–8) and is asking questions as to who the passage might be referring (Acts 8.26–40, esp. v. 34). In a sense Peter himself is in need of the prevenient grace of the Spirit, for he needs to be 'converted' in order to accept Gentiles into the Church fully and without preconditions. Before this happens, he refuses to engage in table fellowship with non-Jews. The story of his dream in which all foods are declared clean (10.4–16) takes place sandwiched within the story of Cornelius's conversion (10.1–48).

There have been many instances since New Testament times, showing evidence of the Holy Spirit's work before a Christian mission arrives on the scene. The first Methodist missionaries to the Cote d'Ivoire were surprised to discover a functioning Christian movement numbered in the thousands before they even began to preach the gospel. The colourful African 'preacher' known as 'Prophet Harris' (William Wade Harris) had been educated at a mission school in nearby Liberia, where he distinguished himself only as a wayward and disobedient boy. Later, he was converted and then took it upon himself to conduct his own preaching tour in neighbouring Cote d'Ivoire. He prophesied the coming of a white missionary and told those who received his message to keep the faith and wait. Nine years later, in 1924, the Methodist missionaries were given a rapturous welcome, as can be imagined, and the main work began with mass baptisms and then training classes to nurture the 'converts' in a more thoroughgoing understanding of their faith, and to organize an indigenous church.[136]

It should be recognized, however, that it is not only in preparing people for conversion that the work of the Spirit may be discerned. It might be seen in the enabling of new dialogue or new relations between Muslims and Christians; it might be seen in forging reconciliation between so-called Catholic and Protestant communities in Northern Ireland; it might be in the encouraging and upholding of the Church during times of persecution – as in the eastern bloc of Europe before 1989. There are also small and personal ways – perhaps 'coincidences' – in which the encouragement of the Spirit can be experienced. An openness to the Spirit can mean many signs of God's grace in the course of the work of mission. A professional and systematic approach to the undertaking of mission is certainly necessary, but over-planning and over-slick presentation can be counter-productive and can squeeze out the spontaneity and wonder of the Holy Spirit's participation and co-operation in Christian mission.

The importance of discerning the Holy Spirit's mind and will can hardly be overstated; and in an age of constant busyness and activity, the Church needs to relearn the art of prayer and contemplation. Further, Christians need to become more godly and spiritual in themselves, in order to discern the moving and prompting of the Holy Spirit. The attraction of retreats for times of prayer and peaceful recollection is becoming more widespread, and the notion of being 'spiritual' is seen as something desirable (unlike the notion of being 'religious'). Time also needs to be given to devotional study and the reading of the Bible if God's mind and will are to be discerned.

There is a strong inclination today to control and manipulate events so that nothing is left to chance. The management mentality of the secular world has its advantages in terms of efficient working, understanding of human psychology, creation of the right image, modernization of structures, etc., but this model – it must be borne in mind – is not a biblical one; and the world of secular work also has much to learn from the Christian Church about detached reflection, listening and consultation, bringing gifts into a harmonious working together, and, above all, doing things in the right spirit, that is, with cheerfulness, respect, love and selflessness and a desire to please God – in other words, in accordance with the Holy Spirit.

Matthew – Christian discipline

Matthew's Gospel has much to contribute to our understanding of mission today. The emphasis in Matthew on the church life – notably on baptism, discipleship, living a righteous life, learning and training – might, after Luke–Acts, seem rather institutionalized and dull. Worse, it could appear to be like a domestication of the Holy Spirit's work. Indeed, fairly soon after the Gospel's appearance, and certainly from the second century onwards, the Spirit's work was indeed viewed largely in terms of confirming faith at baptism, bestowing gifts at ordination, ensuring orthodoxy through the apostolic succession. However, Matthew's Gospel itself is not in the mindset of the second century.

Matthew's understanding of training, education and discipleship has more to do with deepening of faith and commitment. To use a metaphor, it is the putting down of roots in a fertile soil which matters to the evangelist – so that growth can be healthy, steady and strongly founded. If some forms of Christianity rather encouraged faith to shoot up quickly and to blossom like a hothouse flower, Matthew's version of faith contrasts with this and seeks to ensure that the roots are set first so that a deep and solid faith is established, and an upright moral life encouraged to emerge, just as the plant with good roots will develop thick and straight branches from which flowers could bud and blossom in their due season.

The style of churches like Matthew's would later have considerable influence on the Church universal, for eventually great stress was laid upon the catechism and upon baptismal preparation. And such training was viewed as two-pronged – both doctrinal and ethical – attempting to ensure right understanding (orthodoxy) as well as right behaviour (orthopraxy). There was an earthing and deepening of faith and an inculturation to the liturgy and worship of the Church; but there was also a strenuous desire to ensure the moral rectitude of the believer.

Now moral rectitude is not a term which would appeal to many people in the Church or society today. Nevertheless, there is a need for the Church to maintain standards and to establish its distinctive witness to a holy lifestyle and to promote a disciplined approach to personal morality. Integrity is a word with a more popular ring, and this should be a watchword in the life of the Church. There is now all too little emphasis on ethical teachings and understandings in the Church of the twenty-first century, with the possible exception of the Roman Catholic Church. Neither is there much emphasis on understanding one's own church traditions of faith and the background to the Church's worship and liturgy. To take one example, in June of 2003, the Methodist Conference received a report on the church's theological understanding of Holy Communion (entitled *His Presence Makes the Feast*). This was the first time in many years that such a common understanding had been sought on behalf of church members and perhaps the first time that such an overview had been attempted in a thoroughgoing manner. Earlier reports had concentrated on practicalities such as the presence of children at Communion, lay presidency at Communion and extended Communion. All of these were useful, but no overarching common understanding had been reached as to what Communion itself meant.

Matthew's call for observance of the commandments (5.17–20), his arrangement of Jesus' teaching into five blocks of material, and his references to Church discipline (e.g. 18.15–17) might at first glance strike a discordant note with those who want a theologically plural Church and discussion of individual perceptions rather than authoritative teaching. But it is part of the nature of the Church to be like a city on a hill – observed and judged in the world outside. It must sound a clear note when it speaks. Furthermore, individual Christians should be seen as those who can be trusted and relied upon.

With regard to Matthew's emphasis on the discipline of training for discipleship, there is now in the Church a welcome concentration on training, with many new initiatives to establish the Church as a locus for the training of lay people as well as of those entering ordained ministry. A great many schemes and courses have come into being for the training of readers, local preachers, lay workers, lay pastoral visitors, bereavement counsellors and so on. The Methodist Church has introduced Training and Development Officers across all its Districts (usually one to every two Districts) and has instituted Foundation Training for those who wish to explore their vocation – be it to lay or ordained ministry, prior to deciding which aspect of ministry to candidate for. There is not only an encouragement of training across a wide spectrum of Church life from the Church authorities, but there is a new emphasis on the ministry of the whole people of God. The variety of recognized ministries within the life of the Church is on the increase. The report sent to General Synod of the Church of England and passed with a large majority in 2003, called *Formation for Ministry within a Learning Church*, envisaged not only a rationalization and a regionalization of ordination training but also increased access to and the development of lay training as well. All this should take place within a single institution known as a 'Regional Training Partnership'.

The study of religion – or religions – has become a popular discipline once again in universities and colleges, and there are a good number of people in ministry training courses who are self-sponsored: in other words, training because they wish to understand their faith better and to deepen their knowledge of the Bible and Theology and Pastoral Practice and possibly of World Religions as well.

The yearning for roots and a deeper sense of identity has become the catalyst for many aspects of learning and training in the present rapidly changing and shifting world – which itself has largely lost its understanding of the processes of history. The Church needs to capitalize on this yearning: it has a long and fascinating history (though not all glorious); its theology addresses the real and important questions and issues of life; its search for ethical foundations and principles can make a valuable contribution to the search for objective standards and values upon which to build a civilized society.

The training and education of the laity is a tool for mission. If every Church member is able to become informed and articulate, then the Church has a vast new body of witnesses who are capable of giving a reason for the hope that is in them. Where in the past the trained clergy alone were relied upon to teach, preach and propagate the faith, now the time has come to return to Matthew's kind of church, where every member is like a scribe who takes out of his treasure store things old and new.

Sharing in mission – with others

One final and vital principle for mission worth noting and deriving from Matthew's Gospel especially is the insistence that mission is a shared concern. First, it is an activity of the whole Church community. There should be no one who stands aside, for all are called to be witnesses. Conversely, there should be none who feel isolated as 'the only one' interested in mission in any given church. This is no exaggeration – there are many churches which have such a narrow and prejudiced understanding of mission that the members prefer to avoid even the mention of the word.

Matthew makes it abundantly clear in the Great Commission culminating the Gospel that Jesus is addressing a group – and to some extent an indeterminate and open group. Although he speaks ostensibly to 'the eleven' on the mountain in Galilee, there is a sense in which all who read his exhortation to mission are drawn into this inner circle and are addressed along with them. The idea of baptizing and teaching in the list of instructions is evidently an appeal to the Church as a whole to engage in mission as a collective body in solidarity with any who make disciples.

In Matthew the calling of the twelve disciples is immediately followed up with a mission in which the twelve are sent out to the towns and villages of Israel to seek 'the lost sheep' (10.1–4, 5–15). They are instructed as a body; presumably they are to go out as a body, and everyone is to follow the same set of rules. When Matthew describes the feeding of the five thousand (14.13–21) he has Jesus tell the disciples, 'You give them something to eat'. Once again it is assumed that they will act in solidarity with one another. United they will stand – despite their fearfulness: they stutter, 'We have nothing here but five loaves and two fish' (14.17). Yet when the disciples have distributed these the mood changes: 'And all ate and were filled' (14.20). When the disciples try to establish an individual hierarchy or pecking order by asking, 'Who is the greatest in the kingdom of heaven?' Jesus rebukes them by teaching, 'Whoever becomes humble like this child is the greatest in the kingdom of heaven' (18.4). In other words, they are to honour one another and to work unselfishly for one another.

This way of 'doing mission' is the way of encouragement and mutual helpfulness. To act together builds the believers in fellowship and mutual support. It means that nobody is carrying too heavy a burden; all things can be shared and a common mind sought. Mission enacted on a broad front like this also means that no one is under criticism or attack on their own. The indifference and occasional hostility or mockery from the world will strike like poisoned arrows if Christians are acting from positions of isolation and separateness. The concerted effort of a team works like a protective shield; all protect and support their fellow workers, all uphold the one with doubts or fears. Even in the commissioning passage, Matthew significantly adds a careful rider to the comment that the gathered disciples worshipped the risen Christ – 'but some doubted' (28.17). Those who feel at sea on mission, or those who are not at all sure about some aspects of mission, should still be involved, for they are called to be witnesses alongside the others.

Sharing in mission – with the risen Christ

The worship of the risen Lord points us to the other side of mission as a shared concern. All Christian mission is shared with Jesus Christ, the instigator and motivator of mission. Because he leads Christian mission and sends out disciples, mission is therefore conducted in the context of prayer and worship. Matthew has little to say about the Holy Spirit's role in mission, but from the outset of his Gospel he is convinced that the coming of Christ means that God is with us. He quotes from Isaiah 7.14: '"The virgin shall conceive and bear a son, and they shall name him Emmanuel", which means, "God is with us"' (1.23). This indicates that the mission of the Church today is directed by Jesus as the risen Lord and is carried out in his presence. The question of the *Parousia* – Christ's coming again – is not in question here. The Son of Man quotations and the apocalyptic words in Matthew 24.1–44 as well as the parable of the Last Judgement (in 25.31–46) demonstrate clearly that Matthew anticipated a culmination point in history – but the age of the Church is the time when Christ's power is present and directly mediated through the new conditions created by his resurrection life. His authority now has a universal and 'abiding' application.

So much worship in Western Europe today is lacking a real sense of the presence of the risen Christ. This reality – so vividly experienced in the Early Church – is the very thing which brings uplift and inspiration to worship – and to mission. It is the presence of the risen Lord which makes the difference between dutiful obedience and joyful response.

Gerard Hughes draws attention to the reality of the risen Christ behind both doctrine and Scripture:

The Scriptures and church doctrine are given to us, not primarily as records of past events, but as a means of helping us to recognise God at work in our lives now. If it is true that Christ is risen and that we, too, are to rise again, then that truth is given in order to help us to live now . . . Therefore, the resurrection is a source of endless help and reassurance. If we are to live by that spirit, then no crisis, no loss, no failure can ever shatter us. Belief in the resurrection is not simply a hope for the future, but also a power in the present, but also a power which enables us to move from self-preoccupation to selflessness, from timidity to courage, from despair to hope, from sadness to joy . . . [137]

At certain times in the past the Great Commission has been regarded as a command to obey and to accept: the duty laid on all Christians by an authoritative Christ. While this approach might motivate some, for others it instils fear and trepidation about mission. The spirit in which mission should be put into effect is that which Gerard Hughes counsels – a spirit of selflessness, courage and joy. This is a response to the experienced reality of Christ's resurrection. Mission should therefore come, as Paul has it, from the constraint of love: 'For the love of Christ urges us on, because we are convinced that one has died for all; therefore all have died. And he died for all, so that those who live might live no longer for themselves, but for him who died and was raised for them' (2 Corinthians 5.14). Paul also speaks of carrying treasure in clay jars and describes our experience as light 'shining in our hearts to give the light of the knowledge of the glory of God in the face of Jesus Christ' (2 Corinthians 4.6).

Matthew may not use such poetic language, but he would concur with these sentiments; it is devotion and love for the risen Lord which provides the motive force for the Christian life and for Christian mission.

In Matthew we see a link between the awareness of Christ as living Lord and Christ as the one who empowers the mission of the Church to 'make disciples of all nations'. The worship of Christ as risen Lord therefore has an end beyond worship: it leads on to an involvement in mission, in reaching out to others. In this way, Jesus' incarnation continues in the disciples' self-giving to the world. David Bosch once more has an apposite word about the end of Matthew's Gospel: 'The experience of the presence of Christ is so overpowering that it embraces the future.'[138] The coming again of Christ at the end is almost subsumed under the present reality of his being with his disciples. The Church is at once sustained and challenged by the abiding presence of Christ in its midst. And the resurrection of Christ carries the people of God into the final age of salvation history.

If present-day disciples were able to recapture this intense experience described in Matthew's Gospel, that of the immediate and comforting presence of the risen Christ (both in worship and in mission), then they would recover the motivation and boldness to break through barriers of timidity and fear in order to go into the world and make disciples. The dynamic thrust of Matthew's Great Commission would then regain its power to inspire new ventures of faith and new acts of great courage.

It seems fitting to end with Hugh Sherlock's hymn, written out of the Caribbean experience, but summing up both the universal mission imperative and the breadth, height and depth of mission activity:

> Lord, thy church on earth is seeking
> Thy renewal from above;
> Teach us all the art of speaking
> With the accent of thy love.
> We would heed thy great commission:
> Go ye into every place –
> Preach, baptize, fulfil my mission,
> Serve with love and share my grace.
>
> Freedom give to those in bondage,
> Lift the burdens caused by sin.
> Give new hope, new strength and courage,
> Grant release from fears within:
> Light for darkness; joy for sorrow;
> Love for hatred; peace for strife.
> These and countless blessings follow
> As the Spirit gives new life.
>
> In the streets of every city
> Where the bruised and lonely dwell,
> Let us show the Saviour's pity,

Let us of his mercy tell.
In all lands and with all races
Let us serve, and seek to bring
All the world to render praises,
Christ to thee, Redeemer, King.[139]

Notes

1. W. Horbury, 'The Jewish Dimension' in I. Hazlett (ed.), *Early Christianity: Origins and Evolution to AD 600*, London: SPCK, 1991, pp. 40–51.

2. Flavius Josephus, *Contra Apion* 2.282.

3. Augustine, *City of God* 6.11.

4. W. H. C. Frend, *The Rise of Christianity* London: Darton, Longman & Todd, 1984, p. 16.

5. Flavius Josephus, *Jewish Wars* 3.8.9.

6. I. Levy, *The Synagogue: Its History and Function*, London: Vallentine Mitchell, 1964, ch. 1.

7. See A. J. Saldarini, *Matthew's Christian-Jewish Community*, Chicago: University Press of Chicago, 1994, pp. 13–14. See also, John J. Rousseau and R. Arav, *Jesus and His World: An Archaeological and Cultural Dictionary*, Minneapolis: Fortress Press, 1995, pp. 268–72.

8. See Chapter 6, pp. 185–94.

9. R. De Ridder, *Discipling the Nations*, Grand Rapids, MI: Baker Books, 1971.

10. A. Le Grys, *Preaching to the Nations: The Origins of Mission in the Early Church*, London: SPCK, 1998, p. 5.

11. J. Muddiman, 'The First Century Crisis: Christian Origins', in J. Houlden (ed.), *Judaism and Christianity*, London: Routledge, 1991, pp. 29–48 (42).

12. Muddiman, 'First Century Crisis', p. 45.

13. Levy, *The Synagogue*, ch. 1.

14. Flavius Josephus, *Jewish Wars*, in *Complete Works*, 2 vols, London: Heinemann, 1958, 1965, vol. 2, p. 560.

15. A. Harnack, *Mission und Ausbreitung des Christentums in der ersten drei Jahrhundert*, Leipzig, 1924; J. Jeremias, *Jesus' Promise to the Nations*, London: SCM Press, 1958.

16. S. McKnight, *A Light among the Gentiles: Jewish Missionary Activity in the Second Temple Period*, Minneapolis: Fortress Press,

1991; M. Goodman, 'Proselytising in Rabbinic Judaism', *Journal of Jewish Studies*, 40.2, 1989, pp. 175–85; I. Levinskaya, *The Book of Acts in Its First Century Setting: vol. 5, The Diaspora Setting*, Carlisle: Paternoster, 1996.

17. See comments on this in J. Marcus, 'The Jewish War and the Sitz im Leben of Mark', *Journal of Biblical Literature*, 111, 1992, pp. 441–62.

18. Frend, *Rise of Christianity*, p. 120.

19. See W. Rordorf, W., *Sunday: The History of the Day of Rest and Worship in the Earliest Centuries of the Church*, London: SCM Press, 1968.

20. Matthew 8.22 sounds like an incitement to break the Law. Jesus' own practice, while showing great respect for the Law as written in Scripture, is clearly at odds with the Pharisees' practice (cf. Matthew 8.3 with Leviticus 5.3 or Matthew 9.20–2 with Leviticus 12.5 and 15.19–25).

21. See Matthew 5.31–2, 33–7, 38–42. For the background to this, see W. D. Davies and D. C. Allison, *Matthew*, ICC, Edinburgh: T&T Clark, 1988, vol. 1, pp. 505–9.

22. A. Kostenberger and P. T. O'Brien, *Salvation to the Ends of the Earth: A Biblical Theology of Mission*, Loughborough: IVP/Apollos, 2001, p. 87.

23. Saldarini, *Matthew's Jewish-Christian Community*, p. 69.

24. See J. M. G. Barclay, *Jews in the Mediterranean Diaspora – From Alexander to Trajan 323 BCE–117 CE*, Edinburgh: T&T Clark, 1996.

25. Saldarini, *Matthew's Jewish-Christian Community*, p. 71.

26. Le Grys, *Preaching to the Nations*, see pp. 42–5 especially.

27. W. D. Davies and D. C. Allison, *Matthew*, ICC, Edinburgh: T&T Clark, 1997, vol. 3, pp. 573–7 (576).

28. For example, Matthew's misquote about Bethlehem. Instead of being of little importance, as in the original, Matthew has it that Bethlehem is 'by no means least among the rulers of Judah' (2.6).

29. On this, see G. von Rad, 'Die Stadt auf dem Berge', *Evangelische Theologie*, 8, 1948–9, pp. 439–47.

30. See Jeremias, *Jesus' Promise to the Nations*, p. 69 note 1.

31. Kostenberger and O'Brien, *Salvation to the Ends of the Earth*, p. 87.

32. Le Grys, *Preaching to the Nations*, p. 687.

33. On this, see W. Carter, *Matthew and the Margins: A Socio-Political and Religious Reading*, Sheffield: Sheffield Academic Press, 2000, pp. 552–3.

34. Carter, *Matthew and the Margins*, pp. 30–43, 77–8.

35. Saldarini, *Matthew's Christian-Jewish Community*, p. 81.

36. Davies and Allison, *Matthew*, vol. 3, pp. 688–9.

37. On this, see S. Moyise, *The Old Testament in the New: An Introduction*, London: Continuum, 2001, pp. 21–2.

38. J. Marcus, *The Gospel according to Mark*, Anchor Commentary, New York: Doubleday, 2001, vol. 1, p. 491.

39. See, for example, T. J. Weedon, *Mark: Traditions in Conflict*, Philadelphia: Fortress Press, 1971.

40. Marcus, *Gospel according to Mark*, vol. 1, pp. 33–7.

41. Marcus, *Gospel according to Mark*, vol. 1, p. 38.

42. Marcus, *Gospel according to Mark*, vol. 1, p. 354.

43. Ben Witherington III, *Mark: A Socio-Rhetorical Commentary*, Cambridge, MA: Eerdmans, 2001, p. 209.

44. This is suggested by Marcus, *Gospel according to Mark*, vol. 1, p. 490.

45. Marcus, *Gospel according to Mark*, vol. 1, p. 462.

46. Donald Senior and Carroll Stuhlmueller, *The Biblical Foundations for Mission*, London: SCM Press, 1983, p. 220.

47. Senior and Stuhlmueller, *Biblical Foundations for Mission*, p. 223.

48. Morna Hooker, *A Commentary on the Gospel according to St Mark*, London: A. & C. Black, 1991, pp. 393–4.

49. R. Gundry, *Mark: A Commentary on his Apology for the Cross*, Grand Rapids, MI: Eerdmans, 1993.

50. Quoted in P. Esler, *Community and Gospel in Luke–Acts: The Social and Political Motivations of Lucan Theology*, Cambridge: Cambridge University Press, 1987, p. 31.

51. S. G. Wilson, *The Gentiles and the Gentile Mission in Luke–Acts*, Cambridge: Cambridge University Press, 1973, p. 232.

52. E. Haenchen, *The Acts of the Apostles*, Oxford: Blackwell, 1971 (German edn 1965), p. 100.

53. D. Bosch, *Transforming Mission: Paradigm Shifts in the Theology of Mission*, Maryknoll, New York: Orbis Books, 1991, p. 85.

54. J. Jervell, *The Theology of the Acts of the Apostles*, Cambridge: Cambridge University Press, 1996, p. 5.

55. The German Commentary of 1953 – translated as Hans Conzelmann, *The Theology of St Luke*, London: Faber & Faber, 1960.

56. Conzelmann, *The Theology of St Luke*, p. 95.

57. Bosch, *Transforming Mission*, p. 88.

58. Bosch, *Transforming Mission*, p. 113.

59. Jeremias, *Jesus' Promise to the Nations*, pp. 41–6.

60. Bosch, *Transforming Mission*, pp. 110–13.

61. Bosch, *Transforming Mission*, p. 112.

62. Esler, *Community and Gospel in Luke–Acts*, see especially pp. 71–109.

63. On this, see M. Douglas, 'Deciphering a Meal', *Implicit Meanings: Essays in Anthropology*, London: Routledge, 1975, pp. 249–75.

64. On this, see J. D. G. Dunn, 'The Incident at Antioch – Galatians 2.11–18', *Journal for the Study of the New Testament*, 18, 1983, pp. 3–75.

65. Esler, *Community and Gospel in Luke–Acts*, p. 77.

66. *Historiae* V.52.

67. M. Bockmuehl, *Jewish Law in Gentile Churches*, Edinburgh: T&T Clark, 2000, pp. 145–73.

68. J. Fitzmyer, *The Gospel according to Luke*, Anchor Bible, New York: Doubleday, 1981, vol. 1, pp. 823–7.

69. On this, see T. W. Manson, *The Sayings of Jesus*, London: SCM Press, 1977, p. 130.

70. C. F. Evans, *Saint Luke*, London: SCM Press, 1990, p. 697.

71. Ben Witherington III, *The Acts of the Apostles: A Socio-Rhetorical Commentary*, Carlisle: Paternoster, 1998, p. 107.

72. See E. Pagels, *The Johannine Gospel in Gnostic Exegesis*, SBLMS, 17, Nashville: Abingdon Press, 1973.

73. See Eusebius, *Historia Ecclesiastica* 6.14.5, in J. Stevenson (ed.), *A New Eusebius*, London: SPCK, 1977, pp. 196–7.

74. D. Rensberger, *Overcoming the World: Politics and Community in the Gospel of John*, London: SPCK, 1989, p. 17.

75. C. H. Dodd, *Historical Tradition in the Fourth Gospel*, Cambridge: Cambridge University Press, 1963.

76. C. K. Barrett, *The Gospel according to St John*, London: SPCK, 1955 (1st edn) and 1978 (2nd edn).

77. R. E. Brown, *The Gospel according to John*, 2 vols, Anchor Bible, New York: Doubleday, 1966, 1970; see also his *The Community of the Beloved Disciple*, New York: Paulist Press, 1979.

78. J. L. Martyn, *History and Theology in the Fourth Gospel*, Nashville: Abingdon Press, 1979.

79. O. Cullmann, *The Johannine Circle*, London: SCM Press, 1976.

80. R. Alan Culpepper, *Anatomy of the Fourth Gospel: A Study in Literary Design*, Philadelphia: Fortress, 1983.

81. C. H. Talbert, *Reading John*, London: SPCK, 1992.

82. M. Stibbe, *John as Storyteller*, Cambridge: Cambridge University Press, 1992.

83. John Ashton, *Understanding the Fourth Gospel*, Oxford: Clarendon Press, 1991.

84. Gary Burge, *Interpreting the Gospel of John*, Grand Rapids, MI: Fortress, 1996.

85. Maurice Casey, *Is John's Gospel True?*, London: Routledge, 1996.

86. Richard Bauckham, *The Gospels for all Christians: Rethinking the Gospel Audience*, Edinburgh: T&T Clark, 1998, see Chapter 5, pp. 147–72.

87. See on this, especially W. Meeks, 'The Man from Heaven in Johannine Sectarianism', *Journal of Biblical Literature*, 91, 1972, pp. 44–72.

88. On the God of John's Gospel, see particularly Marianne Meye Thompson, *The God of the Gospel of John*, Cambridge: Eerdmans, 2001.

89. Thompson, *The God of the Gospel of John*.

90. Richard A. Burridge, *What Are the Gospels? A Comparison with Graeco-Roman Biography*, Cambridge: Cambridge University Press, 1992.

91. M.-A. Boismard, *L'Evangile de Jean*, Paris: Cerf, 1977.

92. D. A. Carson, *The Gospel according to John*, Cambridge: Eerdmans, 1991, p. 234.

93. On this, see further, Brown, *Gospel according to John*, vol.1, pp. 192–6.

94. Brown, *Gospel according to John*, vol.1, p. 192.

95. Brown, *Gospel according to John*, vol.1, p. 197.

96. Brown, *Gospel according to John*, vol.1, p. 198.

97. See Richard A. Burridge, *Four Gospels, One Jesus*, London: SPCK, 1994.

98. Talbert, *Reading John*.

99. Talbert, *Reading John*, pp. 111–20.

100. Talbert, *Reading John*, pp. 105–10.

101. Talbert, *Reading John*, p. 111.

102. Talbert, *Reading John*, p. 117.

103. Talbert, *Reading John*, p. 119.

104. On this, see I. de la Potterie, 'Truth in John', in John Ashton (ed.), *The Interpretation of John*, London: SPCK, 1986, pp. 53–66.

105. Brown, *Gospel according to John*, vol. 2, p. 1036.

106. Kostenberger and O'Brien, *Salvation to the Ends of the Earth*, p. 212.

107. See further on this, Carson, *Gospel according to John*, pp. 661–3.

108. Bauckham, *Gospels for all Christians*, pp. 28–9.

109. Bauckham, *Gospels for all Christians*, pp. 28–9.

110. Senior and Stuhlmueller, *Biblical Foundations for Mission*, p. 269.

111. J. Moltmann, *The Church in the Power of the Spirit*, London: SCM Press, 1977, p. 65.

112. Bosch, *Transforming Mission*, p. 390.

113. R. Williams, *On Christian Theology*, Oxford: Blackwell, 2000, p. 180.

114. Williams, *On Christian Theology*, p. 180.

115. Kenneth Leech, *Through the Long Exile*, London: DLT, 2001, p. 155.

116. N. T. Wright, *Jesus and the Victory of God*, London: SPCK, 1996, p. 431.

117. Moltmann, *Church in the Power of the Spirit*, p. 249.

118. Moltmann, *Church in the Power of the Spirit*, pp. 257–8.

119. See E. Glenn Hinson, *Evangelization in the Roman Empire*, Macon: Mercer University Press, 1981, p. 75.

120. L. Hurtado, 'The Origin and Development of Christ-Devotion: Forces and Factors', in K. J. O'Mahony, *Christian Origins: Worship, Belief and Society*, Sheffield: Sheffield Academic Press, 2003, pp. 52–82.

121. Hurtado, 'Origin and Development of Christ-Devotion', p. 54.

122. Hurtado, 'Origin and Development of Christ-Devotion', p. 62.

123. See on this, N. T. Wright, *The Resurrection of the Son of God*, London: SPCK, 2003, Chapter 2, pp. 32–84.

124. J. A. Kirk, *What Is Mission? – Theological Explorations*, London: DLT, 1999, p. 26.

125. E. Castro, in Charles van Engen, Dean S. Gilliland and Paul Pierson (eds), *The Good News of the Kingdom: Mission Theology for the Third Millenium*, Maryknoll, New York: Orbis, 1993, p. 133.

126. 'The five marks of mission' are listed as follows: 1. To proclaim the Good News of the Kingdom; 2. To teach, baptize and nurture new believers; 3. To respond to human need by loving service; 4. To seek to transform unjust structures of society; 5. To strive to safeguard the integrity of creation and sustain and renew the earth. These are discussed in Churches Together in Britain and Ireland with the Board of Mission of the Archbishops' Council, *Presence and Prophecy: A Heart for Mission in Theological Education*, London: Church House Publishing, 2002.

127. Kirk, *What Is Mission?*, p. 28.

128. Bosch, *Transforming Mission*, p. 392.

129. Bosch, *Transforming Mission*, p. 390.

130. The main document on mission emerging from the Second Vatican Council was entitled *Ad Gentes*, from which this quote is taken.

131. C. Lacugna, *Freeing Theology*, San Francisco: Harper, 1993, p. 106.

132. For discussion of this variant – i.e. between *orgistheis* and *splagchnistheis*, see Bruce M. Metzger, *Textual Commentary on the Greek New Testament*, London: United Bible Societies, 1975, pp. 76–7.

133. Andrew Wingate, *Free to Be: Discovering the God of Freedom*, London: DLT, 2002, pp. 1–2.

134. Bosch, *Transforming Mission*, p. 118.

135. Bosch, *Transforming Mission*, p. 114.

136. C. Davey, *The March of Methodism*, London: Epworth Press, 1951, pp. 155–9.

137. G. Hughes, *God, Where Are You?*, London: DLT, 1997, p. 142.

138. D. Bosch, *Transforming Mission*, p. 81.

139. *Hymns and Psalms*, no. 744 Copyright: Trustees for Methodist Church Purposes.

Bibliography

General works

Barton, S., *The Spirituality of the Gospels*, London: SPCK, 1992.

Bauckham, Richard (ed.), *The Gospels for All Christians: Rethinking the Gospel Audience*, Edinburgh: T&T Clark, 1998.

Bosch, D., *Transforming Mission: Paradigm Shifts in the Theology of Mission*, Maryknoll, New York: Orbis, 1991.

Burridge, Richard A., *Four Gospels: One Jesus*, London: SPCK, 1994.

Burridge, Richard A., *What Are the Gospels? A Comparison with Graeco-Roman Biography*, Cambridge: Cambridge University Press, 1992.

Hahn, F., *Mission in the New Testament*, London: SCM Press, 1965.

Hall, S., *Doctrine and Practice in the Early Church*, London: SPCK, 1991.

Harnack, A., *Mission und Ausbreitung des Christentums in der ersten drei Jahrhundert*, Leipzig, 1924.

Harrington, D., *Light of all Nations: Essays on the Church in New Testament Research*, Wilmington, DE: Glazier, 1982.

Jeremias, J., *Jesus' Promise to the Nations*, London: SCM Press, 1958.

Kostenberger, A., and P. T. O'Brien, *Salvation to the Ends of the Earth: A Biblical Theology of Mission*, Leicester: IVP/Apollos, 2001.

Lohse, E., *The New Testament Environment*, London: SCM Press, ET 1976 (1974).

Longenecker, R. (ed.), *Patterns of Discipleship in the New Testament*, Cambridge: Eerdmans, 1996.

McKnight, S., *A Light among the Gentiles: Jewish Missionary Activity in the Second Temple Period*, Minneapolis: Fortress Press, 1991.

Meeks, Wayne A., *The First Urban Christians: The Social World of the Apostle Paul*, New Haven and London: Yale University Press, 1983.

Moule, C. F. D., *Worship in the New Testament*, Nottingham: Grove Books, 1977.

Nash, R. H., *Christianity in the Hellenistic World*, Grand Rapids, MI: Zondervan, 1987.

Riches, J., *Jesus and the Transformation of Judaism*, London: Darton, Longman & Todd, 1980.

Rousseau, John J., and R. Arav, *Jesus and His World: An Archaeological and Cultural Dictionary*, Minneapolis: Fortress Press, 1995.

Rowland, Christopher, *Christian Origins*, London: SPCK, 1985.

Senior, Donald, and Carroll Stuhlmueller, *The Biblical Foundations for Mission*, London: SCM Press, 1983.

Stevenson, J. (ed.), *A New Eusebius*, London: SPCK, 1977.

Tuckett, C., *Christology in the New Testament*, Edinburgh: Edinburgh University Press, 2001.

Witherington III, Ben, *Women in the Earliest Churches*, Cambridge: Cambridge University Press, 1988.

1. *Jewish mission as the springboard for Christian mission*

Barclay, J. M. G., *Jews in the Mediterranean Diaspora – From Alexander to Trajan 323 BCE–117 CE*, Edinburgh: T&T Clark, 1996.

Burtchaell, J. T., *From Synagogue to Church*, Cambridge: Cambridge University Press, 1992.

Chilton, B. D., *A Galilean Rabbi and His Bible: Jesus' Use of the Interpreted Scriptures*, Wilmington, DE: Glazier, 1984.

Cochrane, C. N., *Christianity and Classical Culture*, Oxford: Clarendon Press, 1940.

Crossan, J. D., *The Birth of Christianity*, Edinburgh: T&T Clark, 1999.

Crossan, J. D., and J. L. Reed, *Excavating Jesus: Beneath the Stones, Behind the Texts*, London: SPCK, 2001.

De Ridder, R., *Discipling the Nations*, Grand Rapids, MI: Baker Books, 1971.

Dunn, J. D. G., *The Partings of the Ways between Christianity and Judaism*, London: SCM Press, 1991.

Elwell, Walter A., and Robert W. Yarborough (eds), *Readings from the First-Century World: Primary Sources for New Testament Study*, Grand Rapids, MI: Baker Books, 1998.

Frend, W. H. C., *The Rise of Christianity* London: Darton, Longman & Todd, 1984.

Hazlett, I. (ed.), *Early Christianity: Origins and Evolution to AD 600*, London: SPCK, 1991.

Hengel, Martin, *Earliest Christianity*, London: SCM Press, 1986.

Houlden, J. L. (ed.), *Judaism and Christianity*, London: Routledge, 1991.

Flavius Josephus, *Complete Works*, 2 vols, London: Heinemann, 1958, 1965.

Le Grys, A., *Preaching to the Nations: The Origins of Mission in the Early Church*, London: SPCK, 1998.

Levine, Lee I. (ed.), *The Synagogue in Late Antiquity*, Philadelphia, PA: ASOR, 1987.

Levinskaya, I. , *The Book of Acts in Its First Century Setting: vol. 5, The Diaspora Setting*, Carlisle: Paternoster, 1996.

Levy, I., *The Synagogue: Its History and Function*, London: Vallentine Mitchell, 1963.

Markschies, C., *Between Two Worlds: Structures of Earliest Christianity*, London: SCM Press, 1999 (1997).

Moyise, S., *The Old Testament in the New: An Introduction*, London: Continuum, 2001.

Nickelsburg, G., and G. W. MacRae, *Christians among Jews and Gentiles*, Philadelphia: Fortress Press, 1986.

Rordorf, W., *Sunday: The History of the Day of Rest and Worship in the Earliest Centuries of the Church*, London: SCM Press, 1968.

Sanders, J. T., *Schismatics, Sectarians, Dissidents, Deviants: The First One Hundred Years of Jewish–Christian Relations*, London: SCM Press, 1993.

Stanton, G., *The Gospels and Jesus*, Oxford: Oxford University Press, 1989.

Stegemann, E., and W. Stegemann, *The Jesus Movement: A Social History of its First Century*, Edinburgh: T&T Clark, 1999.

2. Matthew's Gospel – making disciples

Commentaries

Blomberg, C., *Matthew*, Nashville, TN: Broadman Press, 1992.

Carter, W., *Matthew and the Margins: A Socio-Political and Religious Reading*, Sheffield: Sheffield Academic Press, 2000.

Davies, W. D., and D. C. Allison, *Matthew*, ICC, 3 vols, Edinburgh: T&T Clark, 1988, 1991, 1997.

Gundry, R., *Matthew: A Commentary on His Handbook for a Mixed Church under Persecution*, Grand Rapids, MI: Eerdmans, 1994.

Hagner, D., *Matthew 1–13*, Dallas, TX: Word Books, 1993.

Hagner, D., *Matthew 14–28*, Dallas, TX: Word Books, 1995.

Jones, I., *The Gospel of Matthew*, London: Epworth Press, 1994.

Keener, B., *A Commentary on the Gospel of Matthew*, Grand Rapids, MI: Baker, 1999.

Long, T., *Matthew*, London: Westminster John Knox (WJK), 1997.

Luz, U., *Matthew*, 2 vols, Minnesota: Augsburg Fortress; and Edinburgh: T&T Clark, 1989, 1990.

Schnackenburg, R., *The Gospel of Matthew*, Cambridge: Eerdmans, 2002.

Senior, D., *Matthew*, Nashville, TN: Abingdon Press, 1998.

Other useful works

Allison, D. C., *The New Moses: A Matthaean Typology*, Edinburgh: T&T Clark, 1993.

Brooks, S. H., *Matthew's Community*, JSNT Supplement, Sheffield: Sheffield Academic Press, 1987.

France, R. T., *Matthew, Evangelist and Teacher*, Exeter: Paternoster Press, 1989.

Kingsbury, J. D., *Matthew as Story*, Philadelphia: Fortress Press, 1986.

Levine, A.-J. (ed.), *A Feminist Companion to Matthew*, Sheffield: Sheffield Academic Press, 2001.

Luz, U., *The Theology of the Gospel of Matthew*, Cambridge: Cambridge University Press, 1995.

Meier, J., *The Vision of Matthew: Christ, Church and Morality in the First Gospel*, New York: Paulist Press, 1979.

Minear, P. S., *Matthew: The Teacher's Gospel*, London: Darton, Longman & Todd, 1981.

Riches, J., *Matthew*, Sheffield: Sheffield Academic Press, 1996.

Saldarini, A. J., *Matthew's Christian-Jewish Community*, Chicago: University Press of Chicago, 1994.

Stanton, G., *A Gospel for a New People: Studies in Matthew*, Edinburgh: T&T Clark, 1992.

Stendahl, K., *The School of St Matthew*, Philadelphia: Fortress Press, 1968.

3. Mark's Gospel – the kingdom revealed

Commentaries

Edwards, J. R., *The Gospel according to Mark*, Cambridge: Eerdmans, 2002.

Evans, C., *Mark 8:27 – 16:20*, Dallas, TX: Word Books, 2001.

Guelich, R. A., *Mark 1 – 8:26*, Dallas, TX: Word Books, 1989.

Gundry, R., *Mark: A Commentary on His Apology for the Cross*, Grand Rapids, MI: Eerdmans, 1993.

Hare, D., *Mark's Gospel*, Kentucky: WJK Press, 1996.

Hooker, Morna, *A Commentary on the Gospel according to St Mark*, London: A. & C. Black, 1991.

Hurtado, L., *Mark*, Massachusetts: Peabody, 1989.

Juel, D. H., *The Gospel of Mark*, Nashville, TN: Abingdon, 1999.

Lane, W., *The Gospel of Mark*, Cambridge: Eerdmans, 1974.

Marcus, Joel, *Mark 1—8*, New York: Doubleday, 2000.

Myers, C., *Binding the Strong Man: A Political Reading of Mark's Story of Jesus*, Maryknoll, NY: Orbis Books, 1988.

Rhoads, D., J. Dewey and D. Michie, *Mark as Story*, 2nd edn, Philadelphia: Fortress Press, 1999.

Telford, W. R., *Mark's Gospel*, Sheffield: Sheffield Academic Press, 1995.

Weedon, T. J., *Mark: Traditions in Conflict*, Philadelphia: Fortress Press, 1971.

Witherington III, Ben, *Mark: A Socio-Rhetorical Commentary*, Cambridge: Eerdmans, 2001.

Other useful works

Barton, S., *Discipleship and Family Ties in Mark and Matthew*, Cambridge: Cambridge University Press, 1994.

Black, C. C., *Mark: Images of an Apostolic Interpreter*, Edinburgh: T&T Clark, 2001.

Fenton, J., *More about Mark*, London: SPCK, 2001.

Francis, L. J., and P. Atkins, *Exploring Mark's Gospel*, London: Continuum, 2001.

Hengel, Martin, *Studies in the Gospel of Mark*, London: SCM Press, 1985.

Kee, H. C., *The Community of the New Age*, London: SCM Press, 1977.

Kingsbury, J. D., *Conflict in Mark*, Minneapolis: Augsburg Fortress, 1989.

Levine, A.-J., *A Feminist Companion to Mark*, Sheffield: Sheffield Academic Press, 2001.

Painter, J., *Mark's Gospel: Worlds in Conflict*, London: Routledge, 1997.

Swartley, W. M., *Mark: The Way for All Nations*, Scottdale, PA: Herald Press, 1981.

Telford, W. R. (ed.), *The Interpretation of Mark*, 2nd edn, Edinburgh: T&T Clark, 1985.

4. Luke–Acts – the fulfilment of God's mission

Commentaries

Bock, D. L., *Luke 1:1–9:50*, Grand Rapids, MI: Baker Books, 1994.

Bock, D. L., *Luke 9:51–24:52*, Grand Rapids, MI: Baker Books, 1996.

Bovon, F., *Luke Chapter 1*, Minneapolis: Hermeneia, Augsburg Fortress, 2002.

Bruce, F. F., *The Acts of the Apostles*, 3rd edn, Leicester: Apollos; and Grand Rapids, MI: Eerdmans, 1990.

Conzelmann, H., *Acts of the Apostles*, Hermeneia, Philadelphia: Fortress Press, 1987 (German edn 1972).

Conzelmann, Hans, *The Theology of St Luke*, London: Faber & Faber, 1960 (German edn 1953).

Evans, C. F., *Saint Luke*, London: SCM Press, 1990.

Fitzmyer, J., *The Gospel according to Luke*, 2 vols, New York: Doubleday, 1981, 1985.

Fitzmyer, J., *The Acts of the Apostles*, New York: Doubleday, 1998.

Green, J., *The Gospel of Luke*, Grand Rapids, MI: Eerdmans, 1997.

Haenchen, E., *The Acts of the Apostles*, Oxford: Blackwell 1971 (German edn 1965).

Lieu, J., *The Gospel of Luke*, Peterborough: Epworth Press, 1997.

Nolland, J., *Luke 1–9:20*, Dallas, TX: Word Books 1989.

Nolland, J., *Luke 9:21–18:34*, Dallas, TX: Word Books 1993.

Nolland, J., *Luke 18:35–24:53*, Dallas, TX: Word Books 1993.

Tannehill, R., *Luke*, Nashville: Abingdon, 1996.

Witherington III, Ben, *The Acts of the Apostles: A Socio-Rhetorical Commentary*, Carlisle: Paternoster, 1998.

Other useful works

Bockmuehl, M., *Jewish Law in Gentile Churches*, Edinburgh: T&T Clark, 2000.

Brawley, R., *Luke–Acts and the Jews: Conflict, Apology and Conciliation*, Atlanta, GA: Scholars Press, 1987.

Douglas, M., *Implicit Meanings: Essays in Anthropology*, London: Routledge, 1975.

Esler, P. F., *Community and Gospel in Luke–Acts: The Social and*

Political Motivations of Lucan Theology, Cambridge: Cambridge University Press, 1987.

Green, J., *The Theology of the Gospel of Luke*, Cambridge: Cambridge University Press, 1995.

Jervell, J., *The Theology of the Acts of the Apostles*, Cambridge: Cambridge University Press, 1996.

Manson, T. W., *The Sayings of Jesus*, London: SCM Press, 1977.

Penney, J. M., *The Missionary Emphasis of Lucan Pneumatology*, Journal of Pentecostal Theology Supp. 12, Sheffield: Sheffield Academic Press, 1997.

Pilgrim, W. E., *Good News to the Poor*, Minneapolis: Augsburg Press, 1981.

Richardson, N., *The Panorama of Luke*, London: Epworth Press, 1982.

Sanders, J., *The Jews in Luke–Acts*, London: SCM Press, 1987.

Talbert, C. H., *Reading Luke*, New York: Crossroad Publishing, 1982.

Tannehill, R., *The Narrative Unity of Luke–Acts*, Minneapolis: Augsburg Fortress, 1986, 1990.

Tyson, J. B., *Luke–Acts and the Jewish People*, Minneapolis: Augsburg Press, 1988.

Wilson, S. G., *The Gentiles and the Gentile Mission in Luke–Acts*, Cambridge: Cambridge University Press, 1973.

Witherington III, Ben (ed.), *History, Literature and Society in the Book of Acts*, Cambridge: Cambridge University Press, 1996.

5. John's Gospel – as the Father sent me, so I send you

Commentaries

Barrett, C. K., *The Gospel according to St John*, 2nd edn, London: SPCK, 1978.

Beasley-Murray, G. R., *The Gospel of John*, Dallas, TX: Word Books, 1987.

Boismard, M., *L'Evangile de Jean*, Paris: Cerf, 1977.

Brown, R. E., *The Gospel according to John*, 2 vols, New York: Doubleday, 1966, 1970.

Bultmann, R., *The Gospel of John: A Commentary*, Oxford: Blackwell, 1971.

Burge, G., *Interpreting the Gospel of John*, Grand Rapids, MI: Baker Books, 1992.

Carson, D. A., *The Gospel according to John*, Cambridge: Eerdmans, 1991.

Kysar, R., *John*, Philadelphia: Fortress, 1986.

Schnackenburg, R., *The Gospel according to St John*, 3 vols, London: Burns & Oates, 1968, 1971, 1975.

Stibbe, M., *John: Readings*, Sheffield: Sheffield Academic Press, 1993.

Talbert, C. H., *Reading John*, London: SPCK, 1992.

Whiteacre, R. A., *John*, Leicester: IVP, 1999.

Witherington III, Ben, *John's Wisdom*, Cambridge: WJK Press, 1995.

Other useful works

Ashton, John (ed.), *The Interpretation of John*, London: SPCK, 1986.

Ashton, John, *Understanding the Fourth Gospel*, Oxford: Clarendon Press, 1991.

Barrett, C. K., *The Gospel of John and Judaism*, London: SPCK, 1975.

Barrett, C. K., *Essays on John*, London: SPCK, 1982.

Boismard, M.-A., *L'Evangile de Jean*, Paris: Cerf, 1977.

Brown, R. E., *The Community of the Beloved Disciple*, London: G. Chapman, 1979.

Burge, Gary, *The Anointed Community*, Cambridge: Eerdmans, 1987.

Casey, Maurice, *Is John's Gospel True?*, London: Routledge, 1996.

Cullmann, O., *The Johannine Circle*, London: SCM Press, 1976.

Culpepper, R. A., *Anatomy of the Fourth Gospel: A Study in Literary Design*, Philadelphia: Fortress, 1983.

Dodd, C. H., *Historical Tradition in the Fourth Gospel*, Cambridge: Cambridge University Press, 1963.

Evans, C., *Word and Glory*, Sheffield: Sheffield Academic Press, 1993.

Fortna, R. T., *The Fourth Gospel and Its Predecessors*, Philadelphia: Fortress, 1988.

Hengel, Martin, *The Johannine Question*, London: SCM Press, 1989.

Kostenberger, A. J., *The Missions of Jesus and the Disciples according to the Fourth Gospel*, Grand Rapids, MI: Eerdmans, 1998.

Kysar, R., *The Maverick Gospel*, London: WJK Press, 1993.

Martyn, J. L., *History and Theology in the Fourth Gospel*, Nashville: Abingdon, 1979.

Pagels, E., *The Johannine Gospel in Gnostic Exegesis*, SBLMS, 17, Nashville: Abingdon 1979.

Porter, S., and C. Evans (eds), *The Johannine Writings*, Sheffield: Sheffield Academic Press, 1995.

Rensberger, D., *Johannine Faith and Liberating Community*, Westminster: WJK, 1988.

Rensberger, D., *Overcoming the World: Politics and Community in the Gospel of John*, London: SPCK 1989.

Smalley, S., *John: Evangelist and Interpreter*, Exeter: Paternoster, 1978.

Smith, D. Moody, *The Theology of the Gospel of John*, Cambridge: Cambridge University Press, 1995.

Stibbe, M., *John as Storyteller*, Cambridge: Cambridge University Press, 1992.

Thompson, M. Meye, *The God of the Gospel of John*, Cambridge: Eerdmans, 2001.

6. The life and mission of the Early Church

Beyerhaus, P., and C. F. Hallencreutz (eds), *The Church Crossing Frontiers: Essays on the Nature of Mission*, Uppsala, Sweden: Almqvist & Wiksells, 1969.

Bockmuehl, M., *Jewish Law in Gentile Churches: Halakah and the Beginnings of Christian Public Ethics*, Edinburgh: T&T Clark, 2000.

Bockmuehl, M., and M. Thompson (eds), *A Vision for the Church: Studies in Early Christian Ecclesiology*, Edinburgh: T&T Clark, 1997.

Bolt, P., and M. Thompson (eds), *The Gospel to the Nations*, Leicester: IVP, 2000.

Bradshaw, P. F., *Daily Prayer in the Early Church*, London: SPCK, 1981.

Brown, R. H., and J. P. Meyer, *Antioch and Rome: Cradles of Catholic Christianity*, London: G. Chapman, 1983.

Christopherson, A., C. Claussen, J. Frey and B. Longenecker (eds), *Paul, Luke and the Graeco-Roman World*, Sheffield: Sheffield Academic Press, 2002.

Dunn, J. D. G., *Christology in the Making*, London: SCM Press, 1980.

Fuller, R. H., *The Foundations of New Testament Christology*, London: Collins, 1969.

Gloer, W. H. (ed.), *Eschatology and the New Testament*, Massachussetts: Hendrickson, 1988.

Goodman, M., *The Roman World: 44 BC–AD 180*, London: Routledge, 1997.

Green, M., *Evangelism in the Early Church*, London: Hodder & Stoughton, 1970.

Hays, R. B., *The Moral Vision of the New Testament: A Contemporary Introduction to New Testament Ethics*, Edinburgh: T&T Clark, 1996.

Hazlett, I. (ed.), *Early Christianity: Origins and Evolution to AD 600*, London: SPCK, 1991.

Hinson, E. Glenn, *The Evangelization of the Roman Empire*, Macon: Mercer University Press, 1981.

Hunt, S. (ed.), *Christian Millenarianism*, London: Hurst, 2001.

Hurtado, L., *One God, One Lord: Early Christian Devotion and Ancient Jewish Monotheism*, London: SCM Press, 1988.

Johnson, L., *Religious Experience in Earliest Christianity*, Minneapolis: Fortress, 1998.

Johnson, M. E. (ed.), *Living Water: Sealing Spirit*, Collegeville: Liturgical Press, 1995.

Leech, Kenneth, *Through the Long Exile*, London: DLT, 2001.

Mazza, E., *The Origins of the Eucharistic Prayer*, Collegeville: Liturgical Press, 1995.

McCulloch, D., *Groundwork of Christian History*, Peterborough: Epworth Press, 1987.

McKechnie, P., *The First Christian Centuries: Perspectives on the Early Church*, Leicester: IVP/Apollos, 2001.

Meeks, W. A., *The Origins of Christian Morality*, New Haven and London: Yale University Press, 1993.

Millard, A., *Reading and Writing in the Time of Jesus*, Sheffield: Sheffield Academic Press, 2000.

O'Mahoney, K. J. (ed.), *Christian Origins: Worship, Belief and Society*, Sheffield: Sheffield Academic Press, 2003.

Stambaugh, J., and D. Balch, *The New Testament in Its Social Environment*, Philadelphia: Westminster Press, 1986.

Stewart-Sykes, A., and J. Newman, *Early Jewish Liturgy*, Nottingham: Grove Books, 2001.

Theissen, G., *The Gospels in Context: Social and Political History*, Edinburgh: T&T Clark, 1992.

Theissen, G., *Social Reality and the Early Christians*, Edinburgh: T&T Clark, 1993.

Walls, A., *The Missionary Movement in Christian History*, New York: Orbis; and Edinburgh: T&T Clark, 1996.

Walls, A., *The Cross-Cultural Process in Christian History*, New York: Orbis; and Edinburgh: T&T Clark, 2002.

Witherington III, Ben, *New Testament History: A Narrative Account*, Grand Rapids, MI: Baker Books; and Carlisle: Paternoster Press, 2001.

Witherington III, Ben, *Women and the Genesis of Christianity*, Cambridge: Cambridge University Press, 1990.

Wright, N. T., *Jesus and the Victory of God*, London: SPCK, 1996.

Wright, N. T., *The New Testament and the People of God*, London: SPCK, 1990.

Wright, N. T., *The Resurrection of the Son of God*, London: SPCK, 2003.

7. *The Gospels and mission today*

Bowen, R. *So I send you: A Study Guide to Mission*, London: SPCK, 1996.

Churches Together in Britain and Ireland with the Board of Mission of the Archbishops' Council, *Presence and Prophecy: A Heart for Mission in Theological Education*, London: Church House Publishing, 2002.

Comby, J., *How to Understand the History of Christian Mission*, London: SCM Press, 1996 (French 1st edn 1992).

Davey, C., *The March of Methodism*, London: Epworth Press, 1951.

Drane, J., *The McDonaldization of the Church: Spirituality, Creativity and the Future of the Church*, London: DLT, 2000.

Edwards, D. L., *The Church That Could Be*, London: SPCK, 2002.

Hughes, G., *God, Where Are You?*, London: DLT, 1997.

Kirk, J. A., *What Is Mission?* – Theological Explorations, London: DLT, 1999.

Lacugna, C., *Freeing Theology*, San Francisco: Harper, 1993.

Larkin, W., and J. Williams (eds), *Mission in the New Testament*, New York: Orbis, 1999.

Metzger, Bruce M., *Textual Commentary on the Greek New Testament*, London: United Bible Societies, 1975.

Newbigin, L., *The Gospel in a Pluralist Society*, London: SPCK, 1989.

Newbigin, L., *The Open Secret*, London: SPCK, 1995.

Marsh, C., *Christianity in a Post-Atheist Age*, London: SCM Press, 2002.

Moltmann, J., *The Church in the Power of the Spirit*, London: SCM Press, 1977.

Riddell, M., *Threshold of the Future*, London: SPCK, 1998.

Sanneh, L., *Translating the Message: The Missionary Impact on Culture*, New York: Orbis, 1989.

Schussler-Fiorenza, E., *In Memory of Her*, London: SCM Press, 1983.

van Engen, Charles, Dean S. Gilliland and Paul Pierson (eds), *The Good News of the Kingdom: Mission Theology for the Third Millenium*, Maryknoll, NY: Orbis, 1993.

Wallis, J., *Lessons on Spirituality and Social Action*, London: SPCK, 2002.

Williams, R., *On Christian Theology*, Oxford: Blackwell, 2000.

Williamson, R., *For Such a Time as This: Sharing in the Mission of God Today*, London: DLT, 1996.

Wingate, Andrew, *Free to Be: Discovering the God of Freedom*, London: DLT, 2002.

Index of Bible references

Index of subjects